1595
0S

‖‖‖‖‖‖‖‖‖‖‖‖‖‖‖‖‖

D0947391

The Practice of Questioning

International Series on Communication Skills

Edited by Owen Hargie

Owen Hargie is a Senior Lecturer and Head of the Social Skills
Centre at the University of Ulster

The Practice of Questioning

J.T. Dillon

Routledge
London and New York

First published 1990
by Routledge
11 New Fetter Lane, London EC4P 4EE

Simultaneously published in the USA and Canada
by Routledge
a division of Routledge, Chapman and Hall, Inc.
29 West 35th Street, New York, NY 10001

© 1990 J.T. Dillon

Page-set and laser printed by
NWL Editorial Services, Langport, Somerset, England

Printed and bound in Great Britain by
MacKays of Chatham PLC, Chatham, Kent

British Library Cataloguing in Publication Data

Dillon, J.T.
 The practice of questioning. – (International series on
 communication skills)
 1. Conversation. Questioning
 I. Title II. Series
 808.56

Library of Congress Cataloging in Publication Data

Dillon, J.T.
 The practice of questioning / J.T. Dillon
 p.   cm. — (International series on communication skills)
 Bibliography: p.
 Includes index.
 1. Questioning. 2. Interpersonal communication. I. Title.
 II. Series.
 P95.52.D55   1989   89-6307
 302.2'24—dc20   CIP

ISBN 0-415-04378-6 (hbk)
ISBN 0-415-04379-4 (pbk)

Contents

List of tables

Editorial introduction

International Series on Communication Skills

In recent years increasing attention has been devoted to the analysis of social interaction in terms of the communicative competence of the participants. In particular, the conceptualization of interpersonal communication as skilled performance has resulted in a veritable flood of empirical, scientific, and descriptive publications regarding the nature of social skills. However, these publications have been disseminated over a wide spectrum of discipline areas including psychology, communication, sociology, education, business, and counselling. As a result, there is a need for a new series of books designed specifically to draw together this material, from disparate sources, into a meaningful evaluation and analysis of a range of identified communication skills.

Each book in this series contains a blend of theory, research, and practice pertaining to a particular area of communication. However, the emphasis throughout the series is on the practical application of communication skills to social interaction *per se*. The books are written by authors of international repute, chosen specifically for their depth of knowledge and extensive publications in the scientific topic under consideration. As such, this series will make a significant contribution to the rapidly expanding field of interpersonal communication.

The books in this series therefore represent a major addition to the literature and will be of interest to students and researchers in psychology, communication, and other disciplines. They will also prove invaluable to the vast range of people in the 'interpersonal professions' (doctors, nurses, therapists, social workers, and so on), whose day-to-day work so much depends on effective communication skills.

Taken as a whole, this series represents an encyclopaedia of information on the current state of our knowledge of skilled communication. It is certainly the most comprehensive attempt to date to chart the existing state of this field of study. As such, it is both a privilege and a pleasure to have been involved in the conception and execution of this series.

The Practice of Questioning

The study of the nature and functions of questions during interpersonal communication has developed rapidly during the past decade. Texts have been devoted to this topic in a wide range of fields, including linguistics, logic, counselling, psychology, survey interviewing, teaching, law, and journalism. Furthermore, a voluminous number of papers, articles, and book chapters have been devoted to the study of questions.

Drawing together all of the separate elements from this wide and varied data bank on the practice of questioning is clearly a difficult task. However, in this book, Jim Dillon has managed to produce a rich and meaningful tapestry, using all of the available questioning strands. This is not surprising, given that he is a recognized world authority in this sphere, having published a vast amount of material on the subject of questioning. He was also instrumental in initiating, and is the editor of, a new journal entitled *Questioning Exchange* which was established to foster a multidisciplinary approach to the study of questions.

In this volume, Dillon offers to take the reader on a journey through the 'whole world of questioning', and it is an offer which should readily be accepted. In Part one, eight separate fields, within which questioning research has been conducted, are covered; namely, teaching, law, psychotherapy, medicine, personnel interviewing, interrogation, journalism, and survey interviewing. The coverage here is comprehensive, with a measured blend of theory, research, and practice. Part two of the book then examines a range of elements of questioning and alternatives to the use of questions. This information is central to a deeper understanding of the subtleties and complexities of this developing area of study.

Thus the contents of this book provide the most detailed analysis and evaluation to date of the practice of questioning during interpersonal communication. Since the ability to use questions effectively is central to effective functioning in most social contexts, the information presented should be of considerable benefit to professionals in a wide range of settings. At the same time, the theoretical perspectives and research material covered result in a fine balance of academic and applied perspectives on the study of questioning.

Owen Hargie
Head of the Department of Communication
University of Ulster

Chapter one

The world of questioning

All around our own little circle of affairs turns a whole world of questioning where people think and do marvellous things with question and answer. Let us take a tour of this world together.

First we will spread out the maps and guidebooks to get an overview of the world (this chapter). Then we will visit eight selected domains of questioning (Part one), much as we might take a package tour of Europe seeing eight countries in five days. Frazzled but exhilarated, we come home remembering scattered sights of interest, bringing lucky finds and insights to our own tired thought and practice of questioning (Part two).

As a device for our tour, we will divide the world into realms of practice and realms of theory. Points of practice might interest us most to see, but the most interesting sights and useful pointers lie undetected in realms of theory.

Table 1.1 maps the realms of practice, with books as our guide. A manual of practice is listed for each of over a dozen fields of questioning, along with a report of research on practice.

The pairing of books within each field tells us at a glance that practice is not a matter of brute action but conception and reflection. It is knowledge-in-action, an enactment that is informed by an understanding at once theoretical and empirical and practical. Hence the far-off realms of theory, separated by artifice into another table, are nearer to practice than we may have guessed. They are not worlds apart. They form the one world of questioning. It's just hard to see the whole world at once.

Realms of theory are mapped in Table 1.2, again with books as our guide. A representative book is listed for each of a dozen disciplines of thought and study about questioning. In very recent years some scholars have been turning to several disciplines to study various aspects of questioning. Table 1.2 also lists multidisciplinary anthologies and bibliographies, and a new journal devoted to questioning in all fields of endeavour.

From these domains of theory come intriguing and useful models of question–answer. They explain what we are doing when we ask and answer, offering an understanding that can inform practice. Without that understanding

Table 1.1 Realms of practice

Field	Manual of practice	Report of research
Education		
	Questioning and Teaching (Dillon 1988a)	Questioning and Discussion (Dillon 1988b)
Law		
	Questioning Techniques and Tactics (Kestler 1982)	Strange Language: Child Victims under Cross-examination (Brennan and Brennan 1988)
Psychotherapy		
	Questioning: Skills for the Helping Process (Long et al. 1981)	'A question classification scale for marriage and family therapy' (Baldwin 1987)
Medicine		
	'The role of the question in medical psychiatric diagnosis' (Lazarescu 1988)	Discourse of Medicine (Mishler 1984)
Personnel		
	The Appraisal Interview (Maier 1958)	'Effects of question type in the employment interview' (Tengler and Jablin 1983)
Interrogation		
	Interviews and Interrogations (Buckwalter 1983)	Scientific Interrogation (Taylor 1984)
Journalism		
	Creative Interviewing (Metzler 1988)	News Interviews (Jucker 1986)
Surveys		
	Asking Questions (Sudman and Bradburn 1982)	Questions and Answers in Attitude Surveys' (Schuman and Presser 1981)
Library		
	Informational Interviews and Questions (Slavens 1978)	'Reference interviews in public libraries' (Lynch 1978)
Management		
	Smart Questions (Leeds 1987)	'Questioning and management' (Fischer 1987)
Sales	Professional selling skills (Xerox 1976)	'On questions ... in service encounters' (Merritt 1976)
Parliament		
	Questions in Parliament (Chester and Bowring 1962)	Questions in the House (Howarth 1956)
Science		
	What to Study (Campbell et al. 1982)	Scientific Method as a ... Question-answering Technique (Hintikka 1981)
Religion		
	Questions are the Answer (Robinson 1980)	Theologie der Frage (Bastian 1970)
Personal life		
	The Book of Questions (Stock 1987)	Homo Quaerens: The Seeker and the Sought (Feldstein 1978)
Everyday life		
	Questioning Techniques (Kaiser 1979)	Questions and Responses in English Conversation (Stenstroem 1984)

our practice could remain ignorant, as we might not know what we are doing nor how to do it better.

Having glanced over the maps and literature, we select eight interesting places to visit. For our convenience the eight domains on our tour are scheduled as the first eight listed in Table 1.1 – education, law, psychotherapy, medicine, personnel interviewing, interrogation, journalism, and surveys or opinion-polling (Chapters 2–9). All of these domains differ in purposes, circumstances, and habits of question–answer. Each domain offers a novel sight and at least one new insight into questioning. At the same time all eight domains let us see familiar sights in novel perspectives.

We will see three major sights at each stop. First, we will explore the surroundings – the environment or circumstance wherein questioning occurs. For instance, we will take a look inside a classroom and a courtroom and a clinic to see what it's really like in there. We will watch questions being used, seeing how they are actually asked and answered in these strange places. For instance, we will watch a lawyer cross-examining a witness. And we will look over the scheme of action in that domain, noting how practitioners go about doing what they do, especially those who do it better than others. For instance, we will see opinion-pollsters preparing and testing their questions before asking them in a survey. These major sights could be posted as theory, research, and practice, but the signs would only mislead us; for in reality we are seeing a mix of the three everywhere we go.

As a brochure for our visit, we will have in hand a transcript of questioning in each domain. These can be picked up in the Appendix. The transcript illustrates all the pointers being made by our guide.

As a souvenir of our visit, we may be tempted to take home some exotic technique of questioning. But all techniques are better left just where we have found them. That is their rightful place, the one place where they can do any good. Back home we would only look foolish using some outlandish technique.

The smart thing to bring home is some *understanding* – theoretical notions that enliven practical actions. Having seen how questioning serves to various purposes in various circumstances – and having also been to enough places where the service is terrible – we come home with a new understanding of how to turn the elements of questioning to our purposes in our circumstances (Part two).

Only the best impressions remain from our tour, so luckily enough we do not have too much to carry with us into our own question–answer practice. To grasp the notion of questioning (Chapter 10) we recall that something is involved before and after the question itself – assumptions and answers. The action of questioning (Chapter 11) also has three ordered elements, with practical steps to take before and after putting the questions – preparation and reflection. Reflection leads to redesign of the questioning, on the promise of doing it better next time.

As we rework our scheme of action we recall having seen on our tour a dozen practical alternatives to questioning (Chapter 12). Now we look at the research to see how a mix of questions and alternatives might enact the best practical choice we can make (Chapter 13). Later we can reflect on the consequences of our enacted choice, again pondering the questions which we have prepared and put to purpose. That is good practice of questioning.

Our travels can make us wise to the ways of the world of questioning. Bon voyage; then, welcome home!

Table 1.2 Realms of theory

Discipline	Representative Source
Logic	*The Logic of Questions and Answers* (Belnap and Steel 1976)
Psychology	*The Psychology of Questions* (Graesser and Black 1985)
Philosophy	*Perplexity and Knowledge* (Clark 1972)
Philosophy of science	*Empirical Inquiry* (Rescher 1982)
Anthropology	*Questions and Politeness* (Goody 1978)
Linguistics	
English	*Questions and Answers in English* (Pope 1976)
other languages	*Interrogativity* (Chisholm 1984)
Sociolinguistics	*Questioning Strategies in Sociolinguistics* (Churchill 1978)
Discourse analysis	*Dialogue Games* (Carlson 1983)
Literature	*Meaning and Reading* (Meyer 1983)
Semantics	*The Semantics of Questions* (Hintikka 1976)
Computer science	*Natural Language Question Answering Systems* (Bolc 1980)
Multiple disciplines	
anthologies	*Questions* (Hiz 1978)
	Questions and Answers (Kiefer 1983)
	Questions and Questioning (Meyer 1988)
bibliographies	'Bibliography of questions and answers' (Egli and Schleichert 1976)
	'Categories of literature on questioning' (Dillon 1981)
	'Multidisciplinary perspectives on question–answer' (Romero 1985)
	'Annotated bibliography on question-asking' (Dillon *et al.* 1988)
journal	*Questioning Exchange: a Multidisciplinary Review* (London: Taylor and Francis)

Domains of Questioning

Chapter two

Classroom questioning

'Well then,' proposed Socrates, 'if you should ever be charged in actual fact with the upbringing and education of these imaginary children of yours, ... so you will make a law that they must devote themselves especially to the technique of asking and answering questions.'

'Yes, I will, with your collaboration.'

(Republic VII:534)

To the example of Socrates the tradition of classroom questioning traces itself, waveringly. With no help from Socrates, children everywhere are schooled to become masters at answering questions and to remain novices at asking them. Normal practice is to induce in the young answers given by others to questions put by others. It is against the norm for students to ask questions. Hence classroom questioning means teacher questioning.

The same is the norm elsewhere in the world of questioning. It is against the law for witnesses to ask questions in the courtroom. Students and witnesses do not ask questions, and neither do patients in medical clinics, clients in psychotherapy, suspects under interrogation, interviewees in news broadcasts, or respondents in opinion polls. So too with children and other subordinates in school and out. They all must communicate through answers. Someone else will ask the questions. That is the normal question–answer communication.

Classroom researchers repeatedly find 'the dearth of student questions and the deluge of teacher questions' (Susskind 1969: 146). For instance, in both elementary and secondary classrooms they have found these same rates of questioning (studies reviewed by Dillon 1988b):

over the class hour, eighty-four questions from the teacher and two questions from all the students combined in the class;

over the school year, one question per month per pupil.

From Plato's Academy to present-day schools, the tradition has seen questions as useful devices for teaching and learning. But modern practice emphasizes only the use of questioning for teaching. It has forgotten the ancient complementary use of student questions for learning. In that way questioning in school has come to mirror, and thus to serve, questioning in society.

Teacher questioning remains the next oldest and most familiar practice of questioning. Everyone who has been to school recognizes it, and readily falls back into it. The everydayness of this practice, and our long experience with it, may oddly hide from us its peculiarity as a mode of communication and the complexity of the situation in which it transpires. To ask and answer questions in a classroom is easy. But that says nothing about how effective the question–answer is. Its effectiveness turns on its service to educative purpose in classroom circumstance. And the classroom circumstance is complex beyond present understanding.

Classroom contexts

The classroom seems a simple enough place, yet it shows impenetrable complexity. And although it is a single place, the classroom is a complex of multiple contexts. There is no one such thing as 'the classroom context', hence no one such thing as 'the use of classroom questioning'. Rather there are multiple contexts, each entailing a differentially apt use of questions.

One of the distinctive features of classroom questioning is that many people are being asked questions all at once by one other person. All other practices of questioning involve one questioner and one respondent. Some involve several questioners but each with one respondent in a separate setting; others involve several settings but each with one questioner and respondent. Classrooms involve one questioner with multiple respondents all at once, in various and serial settings day after day – all within the same room.

No matter the context, *the classroom circumstance is complex*. It is complex for the large number of people acting within it. And it is complex for six further properties (Doyle 1986):

1 *multidimensionality* – a large number of events and tasks occur within the hour, even the minute;
2 *simultaneity* – these many things are happening at once, not serially;
3 *immediacy* – the pace of events is rapid, with little time to reflect before or after acting;
4 *unpredictability* – events typically take unexpected turns and rarely take intended turns;
5 *publicity* – events are witnessed by a large number or portion of students who may be influenced variously by that which is transpiring between two parties at hand;
6 *history* – students and teacher as a class accumulate a common set of experiences, routines, and norms which provide a foundation for

conducting activities and which enhance or delimit the promise of future activities.

These are the properties of classroom complexity regardless of the activity at hand, say a lecture or seat-work. But they are especially conducive to complexity in lessons where students and teacher talk back and forth.

> Group lessons require that a teacher cope with a complex social system with multiple participants of different abilities and a discontinuous signal system to guide the flow of events, monitor the development of content in an often unpredictable pattern, and provide accurate and appropriate feedback to individual students for their answers
>
> (Doyle 1986: 415).

That is what is going on when a teacher asks questions.

The classroom is *a complex of multiple contexts*. Research in elementary classrooms has distinguished 11 different 'activity structures' (Berliner 1983) and 17 different 'instructional formats' (Stodolsky *et al.* 1981) – all of which can be seen in the *same classroom* at different times during the school day. Activity structures include seat-work, reading circle, one-way presentation (for example, lecture), and two-way presentation (such as recitation). Each activity structure exhibits different features or characteristics that vary on a dozen dimensions: time spent, number of students involved, group stability, role of teacher and of student, student response, teacher and student feedback, evaluation procedures, teacher and student control of content and of process.

Despite this variety of structures and features, we note that all 11 cases are variants of one sole category, *activity*. They're 'activity structures'. There are still other major categories of classroom circumstance. Hence we could make other lists, one for each of the other major categories, thereby constituting further classroom contexts. Let us imagine, say, 11 contexts classified by variations in *purpose* instead of activity; or by students, by teacher, by subject-matter, by result, by milieu.

Further, one of these activity structures, two-way presentation, is distinguished by another list into two different instructional formats called recitation and discussion. Both of these involve question–answer. Research on recitation – one among 17 instructional formats on the list – shows that this single format exhibits different properties varying in six dimensions: group quality, student behaviour, feedback, expected cognitive level, and materials used by students and by teacher. These different properties vary according to the socioeconomic level of the school and the subject-matter within the classroom. More recitation episodes are observed in classrooms in schools at lower than at middle socioeconomic levels, and more at middle than at higher levels; while at all levels there are more recitation episodes in mathematics than social studies lessons within the same classroom in the same school (Stodolsky *et al.* 1981).

What is more, these episodes of the one instructional format – recitation – serve five different instructional purposes: to review past learning; to introduce new material; to practise skill and mastery; to check work; and to clarify understanding. Yet further, several of these purposes can be seen to inform one and the same recitation episode. 'It is very common to find more than one instructional purpose served in a single recitation segment' (Stodolsky *et al.* 1981: 128).

In short, the use of classroom questioning differs as the classroom contexts vary. It differs among 11 activity structures and among 17 instructional formats. It differs between two instructional formats, recitation and discussion, involving the same activity structure. It differs within the one format of recitation, among socio-economic levels of school and between subject-matters within the same classroom and the same school. It differs according to the various purposes for recitation, the various purposes for discussion, and so on for other classroom contexts. And it differs even in the same recitation episode in the same classroom with the same subject-matter, as it serves several different purposes.

All of this may sound as if teachers should use different questions for each different educative purpose in each different classroom circumstance. How complex and how particular! That is a good impression to have of classroom questioning. It would make for good practice of questioning in classrooms and in other domains as well.

Recitation and discussion

Recitation and discussion are two broad types of classroom interaction, each of which can take on many different forms. Both involve teacher and students talking back and forth; both involve questioning and answering, but each in a characteristically different way. To illustrate, transcript no. 1A (Appendix, p. 238) reproduces a snippet of classroom recitation, and no. 1B (p. 238) a discussion.

The two classes are similar except for the fact that one is a recitation and the other a discussion. Both are history classes taught in the very same week in the junior year of secondary school (students aged 16–17). Both are taught by good teachers, and students in both classes have the same verbal ability as measured by standardized tests. So, the differences between them are not due to the skill of the teacher, ability of the students, level of school, time of year, or nature of subject-matter. The difference is due to the processes that teacher and students are engaging in.

Recitation is characterized by one way of talking back and forth, discussion by another. As we compare Mr H's recitation class and Mr T's discussion class

Table 2.1 Questions in classroom processes

Aspect of questioning	Recitation class (transcript no. 1A*) (%)	Discussion class (transcript no. 1B*) (%)
Teacher talk (vs student talk)	69	22
Question turns	78	11
Teacher–student turns (vs student–student)	88	6
'Higher-cognitive' questions (vs 'lower-cognitive')	29	87
Students participating	41	77
Rate of exchanges	6 per minute	1 per minute
Average student response	4 seconds	25 seconds

* See Appendix

(transcript no. 1), we can see how these two processes differ in the predominant speaker, type of exchange, sequence, pace, the kinds of questions asked, answers given, and evaluations supplied. Table 2.1 displays these differences as seen in the two selected classrooms.

The predominant speaker in recitation is the teacher, typically speaking for two-thirds or more of the time. In discussion the predominant speaker may be the teacher, but students typically speak half or more of the time. For example, in our illustrative recitation class, Mr H speaks for 69 per cent of the time; in Mr T's discussion class, students speak for 78 per cent of the time (Table 2.1). In other discussion classes students may speak for less and the teacher more, but never will the teacher speak much more than the students do. Always in recitation the teacher speaks twice as much as the students do.

The characteristic exchange in recitation is question–answer, always teacher–student. It is a three-part exchange involving the same moves by the same speakers:

1 Teacher question;
2 Student answer;
3 Teacher evaluation plus next question.

By contrast, this exchange does *not* characterize discussion, which involves rather a mix of moves by a mix of speakers – questions and statements and responses by students and teacher. For instance, questions account for 78 per cent of Mr H's turns at talk in the recitation, but for only 11 per cent of Mr T's turns in discussion.

The sequence of turns is therefore predictable: 88 per cent of turns in the recitation are teacher–student, compared to 94 per cent student–student turns in the discussion class. Other discussion classes may have far fewer student–student turns, in a mix of teacher–student, student–teacher, student–student exchanges. But recitation classes will always have the same teacher–

student turns, due to the characteristic exchange of (1) teacher question, (2) student answer, (3) teacher evaluation plus next question. Here the teacher necessarily takes two of three turns, and one student cannot speak after another. Partly as a consequence, more students participate in a discussion than in a recitation. In Mr T's discussion 77 per cent of the students spoke, compared to 41 per cent of Mr H's students in the recitation.

The overall pace also differs. In a recitation we typically hear many, brief, and fast exchanges. In a discussion we will hear fewer, longer, and slower exchanges. The pace in a recitation could be slower but the pace in discussion could not be much faster. For example, the pace in Mr H's recitation involves six question–answers per minute, with student responses lasting four seconds at a time, on average. By contrast, Mr T's discussion involves one exchange per minute, with students typically speaking for half a minute at a time.

A striking way to appreciate this difference is to stand in the middle of the school corridor, with H's recitation class on our left and T's discussion on our right. Following the transcripts in the Appendix and using a stop-watch, we are startled to find that by the time T's class is just completing one single exchange, the *whole* of H's recitation episode will already have flashed by. Not only is the question–answer short but it is fast. In the old days it was too fast for trained stenographers to record (Stevens 1912). In modern times it takes computerized chronometric equipment to detect the traces of pausing between the exchanges. Numerous studies have demonstrated that the average pause between the answer and next question is less than one second (for example, Rowe 1974).

The character of question, answer, and evaluation also differs between recitation and discussion. For the recitation question, that which is in question is not actually the question itself as asked. Teacher and student usually know the answer. Something else is in question, such as the student's demonstration of knowledge of the answer and the teacher's appreciation that the student knows the answer in some way. The teacher in a discussion class may also know the answer, but the students usually do not. That is why they are in school, and why the class is a discussion. Here the thing that is in question is typically the question that is being asked. The students do not demonstrate but construct, gain, or use knowledge about the matter in question.

This difference in the questions asked can sometimes – not reliably – be seen in the type of cognitive process inferred behind the question, or inferred to produce the answer. In education the question types of most interest broadly contrast 'higher/lower' cognitive processes: those involving base knowledge, comprehension, and recall compared to those involving loftier matters of analysis, inference, speculation, synthesis, and the like. On this broad division, recitation is cast into the lower and discussion into the higher reaches of cognition. For example, 71 per cent of Mr H's questions are lower-cognitive, and 87 per cent of Mr T's are higher-cognitive (Table 2.1). But that difference is not always of the essence, since students can well discuss facts and recite opinions, just as well as they can discuss opinions and recite facts.

The essential difference in the questions asked cannot easily be seen by looking at the question. But it can easily be heard in what follows upon it. For example, H's recitation class starts with the main question for the hour (not shown in the excerpt): 'Why do you think they won, these 13 colonies?' This looks like a question about the reasons that the American colonies won the Revolutionary War; and it appears that students are being asked to think and to reason through the issue, perhaps to speculate and give their explanations, interpretations, and opinions. But no one in the room believes any of that for a moment; at least, no one acts as if believing it. The question in T's discussion looks very much the same. 'Do you feel that Louis XIV was justified in his treatment of the Huguenots?' That looks as if students are being asked to think things through and come up with reasons and opinions, grounds for and against justification. And that is just what everyone in the room starts doing.

The answers in a recitation class not only are foreknown by teacher and student and not only are right or wrong, but also they are *predetermined* to be right and wrong. The question in discussion is *not* predetermined, whether teacher and students know the answer or not. Furthermore, in recitation there is one and the same predetermined right answer for all students; in discussion there could be a different right answer for each student and even one right answer that all students come up with, but not a predetermined right answer. For example, take the questions in the recitation episode: Why did the colonies win? What made Washington militarily successful? We can easily imagine a conference of historians, British and American, or of political scientists or of military strategists, addressing that question and coming to divergent answers – distinct, perhaps even opposing reasons for victory and success. We can even imagine their concluding to one and the same set of reasons – moreover, the very set of reasons that we hear spoken and affirmed in the recitation class. Yet none of this hemming and hawing will stall the recitation process. The historians discuss the question, whereas the students do not; they may diverge on the answers, whereas the students may not; and whereas they may come to one and the same answer, the students must give the one predetermined right answer. We see the proof in what follows upon the answer.

After a student answers in recitation, we always hear 'right/wrong' in so many words, and always from the teacher. In discussion we hear 'agree/disagree' and we hear it from a student and/or from the teacher. For example, in T's discussion we hear a series of students giving different answers to the question, then we hear a series of 'agree/disagree' both from students and teacher. Mr T never says 'right/wrong'. He says, 'OK, I can see where you're coming from, but I don't know if I can totally agree with that' (exchange 2 in transcript no. 1B). Later he says, 'All right, Marty raised an interesting point' (exchange 4). Thereafter Sean says that Marty was wrong; Marty says that Sean has a good point; Diane disagrees; and Mark says that Diane has a good point. We hear none of that in a recitation. Mr H says 'OK' or 'Very good'. When the answer is not OK or very good, he politely never says, 'You're wrong!' but impolitely ignores the answer and repeats the question until the right answer is produced by someone else (exchanges 4–6 in transcript no. 1A). That is because the answer is predetermined by the teacher (text, curriculum) to be right/wrong.

Pedagogy of questioning

On the principle that pedagogy is *disciplined behaviour in service to educative purpose in classroom circumstance*, the pedagogy of recitation and discussion questions must differ – for these processes vary in purpose and circumstance. So do the other classroom processes that involve questioning (such as reading circle, testing).

The manuals specify a multiplicity of practices, such as five general questioning strategies, 15 specific strategies, and 25 questioning techniques (Hyman 1979). Yet no technique of questioning can serve various purposes and circumstances. In point of fact, the use of questions that is appropriate for one process may be counter-productive to another. Teachers who use recitation questioning with the intent of promoting discussion achieve the effect of preventing discussion. The process turns into a recitation, while students turn to their books in search of the answer. 'Now wait a minute, don't turn to your book!' exclaimed one teacher trying to start a discussion on the Mayflower Compact. 'Let's just think something out here. What did those people agree to before they got off the boat?' The students were right to turn to their books, because this process was not going to be a discussion but a recitation (Dillon 1985).

Better practice can be devised by the individual teacher who examines the purposes and circumstances to be served by the questioning. Particulars of practice are best devised by a scheme of generic action, outlining the general questions that a teacher may answer in preparing, putting, and pondering the specific questions to purpose in circumstance (Dillon, 1988a).

The first act is to *prepare the questions* for the asking. The first step of preparation is to specify to self the purpose in circumstance, so as to devise appropriate questions to serve just that. Why ask? about what? to whom? when? in which manner? and so on. Two generic questions help in preparing the specific questions to ask:

1   What is it that students are to know or to learn from this coming lesson?
2   To which questions does that knowledge or learning represent an answer?

Next, the specific questions are laboriously written out and reformulated. Then they are arranged and rearranged in some promising order according to the series of answers that are desired and anticipated – given the teacher's knowledge of the students, subject-matter, and so forth. Series of related and subordinate questions can be readied by the device of sketching out the alternative answers to each question, then tracing relations among the various alternatives and the appropriate next question. For instance, answers A1 and A2 are sketched for question Q1; then Q2 is formulated to follow from A1 and Q3 from A2.

While actually putting the question, the generic issues run:

1 What do I want the answer *for*?
2 What shall I *do* with the answer?

Therefore the one generic practice at this point is to *listen to the answers*. Like other practitioners, teachers must discipline their behaviour actually to attend to the answers; otherwise they will not appreciate them correctly, or even hear them. Listening gives the information needed to adjudge the kind of answer that is being given, whether in fact it is an answer or some other response, and what to do with it in either case.

After putting the questions, the generic practice is to *ponder the question–answer*. Reflection bears on two generic issues.

1 How did the questions work?
2 Which next questions might work better?

This act of reflection completes the practice of questioning that began in preparing the questions to ask. It issues in a new design of questions that give better promise of serving purpose in circumstance on the morrow. That is good pedagogy, and good practice of questioning in any field.

Do teacher questions achieve the purposes set for student learning? No one quite knows. The very best experimental research has not been able to tell one way or the other (studies reviewed by Winne 1979).

Teacher questions are more surely known to be useful for covering the subject-matter to be learned, for controlling social and verbal behaviour while apparently learning, and for testing what has been learned. They are less certainly known to enhance the cognitive, affective, and expressive processes of students in the classroom. For these purposes alternative, *non*-questioning techniques are demonstrably effective, especially during discussion classes. (Chapters 12–13 describe practice and research on alternatives to questioning.)

One of the obvious alternatives is to use student questions. These lead surely to learning. Teacher questions serve other purposes. Everyone knows that, because everyone has been to school and learned their lesson. This is the lesson we play out as we grow up into the world of questioning.

Chapter three

Courtroom questioning

In 1079 BC, an Egyptian royal commission tried locals for looting the Pharaohs' tombs. The Vizier himself came down to head the enquiry, while Scribe Djutmose conducted the cross-examination:

Vizier: What is the story of this silver which your husband took from the Great Tombs?
Woman: I did not see it.
Scribe: How then did you buy the servants?
Woman: I bought them in exchange for blocks of dates from my palm grove.

Another witness produced a spirited but deadly alibi.

Vizier: What is the story of your going to raid the Great Tombs?
Seka'atiamum: Far be it from me! The Great Tombs! Put me to death for the tombs of Imiotru, for they are the tombs in which I was.

'He was examined further with a stick,' notes the court record. Scribe Djutmose was well prepared to pursue the cross-examination.

Witness: Stop, I will tell you. We took a silver mummy-covering from the tomb and broke it up and put it into a basket and divided it up –
Scribe: The tomb from which you brought away the silver vases is one tomb but the tomb from which you brought away this mummy-covering is another, making two tombs.
Witness: It is false, the silver vases belong to the main treasure of which I have told you already; one tomb and one only was what we opened.

The record notes: 'He was examined again with the birch, the stick and the screw' (Romer 1984: 180–1).

A less antique but more famous trial featured Socrates as the ineffectual cross-examiner of his accuser, Meletus (*Apology*, 24d–27e). An earlier scene, from the Bible, featured Daniel's cross-examination of two elders who had testified to catching Susanna in an adulterous pose (*Daniel* 13: 54–8). Daniel questioned them separately.

Daniel: Now then, since you saw her so clearly, tell me under what tree you
saw them lying?
Elder 1: Under a mastic tree.
Elder 2: Under a holm oak.

Their answers earned them the death penalty, as did Socrates' questions.

These trials from ancient Egypt, Greece and Israel show the antiquity of
courtroom questioning, and many of the themes of practice as well. For instance, they show the use of direct examination and cross-examination, the
adversarial cast of the questioning, the compulsion under law to answer, and
the fallibility of testimony, even eyewitness testimony. All of these themes and
practices also appear in the trial from present-day Australia in transcript no.
2 (Appendix), where young Beverley is cross-examined. She is certain that
Uncle David has molested her repeatedly, but under questioning she cannot
remember when, where, how, why, and the like. Did David molest Beverley?
This is the question that excites depiction in films, novels, television, and
other fantasies. Beverley answers 'yes' and David 'no'. In the tedium of real
courtrooms, questioning is used in peculiar ways to make one of these answers
more acceptable than the other. Whether *or not* David molested Beverley, the
questioning will serve either to acquit or to convict him. The same happened
in bygone millennia to Seka'atiamum, and to Susanna, and to Socrates.

Courtroom contexts

Question–answer is the archetypical means whereby courtroom proceedings
take place. On the whole, communication in courtrooms must take place
through question and answer. The question–answer is schematized to an extreme, constrained by procedural rules (for example, rules of evidence), and
allocated to specified parties at specified times. For instance, lawyers speak in
questions, witnesses in answers; witnesses do not ask, lawyers do not answer.
Yet although the lawyer speaks in almost nothing but questions inside the
courtroom, the great majority of lawyers' questioning occurs outside the
courtroom.

The first context for questioning in this field is extra-courtroom, in interviews and depositions of witnesses, and question–answer rehearsals with witnesses. Since only a quite small proportion of cases (in the USA) actually go
to trial, the deposition is the most significant event in a lawsuit; and lawyers
find it imperative to interview all witnesses before these testify either at a deposition or at a trial (Kestler 1982). Hence not only the most questions but
also the most crucial questioning and most frequently the only questioning
will occur in non-courtroom contexts.

The courtroom represents another place for questioning. But although it is
a single place, the courtroom offers *multiple contexts* for questioning, in which

the features of questioning differ one from another. Hence there is no one such thing as 'the use of questions in courtrooms', any more than there exists such a thing as 'the lawyer's use of questions'.

To illustrate, we have cited the use of questions in extra-courtroom contexts of interview, deposition, and rehearsal of witnesses, in each of which questioning has distinctive features (caused in part by differing purposes and differing rules of procedure). Now we will examine various courtroom contexts – non-trial and trial proceedings. Each of these also presents further contexts for questioning. Non-trial courtroom contexts include pre-and post-trial hearings. Trial contexts include direct-examination and cross-examination episodes. Every one of these contexts displays a distinctive use of questions. For instance, the questions during direct examination and cross-examination differ, and they differ further as they are put by the prosecutor and by the defence attorney as each rises to examine on direct examination and then on cross-examination.

Non-trial proceedings

Three non-trial courtroom proceedings are called Initial Appearance, Change of Plea, and Magistrates' Hearing. In an Initial Appearance (hereafter IA), the questions are used to determine the identity of the defendant, his knowledge of the charge against him, conditions of release, and date of next court appearance. Change of Plea (CP) is an alternative to trial; here the defendant now pleads 'guilty'. The questions ascertain the defendant's knowledge and volition so to plead, and the factual basis for it (for example, that certain evidence is available which might lead a believing jury to convict). In Magistrates' Courts (MC), the process here being described is a hearing in the Arrears and Maintenance division to ascertain the income and expenses of a defendant already charged to pay, but failing to pay, some fine or maintenance; and then to determine the amount to be paid each week.

Who asks the questions? First of all, not the defendant. Nowhere in any legal proceeding in any context does the defendant or any other witness ask questions; defendants and witnesses answer questions. In 42 CP hearings studied (Philips 1984), defendants asked only 1 per cent of all questions, and only 3 per cent in six MC sessions (Harris 1984). The Magistrate asked 42 per cent and the clerk 55 per cent; the lawyers in CP asked 3 per cent and the judge 96 per cent of the questions.

What types of questions are asked? Table 3.1 shows the overwhelming majority of questions in all three proceedings to be yes/no, and the majority of the few wh-questions to be narrow and closed. These types of question characterize all courtroom proceedings. But Table 3.1 also shows a systematic difference between two proceedings held in the same courtroom – IA and CP.

Table 3.1 Questions in non-trial proceedings

Question type	Initial appearance*	Change of plea*	Magistrates' hearing[†]	
yes/no	83%	91%		62%
wh-	17	9		38
of wh- only				
what	58	37	broad	16
how	9	49	narrow	84
other wh-	33	13	–	–

Sources: *Philips 1985; [†]Harris 1984

There are twice as many wh-questions in IA as in CP. As for types of wh-questions, in IA 'what?' predominated and 'how?' questions were negligible; the reverse is the case in CP. Moreover, the use of 'how?' in CP is routinized, and expressed in full sentences with fronting (that is, the 'how' appears at the front). By contrast, the 'what?' in IA is not routinized, and is expressed in both non-sentence and full-sentence forms with both fronting and non-fronting (Philips 1985). These minor linguistic differences follow from the characteristics of the context in which the questions are used, while significant differences follow in turn from them.

For instance, CP is a more routinized hearing than IA, which shows more diversity. As an initial hearing, IA features less information that is already known and already shared among participants. The questions are relatively more open, the answers longer and less predictable, with more requests for elaboration and repair. But the questions are more open for the fact that the talk is primarily among court officers – judge, clerk, lawyers, police. In CP the question–answer is short and routinized because the talk is primarily between judge and defendant. The questions in CP are constraining in order to restrict and to direct the defendant's talk, so that his talk will be neither too much nor the wrong kind. Defendants' speech must be sharply curtailed and controlled lest in their ignorance and inexperience with things legal they damage their own case or ruin the legality of the proceeding (Philips 1984: 230–1). That characterizes trial proceedings as well, and also MC hearings, for further reasons. In MC hearings, marked like the other non-trial proceedings by predominant yes/no and narrow wh-questions, every time a defendant tried to elaborate the minimal response called for, the magistrate was observed to interrupt with a further question (Harris 1984). As a rule, almost with exception, witnesses are advised by their lawyers to answer only as specifically asked and resolutely no more (for example, Kestler 1982; Tierney 1971).

What types of answers are given to the questions? The answer depends not only on the type of question asked and not only on the context wherein it is asked, but also on who has asked it and on who is answering it. Even within a single context the answers will vary accordingly. Table 3.2 shows the different answers given to questions of different types by defendant, lawyers, and judge

Table 3.2 Questions and answers in change of plea proceedings

Questioner/ respondent	Questions			Non-copy responses			Elaborated responses		
	Y/n	wh-	All	Y/n	wh-	All	Y/n	wh-	All
Defendant	88%	12%	1%	5%	13%	5%	2%	5%	2%
Lawyers	94	6	3	32	33	32	21	15	20
Judge	91	9	96	46	50	46	20	(–)	19
All	92	8	100	10	20	10	5	8	5

Source: Philips 1984

as questioner and respondent in CP proceedings. The statistics display the different uses and functions of the *same* question form in the same context, according to who asks and answers.

As seen in Table 3.2, respondents give different answers to the same type of question. The higher the status of respondent relative to questioner, the less the response copies the format of the question and the more it elaborates beyond what is asked. For instance, defendants fail to answer a yes/no question in terms of its form only 5 per cent of the time (and only 13 per cent for wh-questions), whereas one-third of the lawyers' answers and one-half of the judge's fail to conform. Indeed, in all 42 sessions studied, one lone 'yes' was given by a judge to a yes/no question (Philips 1984: 246). Similarly for responses that elaborate: defendants elaborated for 2 per cent and lawyers for 21 per cent of yes/no questions (5 per cent and 15 per cent for wh-questions). Thus, although overall there is very little non-copy and elaboration, there are large and significant variations in both according to who asks and answers the very same type of question.

Trial proceedings

The case is even more complicated in trial proceedings. Here the questions vary not only by questioner but also by phase or episode of the trial. The major phases are direct examination and cross-examination. The major questioners are the prosecuting attorney and the defence attorney. Table 3.3 shows the different questions asked by prosecution and defence during direct examination and cross-examination in a murder trial.

As seen for other legal proceedings, the majority of questions in this trial are of the yes/no type, and the majority of wh-questions are narrow. The types of question are listed in Table 3.3 on a continuum of control, with broad wh-questions less controlling than narrow ones, wh-questions less controlling than yes/no ones, and grammatical yes/no questions less controlling than tag ones. Overall, the questions are of the more-controlling types; two-thirds are yes/no and one-third wh-questions. But the distribution of these broad types

Table 3.3 Questions in a murder trial

Question type	All	Direct examination		Cross examination	
		Prosecution	Defence	Prosecution	Defence
wh-	33%	54%	39%	31%	17%
broad	–	8	3	1	–
narrow	–	46	36	30	17
Yes/no	67	45	59	68	82
grammatical	–	42	32	51	27
prosodic	–	3	23	13	45
tag	–	–	4	4	10

Source: Woodbury 1984

and their sub-types within systematically differs according to questioner and episode of trial.

There are more less-controlling questions on direct examination than on cross-examination, and more by the prosecution than by the defence. There are more more-controlling questions on cross-examination than on direct examination, and more by the defence than by the prosecution. That is, the questions were less controlling of witnesses during direct examination than during cross-examination. More wh-questions were asked by both the prosecution and the defence during direct examination than during cross-examination; and in each case more of the prosecutor's questions than the defence's were of these less-controlling types. More yes/no questions were asked on cross-examination than on direct examination, and in each case more by the defence than by the prosecution.

On direct examination, the prosecuting attorney asked more wh-questions than yes/no questions, and on cross-examination more yes/no than wh-questions; more of his questions on cross-examination than on direct examination were yes/no; and on both direct examination and cross-examination he asked more wh-questions than did the defence attorney. The defence attorney asked more yes/no than wh-questions both on direct examination and cross-examination; more yes/no questions on cross-examination than on direct examination; and more yes/no questions than the prosecutor did on both direct examination and cross-examination.

As to particular types of question, very few broad wh-questions were asked on direct examination and next to none on cross-examination, where the questions are overwhelmingly yes/no. Both the prosecution and the defence asked more prosodic (or intonated) and tag types of yes/no questions on cross-examination than on direct examination, but the defence attorney used tags and especially prosodic questions much more than did the prosecutor. The prosecutor used more of the grammatical yes/no questions than any other types, both on direct examination and cross-examination, and much more than the defence did. While the prosecutor used four times the prosodic questions on cross-examination as he did on direct examination, the defence used four times as many as the prosecutor did. Nowhere did anyone use alternative or disjunctive questions – a further, third type between yes/no and wh-questions, accounting for 1 per cent of the 4,200 questions in this trial. These allow the witness to choose one of the lawyer's alternatives, rather than having to produce another which may be far more damaging or helpful, as the case may be. 'Why give the witness a choice?' ask the manuals. 'Pin the witness down to the answer you want' (Kestler 1982: 75).

All of that suggests 'the strategic use' of questions (Woodbury 1984). Strategic use is made of the same types of question in different ways by different questioners in different contexts of the 'single' context of a trial. Moreover, the same questioner uses the same questions differently in the two processes, and differently according to whether he is questioning a friendly or hostile witness on direct examination or on cross-examination. The study of this trial concludes:

> How questions are used by speakers in court depends partly on their pragmatic properties, partly on the rules of discourse governing different episodes of the trial, partly on the purpose of the activity that is going on, and partly on whether the participants are in an adversary or nonadversary relationship.
>
> (Woodbury 1984: 225)

For instance, wh-questions are more suited to direct examination, where the witness is to tell his story in his own words. On cross-examination, yes/no questions are more suitable because they constrain the witness to confirm or deny propositions set forth by the attorney. Here it is the attorney who tells the story in his own words, while the witness is constrained to answer yes or no.

Of particular types of yes/no questions, the prosodic (or intonated) one is especially suited to the defence, especially on cross-examination, in order to counter this same witness's story given in his own words on direct examination by his own attorney. The prosodic type of yes/no question in particular allows the attorney to word the evidence, to signal his belief about its truth, and also to indicate the expected answer. 'Witnesses' affirmations or denials transform lawyers' utterances into evidence' (Woodbury 1984: 215). If the witness has not given evidence as desired by the other party, the attorney on cross-examination may constrain him to do so by affirming/denying the evidence he proposes in the question – precisely in the way that he proposes it and none other; only for a yes/no answer and no other.

In sum, the use of questions differs between courtroom and non-courtroom contexts, between trials and non-trial courtroom contexts, between non-trial contexts and between contexts within a trial context. One and the same lawyer might use the same questions differently not only in the different proceedings but also within one and the same proceeding, such as a trial, according to whether he plays the role of prosecuting or defence attorney, and as witnesses play friendly or hostile roles, both during direct and cross-examination. In each role, during each episode, with each witness, the same lawyer may use the same set of questions differently.

As a consequence there can be no one practice of questions in the courtroom, nor any one technique that can serve to purposes in circumstances. In fact, the variety of contexts entails not just differences but polar reversals. For instance, the use of leading questions is prohibited on direct examination but permitted on cross-examination. Leading questions are unnecessary and, moreover, unhelpful during direct examination, while they are necessary and most serviceable to purpose on cross-examination.

Cross-examination

Cross-examination represents one context for questioning among the contexts within the trial context within the context of courtroom proceedings which form part of the context for 'the lawyer's use of questions'. Cross-examination is the questioning of a witness who has given testimony on direct examination. The questioning is adversarial, just as the trial process is adversarial.

The witness has testified on direct examination by the attorney for side A in the case. Now the witness is cross-examined by the attorney for side B. (The attorney for side A cross-examines the witness for side B.) The purposes of cross-examination are multiple, reducing to the same generic purpose as for direct examination: to achieve material gain for that side of the case which is conducting the questioning. (Where material gain is not likely, cross-examination is pointless. The good cross-examiner rises to say, 'No questions'.) In general, for side B, that involves either discrediting the witness's testimony for side A, or eliciting from that witness testimony favourable to side B instead of A. That means that the questions must be such as to elicit answers which will weaken the testimony already given in favour of A, and/or which will support the case being made by B.

As a rule, testimony given for A can readily be weakened under cross-questioning and A can readily be made to give testimony for B (not: 'readily give testimony'). That is for the fundamental fact that *testimony is fallible*. This fact is most difficult to appreciate, but it is easy to demonstrate.

We may not appreciate the fallibility of testimony because of our common habits of thought. We may over-esteem what people say in answer to questions, especially when they are compelled by law to answer and swear under penalty to answer truthfully. We may forget that people give untruthful answers when they are not lying, and willy-nilly give partial or slanted answers. And we, like any witness, may over-estimate the factuality of our own answers when testifying to the facts before us. People regularly do not know what they are talking about when they confidently and candidly assert what they know. Even direct eyewitness testimony is fallible. People readily witness to events that have never transpired, much less were ever seen by them. Moreover *they are sure of it*. It is facile beyond belief to supply a person with an event that he has never seen, to which he subsequently becomes a direct eyewitness. The easiest way to do so is to ask him a question about what he saw, although he did not see it. A mountain of psychological research has now demonstrated all of this to the satisfaction of everyone save the eyewitness, who alone among living souls remains convinced that he saw what he saw. (For example, see the studies by Loftus 1979.) Lastly, we may tend to presume without reflection that in a case with two sides, one side must be right (true, correct, factual) and the other wrong – all right and all wrong, one side or the other.

Against these habits of thought let us propose a variety of factors which stimulate the fallibility of testimony. These are the factors put into question on cross-examination.

First, the witness may be *lying* in his direct testimony.

Or the witness may be honestly *mistaken*, or yet *incompetent*. His testimony may be defective because of his ignorance, inability, prejudice, inaccurate perception, faulty memory, wishful thinking, and the rest. (Of course, none of *us* could be mistaken in any of these ways.)

Or the witness may be *partisan*, or otherwise biased in favour of side A or against side B. He exaggerates, minimizes, selects, colours, warps, slants, and edits his testimony – wittingly or no. *All* witnesses are prone to do so because all witnesses are known to be partisan (save for ourselves). It is an adversarial proceeding, and witnesses testify to their side of the case, which is that side calling them to testify. 'The side for which they testify always becomes their side the moment they take the witness chair, and they instinctively desire to see that side win, although they may be entirely devoid of any other interest in the case whatsoever' (Wellman 1936: 176–7). It is the exceptional person, not the everyday witness, who can testify as readily and steadily for one side as for the other, on cross-examination as on direct examination.

Finally there is the simple factor that it is through answers that a witness must give testimony. Hence the testimony depends on *the questions asked*. Remove for one illusory moment from real witnesses all trace of perjury, incompetence, mistakenness, and partisanship. Still the answers will depend on the content and phrasing of the question, and on whether the question has been asked in the first place. The court only hears that which the one side wants it to hear which the other side cannot keep it from hearing (Tierney 1971). Thus, on cross-examination, a question may be asked that was deliberately omitted on direct examination, such that the witness now gives the answer favourable to B (or damaging to A). Or the question may be put in a different way, or the same question put at a different angle, so as to weaken or to qualify the original answer, perhaps explaining it away. Damning answers can be saved by their redeeming qualities – vice-versa, too.

These factors give objectives to cross-examination. Here are various objectives (Busch 1961; Keeton 1954; Wellman 1936):

- to discredit the testimony or to discredit the witness;
- to elicit testimony that discredits unfavourable testimony or that corroborates favourable testimony, given by other witnesses;
- to compel admission of facts contrary to or inconsistent with the witness's direct testimony;
- to weaken the effect of direct testimony by impugning the witness's knowledge, memory, or ability to narrate facts consistently and correctly;
- to reveal the witness's partisanship or willingness to misrepresent (colour, slant, and so on) facts because of some relationship, friendly or hostile, with the parties or for some pecuniary interest or other improper motive;
- to impeach the witness by demonstrating that his previous statements are at variance with his direct testimony, or by showing his previous crimes or other characteristics rendering him unworthy of belief;
- to qualify the witness's story, to show its improbability, or to show that the story is coached and rehearsed;
- to elicit new matter derogatory to the witness or helpful to one's own case.

It follows as a matter of course that cross-examination varies. Multiple methods, approaches, styles, and techniques of questioning serve different purposes with different witnesses in different circumstances. Cross-examination is no one single thing, and no one instance illustrates all the things that cross-examination can be. To illustrate one instance, transcript no. 2 (Appendix) reproduces the cross-examination of a 13-year-old girl named Beverley, who has testified that her stepfather David repeatedly molested her. The attorney for David rises to cross-examine Beverley, putting to her 478 questions in this one sitting. (Were David also to testify, Beverley's attorney would cross-examine him.) The questioning is effective to purpose – namely, to the purpose of the cross-examiner in this circumstance; it is not effective to Beverley's purpose.

We will cite selected portions of Beverley's cross-examination in the course of examining various linguistic features of lawyers' questions during cross-examination. All of these features are revealed in a study of 26 cross-examinations in Australian courtrooms (Brennan and Brennan 1988). All of the cases involve children aged 6–15 being cross-examined about their testimony of sexual victimization.

These cases only make more plain and poignant certain characteristics of questioning in cross-examination everywhere. It is a peculiar use of questioning to particular purpose. So peculiar is the language of questioning that children have been shown not to understand as many as half of the questions actually put in the courtrooms: they cannot even repeat them with any recognizable sense (Brennan and Brennan 1988). So painful is the questioning that the children often enough break down in distress and tears, requiring a recess. Adult witnesses too break down. To break the witness is a common objective of the questioning. Analysis of the language of the questions reveals a dozen and more features that help us to understand two correlated contraries: the difficulty of the witness and the success of the cross-examiner. (All examples are from Brennan and Brennan 1988.)

Negation

It is well known that people find it harder to process negative than positive expressions. For one reason, people commonly first transpose the negative into the corresponding positive before determining their response, next wondering whether their response is to be expressed appropriately in positive or negative terms. Answering hundreds of 'negative' questions is trying. Lawyers use a proliferation of negatives.

1 *Insert:* 'Now you had a bruise, did you not, near one of your breasts, do you remember that?'
2 *Tag:* 'When Mr Smith asked you if you could remember anything about a towel you said you could not remember anything about a towel? The first time? Is that not right?'
3 *Preface:* 'Did not Phoebe have an accident with the horse about ten days before this,. have some bruising? Remember that?'
4 *Multiple negatives:* 'And do you remember another occasion your father, or your stepfather, asked if you were playing sport, did you not say no?' (Answer: 'I don't know.')
5 *Negative terms:* 'Do you deny...?' (Answer: 'What does deny ... ? Objection. Question allowed.')

Juxtaposition

This is the 'hop, skip and jump' approach widely recommended to cross-examiners (for example, Kestler 1982). Any witness will find it confusing and disconcerting to answer strings of questions about different topics that quickly and repeatedly change without rhyme or reason. In sexual assault cases the special feature is that topics shift from the personal to the objective. In the course of answering dozens of questions about sensitive anatomical details, the child is suddenly asked, 'Do you know Frank Murphy?' or 'Was it at Clareville or West Hampton?'

Nominalization

The question objectifies action without mentioning the agent or the recipient. The witness is to answer about personal and distressing acts he has suffered, as if he had been watching a detached event such as 'the taking down of the pants, ... the massage of the breast' and so on.

Specific and difficult vocabulary

The words are understandable only to initiates of the courtroom process or only to sophisticated adult users of the language. A good example is the juridical oddity, 'Now you told His Worship earlier...'. In fact, the witness has not told His Worship anything; he has been speaking to the lawyer. Another oddity runs, 'I suggest to you that all of this is a figment of your imagination.' Such terms appear fleetingly in the midst of rapid questioning and, while readily grasped by experienced court personnel, they pass by on their own odd way beyond a witness's grasp. None the less he must answer, as this 7-year-old had to:

> Well Peter didn't stay and you ran away, you ran away, I mean, I withdraw that. You didn't run away and Peter stay. You say Peter ran away and you stayed?

Such terms are also used on direct examination. When 13-year-old Beverley had just taken the stand, her own lawyer posed to her this quaint question (about her stepfather, the accused):

Q. Beverley, is the person before the Court, David Courtney, known to you?
A. Pardon.
Q. Do you know David Courtney?
A. Yes.

Multifaceted questions

Not only are these questions long and complicated, but also 'they consist of convoluted preambles, confused centres and rhetorical endings' (Brennan and Brennan 1988: 66):

> And did your mother ever say to you that if somebody asks you the questions that I am asking you, you should say that we didn't say what was going to be said?

Some of these questions offer multiple options; the witness must answer 'yes' or 'no' – but to which?

And you told the policeman that Daddy said 'Mum's coming'. Now that is not true is it? Do you remember telling the Court here just a few moments ago, you said 'Mum's coming'. That is true is it not?

As this question suggests, answering 'yes' *or* 'no' to any of the options in question provides the cross-examiner with yet another opportunity later on to refer to that answer and to imply still further unreliability of the witness. Then again will it be the witness who appears confused. Maybe the question is confused.

Well, I know, I understand what you say you have been talking to her today but you see what I am asking you is this, that statement suggests that you said those things that you now say are wrong to the police. Now did you say it to the police or did you not? (Answer: I don't know.)

The references may be clear in the mind of the questioner who has focused on a given item of testimony, but not clear to the witness who has given testimony on dozens of items.

Q. Well you are not sure whether you said those things to the police which are wrong?

A. Mmm.

Referral to police statement

Years before appearing in court, the witness has made a statement to the police about the assault which, in its turn, may date to years earlier. Moreover, in cases of child sexual abuse the victim typically alleges multiple assaults over time; and in any case the witness has given not one but many statements not only to police but also to other parties (counsellor, teacher, investigator, lawyer). Now on the stand the child aged 8 is questioned about some one detail of one statement which he made at age 6 about some detail of one event at age 5. The response is predictable. For example, an 8-year-old boy was asked 101 questions about his statement of the timing of an assault when he was 5 years old, ending with:

Q. So what's the position, did it happen the next day or did it happen the next year?

A. I said the next day but then I must be wrong if it said on my statement.

Q. You made a mistake?

A. Yes.

Q. A big mistake, is that right?

(Child breaks down.)

Quoting of witness's words

These are not questions about what happened, but about what was said about what happened. The lawyer will ask: 'Do you remember that you told us, or do you not remember?'

> Remember that you told us before the lunch break that ... , do you remember saying that, before lunch, do you remember or do you not? [Answer: No.]

To this point the child may have answered 500 questions and now he is being asked about his *response* to one or two of them. The child often answers 'no' or 'I don't remember'. That is actually not to say that the child did not say that and not that it is not true; yet that is not the implication, and its effect is to impugn the testimony or the witness. The witness's credibility is diminished not by ability to testify but by inability to recall the testimony. The impression is all the stronger when formed over the course of a dozen or even a hundred such answers.

Quoting of other people's words

This feature resembles the previous one. The 361st question put to 13-year-old Beverley (transcript no. 2) runs:

> Did you say that – sorry. I suggest to you that Mary – I withdraw that. If I said to you Beverley that Mary had said that you said 'If you follow what I'm doing then we'll get rid of him' what would you say?

Repetition of answer

The lawyer merely repeats the answer, to the effect of possible disbelief.

A: The family.
Q: The family?
A: Yes.

This usage is especially effective in selected cases of 'no' and in most cases of 'don't know' or 'don't remember' and the like. The lawyer has merely to repeat 'You don't know' or 'You don't remember' and then put further questions about minutiae of the event, again repeating the answers, 'You think so', 'You're not certain'. In just that way, one 15-year-old boy answered 'I can't remember' 53 times to a series of questions that began, 'Just to be clear there is no doubt in your mind...'

Beverley's cross-examiner repeatedly uses this tactic, moreover *alternating* series of 'can't remember' questions with other questions that Beverley answers confidently. The 'can't remember' series run from questions 43–8,

54–8, 70–9, 84–94, then 158–75 and again at 246–57 (transcript no. 2). It appears that such a series is introduced at each point that Beverley confidently answers to a critical fact at issue. For instance, answers 245 and 250 are 'certain', but 246 and 251 are 'I don't remember'. Thereafter 252–7:

> Q. You do not remember?
> Q. And do you think it might be 1984?
> Q. You think it was 1984?
> Q. And do you remember whether … ?
> Q. You think it was … and can you remember if … ?

The repetition is especially effective at 158–75, after one single answer at 157 asserting an assault.

> Q. Well, can you tell me how that came to pass?
> Q. Sorry?
> Q. You cannot tell me what led up to?
> Q. You cannot remember?
> Q. You cannot remember anything about it at all?
> Q. You have forgotten everything about it?
> Q. You have forgotten where it took place?
> Q. Apart from the place, there is nothing else you can remember about it?
> Q. Is that, is what I have said correct?
> Q. There is nothing else that you can remember?
> Q. Sorry, keep your voice up?
> Q. Do you remember the day of the week?
> Q. Do you remember whether it was night or day?
> Q. It was night. Do you remember if it was early at night? Or late at night?
> Q. You do not? Do you remember if you were in bed, or were you up?
> Q. You cannot remember. Do you remember who was at home?
> Q. And do you remember where you say he assaulted you? [Answer: No.]

In that one series, Beverley appears 15 times not to remember or to know critical features of an assault, while the cross-examiner adds another dozen times by his repetition.

In an earlier series where Beverley identifies the attacker as her stepfather Uncle David, the cross-examiner introduces an incredible string of 'don't remember' answers and repetitions (83–94):

> Q. And when your Uncle David came in to your room, did he turn the light on?
> Q. You do not know?
> Q. Did he close the door after him?
> Q. And that is when he came in?
> Q. And he closed the door?

Q. And you say you think so?

Q. Are you not sure?

Q. You are not sure. You usually ... ?

Q. Did you hear him come into your room?

Q. You were asleep?

Q. You do not really know?

Q. So you do not remember?

This advantage is then immediately pressed by questions that *delete Uncle David* as the attacker, all the while retailing the attack (102–6):

Q. I see, so you did not know whether it was Uncle David, did you, at that stage?

Q. So somebody came into your room?

Q. And somebody, that person, then pulled the blankets down?

Q. And that person who you do not know, who you did not know at that stage, took your nightie off?

And then (113–14):

Q. And, but you did not know who this person was?

Q. I see. But you had no idea who it was but you thought it was your Uncle David?

This effective use of questioning introduces amidst one or two facts dozens of answers that together leave the impression of unreliable testimony. By analysing these series we can appreciate that the dozens of unreliable answers attach to insignificant, even trivial, details, compared to the one or two confident answers about the terrible main event at issue. But the impression formed by the jury is just the reverse: overall uncertainty compared to one or two minor facts.

Details of multiple events

These are questions about particulars of different times, spaces, and places regarding one or two incidents – selected for trial – among a hundred assaults over some years previously. The witness, especially the child, cannot recall these details accurately, and can be expected to confound them. Questioning will arouse the confusion. An 8-year-old is asked:

But what you've told us here today that the first time when you and Peter tricked him to go upstairs and the second time is when he told you to go upstairs, now they're different aren't they?

One curious aspect is that these selected particulars may be irrelevant, yet time-space-place are popularly regarded as essential *hard facts* which no one could mistake. Hence the predictable confusion of the witness over these peripheral matters is likely to be seen by a jury as unreliability at the very core of the testimony.

Embedding

The lawyer uses certain syntactic devices to wedge in chunks of content and connections that strain the witness's reach for comprehension. For instance, most English sentences are 'right-branching', while many lawyers' questions are 'left-branching'. A 9-year-old is asked:

> Taking you back to the time when you were living in Sydney, when you first met Fred, at that time and throughout the period that Fred was living with your family, he used to work as a baker, didn't he?

Impeachment

In addition to these dozen linguistic features, cross-examiners use several typical approaches or strategies to impeach a witness. Four are particularly effective with children, in view of popular beliefs about children's dispositions.

1 *Lying*. Ask as if the child were telling lies, and question particularly one specific item as a lie. For instance, a 10-year-old is shown to have said 'big fat liar' instead of 'bull artist'. The questioning ended with:

> *Q.* See, you could be mistaken about a lot of the evidence you are giving, could you not?
> *A.* Yes.

2 *Imagination*. Ask as if the child were dreaming up the sexual assault. One 7-year-old was asked 121 questions about her propensity to make up stories, and good stories.

> *Q.* Do you get good marks at school for making up stories?
> *A.* Yes.

3 *Memory*. Ask as if the child cannot remember. After answering 530 questions on that day, an 11-year-old was asked a dozen more questions about the name of the street he lived on when one particular assault took place, trading on a mistaken name in his police statement.

> *Q.* Well, that could be something you'd remember, wouldn't it. You see the position, Donald, I suggest to you, you're not telling the truth?
> *Prosecutor:* Would Your Worship take a short adjournment, the boy's obviously distraught.

4 *Motivation*. Ask as if the child made up the story in order to punish the parent or relation whom he accuses of assault. Beverley has accused her stepfather, Uncle David. The cross-examiner questions her at length (questions 269–325) and she answers that:

she does not like David;
he once saved her life;
he cared for her epileptic fits;
he bought her uniforms for her rugby team;
she loved him at one stage;
he was strict;
he punished her for smoking;
he caught her lying;
he punished her for breaking her sister's arm in a fight;
he threatened to put her into a Home.

There followed two short questioning episodes. One asked if Beverley did not tell her sisters to follow her lead in getting rid of David; the other asked if she had not, in the period at issue, had sexual relations with her schoolmate Steve. Objection! exclaims Beverley's attorney.

Uncle David may well have assaulted Beverley. But that will not be the conclusion of hundreds of question–answers impeaching her motive and memory. Beverley could be right about the central fact. Rightly or wrongly, she answers unreliably about everything else – due, perhaps, not to the truth of the matter but to the strategy of questioning. This questioning is effective to purpose.

Preparation of questions

It may startle us to discover that the questions put by experienced and successful lawyers are prepared well in advance. That isn't what it looks like on TV. Naturally, the less accomplished lawyers are able to ask questions just as these come to mind while facing the witness. But the manuals and lore lay special stress on painstaking preparation.

'Frame your questions in advance', advises a standard textbook on trial tactics (Keeton 1954: 39). Then examine and test them for recommended brevity, simplicity, and clarity – always with the jury in mind. It is to the jury that question–answer will communicate, not to the lawyer and witness who are asking and answering. Formulate and write the questions down, advises another manual; 'at the least, review your questions 2–3 times in your head' (Brown 1987: xvi). 'Write out your questions in detail', advises a third manual (Kestler 1982: 19).

One method is to prepare a comprehensive cross-examination sheet for each witness before the trial. The exemplar is a famed cross-examiner who would start preparing this sheet the moment he was assigned to the case! The sheet first specifies the objective for the examination; then lists the facts to use as building blocks towards that goal; and finally cites a piece of evidence for each fact (Brown 1987). Another planning method begins by identifying a particular issue and asking of it the familiar questions of what? when? where? who? how? and why? Then a detailed written outline is made, combined with the prepared questions. These questions can then be rehearsed with the lawyer's own witnesses, proceeding to a mock but serious cross-examination of one's own witness. This question–answer can be taped for lawyer and witness to evaluate. After the trial, the lawyer does well to study the court transcript of his questioning (Kestler 1982).

As for actually putting the questions, no one scheme of action is useful to follow. The classic authority explains: 'One has to deal with a prodigious variety of witnesses testifying under an infinite number of differing circumstances' (Wellman 1936: 28); 'The infinite variety of witnesses one meets with in court makes it impossible to lay down any set rules applicable to all cases' (p. 148). None the less, despite this principle, other manuals pointlessly specify a multiplicity and variety of inconsistent particular techniques for questioning, each one all too specific to be useful. One manual consists of nothing but 30 maxims for cross-examination (Brown 1987). Another specifies 33 principles of questioning strategy and 44 questioning techniques and tactics (Kestler 1982). Better lessons are taught by a standard textbook (Keeton 1954), that a method of cross-examination which serves one purpose may defeat another; and by the classic treatise (Wellman 1936), which details how using one and the same questioning technique brought victory in one famous case and disaster in another.

The best practice seems to be to prepare the questions with specific purposes in mind for the particular examination of a given witness. One noted prosecutor claimed to have spent 100 hours in preparing the cross-examination of a single witness in a famous case (Brown 1987). Useful lessons can be learned by studying transcripts from notable trials and famed examiners, supplied in plenty by sources in this field (for example, Fordham 1970; Wellman 1936). These questioning episodes are fascinating and wondrously entertaining. But they can remain uninformative and uninstructive. Their study will be useful only if the lawyer takes care to perceive the purposes and circumstances in the example; otherwise the effort is fruitless, while the imitation of exemplars can be disastrous.

Another good guide to practice might be devised by turning round the advice given to witnesses. These are the things that witnesses are told to observe in order to avoid damaging their own case and being over-controlled by the examiner. The lawyer who would control and damage might take this advice for his questioning. Here are some of these items of advice to witnesses (Kestler 1982; Tierney 1971). Pause before answering. Volunteer nothing, but answer only if asked and only as asked. Qualify a yes/no answer, if possible.

Correct the assertions in the question. Incorporate the question into the answer. Stick only to what you know from your five senses. Maintain a sober, even temper, absolutely refusing to be provoked no matter how provocative the questioning. Don't respond to silence or to stares and gestures, nor to any statements; force the lawyer to ask a question before you will say anything.

Once having put the question, the lawyer is best advised to *listen to the answer*. The manuals have to insist on this commonplace. 'You cannot get the answers you need if you fail to listen. ... Not only must you listen carefully to the answer, you must press relentlessly to get the answer you want' (Kestler 1982: 147). Careful listening is critical to witness control and to appropriate sequencing of questions. Those lawyers who think up questions on their feet while the witness is answering the previous question defeat the very purpose of their questioning.

There are only two rules of thumb, and both apply to cross-examination. They are cited everywhere in the manuals and they are tellingly illustrated in trial transcripts and war stories that circulate. *'Don't ask "why?"'* A 'why' question is based on the assumption that the witness has no explanation that would strike the jury as reasonable. It opens the way to any opinion, argument, or inadmissible fact that the witness chooses to state in explanation (Keeton 1954). But this rule is subordinate to an even hoarier one: 'Never ask a question unless you already know the answer.' It is a strict rule, but 'there is the logic of much tragic experience behind it' (Busch 1961: 221). A surprise 'wrong' answer is much more effective and damaging on cross examination than on direct examination, and it alone can lose the case. It impresses the jury more, since the answer is elicited by the very side that does not want it heard. One manual generalizes the rule as: 'When in doubt, don't ask a question. When in doubt, don't cross-examine' (Brown 1987: p. 6).

Beverley's cross-examiner was not in doubt – neither about the answers nor about the gain they could achieve for his case. He put to Beverley 478 questions in a row (transcript no. 2). But according to purpose and circumstance, a cross-examination can as well be quite short. In one case, as prosecutor, Francis Wellman (1936) asked only five questions and won. In another case, as defence, all he needed to win was two. A workman who was suing the railway subsequent to an accident testified that he could no longer raise his arm above his shoulder. Wellman asked him, sympathetically, to show the jury the extreme limit to which he could extend his arm since the accident. Slowly and painfully the witness raised his arm parallel to his shoulder. 'Now show the jury how high you could get it up before the accident.' The man extended his arm all the way up above his head. From the court came peals of laughter plus yet another verdict for this exemplary courtroom questioner.

Good technique, yes. But it will work only if you prepare to question a lying and stupid witness with an uninjured shoulder. Better prepare for questioning to purpose in your circumstance.

Chapter four

Clinic questioning: psychotherapy

Psychological helping interviews – psychotherapy, counselling, psycho-analysis, psychiatry – represent more than just another field for the practice of questioning. This one field contains divergent processes describing *different contexts* for questioning. At least three different cases must be considered, describing three different styles of psychotherapy: the 'rational-emotive', the 'client-centred', and 'eclectic' therapies. (Various approaches within counselling, psychoanalysis, and psychiatry fit within these.) Hence this section, although bearing on only one field, will appear to be describing three different fields of questioning.

Use of questions

The founder of 'rational-emotive' psychotherapy (Ellis 1977) instructs therapists to 'take a Socratic questioning stance rather than making declarative sentences' (p. 192). The founder of 'client-centred' therapy (Rogers 1951) proscribes the use of questions altogether, prescribing instead declarative statements. Proponents of 'eclectic' styles of therapy (Long *et al.* 1981) actively encourage certain uses of questions at certain times, while actively discouraging others.

The use of questions in actual practice seems to follow accordingly – although next to nothing is known for sure due to lack of research on questioning in this field. Consider as examples the published transcripts of sessions from various schools of therapy (Appendix). The rational-emotive therapist (transcript no. 3) uses nothing but questions – 11 out of 12 therapist utterances are questions. The client-centred therapist (no. 4) uses everything but questions – 15 out of 15 utterances are non-questions. The eclectic therapist (no. 5) uses questions half and more of the time.

Therapy	Questions
Rational-emotive	92%
Client-centred	0
Eclectic	61

'Eclectic' therapy itself is not a single process but a variety of practices between the extremes of rational-emotive and client-centred therapies. Hence the use of questions also varies within this range.

Eclectic therapy	Questions
Unspecified	40 %
Gestalt	27
Personal-construct	13
Ego-oriented	6

Sources: studies of transcripts by Long et al. 1981 for unspecified; Stiles 1987 for Gestalt; Neimeyer 1988 for personal-construct and other 'technically eclectic' therapies; and Snyder 1963 for ego-oriented relationship therapy.

Oddly enough, clients or patients do not ask questions. Of the questions in 'personal-construct' and other technically eclectic therapy sessions (Neimeyer 1988), the overwhelming proportion is asked by the therapist:

Therapist – 90 per cent of questions
Client – 10 per cent

As a proportion of their own talk, questions account for even less on the client's part:

Therapy	Client questions (%)
Rational-emotive	0
Gestalt	0
Personal-construct	1.5
Ego-oriented	4.1
Client-centred	0

Sources: transcripts nos. 3 and 4, and studies by Stiles 1987 of Gestalt and client-centred therapy; by Neimeyer 1988 of personal-construct therapies; and Snyder 1963 of ego-oriented relationship therapy.

Whatever the school of therapy, the manuals are unanimous against answering a client's question. Not much need be said about that in view of the apparent lack of questions from clients. But the reasons are reducible to the undesirability of fostering the client's dependence on the therapist, or of his/her displacement of enquiry from self on to the therapist. The therapist can reply or respond to the question but not *answer* it. One rule of thumb is to respond to the feeling or motive of the question rather than to its content, in such a way as not to encourage further questioning of the therapist by the client (Arbuckle 1975). The general therapeutic notion is to encourage enquiry by not answering questions – the client is to explore the question and come to an answer. The therapist helps by sustaining the question. At first paradoxical, this subtle practice and its motivating purpose is of benefit both in therapy and in school settings. The contrary practice, with its confused motives and effects, only *appears* to be helpful: answering the question reassures the superiority of therapist/teacher and reconfirms the dependency of client/student. The answerer feels good but the questioner learns nothing but the same old sad lesson.

Moreover, the grounds proposed for the different uses of questioning also describe polar reversals. The persistent and vigorous use of questions by rational-emotive therapists is noted with approval, on grounds that frequent questions keep the therapist from being dominant, while helping the client to think for him/herself (Ellis 1977: 192; Wessler and Wessler 1980: 175). By contrast, the occasional question found in client-centred transcripts is footnoted with criticism, on grounds that the therapist is being directive, while blocking the client from independent exploration and expression (Curran 1952: 237–340; Rogers 1942: 272, 280). The eclectic therapist's selective use of 'facilitative' questions is encouraged because they are helpful to communication, while 'inappropriate' questions are discouraged because they inhibit it (Long *et al.* 1981: 1 *et passim*).

The case with psychotherapy is yet further differentiated, and complicated, by two other factors. Psychotherapy entails a *series* of interviews rather than a single interview (as, for example, an employment interview); and it consists of stages or *phases* rather than a unitary process. The process of therapy – 'a' case or instance of therapy – progresses through various stages over a number of interviews, as well as each interview proceeding through a number of steps or segments. Each style of therapy conceives of the stages in its own way. For example, one view of eclectic counselling and psychotherapy (Long *et al.* 1981) distinguishes three consecutive phases over a course of therapeutic treatment: exploration, integration, and action. Each phase is marked by a distinctive use of questions, each of various types. For instance, the types of questions required for the second phase are held inappropriate for use in the first phase. These phases thus describe three different *sub-contexts* for questioning within one of the three different contexts of this 'one' field of psychotherapy.

Types of questioning

The types of questions used in psychotherapy may well vary not only among the stages within any one interview or one process of therapy, but also among the different schools or approaches to therapy. For instance, rational-emotive therapists appear to use direct, closed questions bearing on intellectual cognitions ('ideas') of the client, whereas an eclectic therapist with some non-directive orientation might use indirect, open questions about feelings.

In addition to these aspects of form, function and content, a scheme of questions for marriage and family therapy (Baldwin 1987) classifies questions by time frame and membership, because these are important aspects to that process. And, by contrast to other types of questions identified for therapy, types in this scheme are derived from an empirical examination of questions actually asked by family therapists. The scheme seems useful for understanding questions used in other therapeutic approaches as well. Here are the main categories of questions, with examples from family therapy.

1   *Time frame* refers to the tense of focus in the question – past, present, future, and subjective. 'What would happen if she left?' illustrates the subjective type. The time frame of the question importantly determines the time-focus in which the therapeutic dialogue is carried out, varying among different orientations to therapy and different phases of a given therapy, as it explores past determinants of behaviour, present dynamics, or future conditions such as desired changes or anticipated consequences.

2   *Membership* refers to the number of persons in the question – single, dyad, triad, multiple. The number of persons included is important in family therapy and other therapies that bear on interactions and relationships.

3   *Form* refers to syntax of question – indirect or direct, closed or open.

(a)   *Indirect* (elsewhere also called 'embedded') – 'I wonder where the house is?'

(b)   *Direct closed*
  (i)   Yes/no: 'Will you be in town for your appointment?'
  (ii)   Tag: 'You two want to separate, is that it?'
  (iii)   Intonated: 'Your mom never expects your help?'
  (iv)   Alternative: 'Do you want to move out or stay?'

(c)   *Direct open*
  (i)   Simple: 'What ideas do you have?', 'Why did you do that?'
  (ii)   Complex: 'So what is it that happens when she cries?'

(d)   *Function*
  In this scheme, 'Function' refers to semantics of the question, primarily whether its meaning is basic or contextual information-gathering.

(a) *Basic information gathering*
    (i) Information: 'How old is your father?'
    (ii) Closed judgement: 'You like long legs?'
    (iii) Open judgement: 'What's your explanation?'

(b) *Contextual information gathering*
    (i) Relationships: 'How do you two show affection?'
    (ii) Sequence: 'Then what do you do after the blow-up?'
    (iii) Comparisons: 'Is Karen a better helper to you than Tim?'
    (iv) Hypothetical: 'Suppose she were willing to take you back, would you go?'

As with any classification, this scheme serves well to some purposes but not others. For instance, it does not reflect the frequency, pace, or sequence of therapist questions, nor their appropriateness, nor yet anything about the client's response or the effect of the questions on the process or the client. That is the general case in certain other fields as well, where little or no research is done either on (1) the actual use of questions by practitioners or (2) the effectiveness of the questions to communicative purposes, processes, or outcomes.

On the other hand, the scheme is useful for examining the questions actually used by various therapists, and for comparing this usage against the advice and claims about questioning in this field. Better still, it may inspire different schemes to be constructed that reflect different purposes and practices of questioning. And most usefully of all, this scheme helps any individual therapist to examine his/her own questioning practices, say with a tape-recorder. 'When ineffective questions occur, or the novice is baffled with the responses of the family, an analysis of the questions asked could prove very fruitful in correcting the therapist's questioning approach to the family' (Baldwin 1987: 384). That is sound advice and excellent practice for therapists of other schools and for practitioners in other fields who use questioning.

In the field of psychotherapy, various therapists systematically use continuous questioning, deliberate non-questioning, or selective questioning (and non-questioning).

Continuous questioning

The rational-emotive therapist (transcript no. 3) uses nothing but questions. 'The therapist takes a Socratic questioning stance' (Ellis 1977: 192). Once his questions have uncovered and clarified the client's irrational ideas or philosophic assumptions, 'he tries in a hard-nosed and persistent manner to annihilate them' by repeated and vigorous questioning. The transcript is used to illustrate how the therapist 'challenges the client to think about the validity of his assumptions and pushes him to think for himself instead of merely parroting rational phrases' (ibid.). He puts this series of questions:

1   Why?
2   Why?
3   Why?
4   Why?
5   What is the logic?
6   Why doesn't it?
7   Why does it not?
8   Is that possible?
9   What does that mean?

This excerpt looks like a classroom recitation. Indeed, rational-emotive sessions refer to books read and homework to do; the questioning is cognitive and factual, and the answering co-operative and agreeable. It is 'rational' therapy, resembling the view of education as correcting the wrong answers and getting the right answers about the subject-matter. The subject-matter in this style of therapy is self's ideas related to self. The therapy is called 'rational-emotive' in that self's disturbing feelings are attributed to self's disturbed ideas. The questioning is used first to display the deficient ideas that disturb feelings, next to challenge and dispute their rightness, and then to dissuade the client from the incorrect ideas and to guide him to the correct ones – to right thinking.

Probing questions are prolifically used to search out components of the client's irrational thinking, and they are persistently used until the complete irrational idea is displayed, since the eventual purpose is to change the complete idea and not some one or two components of it (Wessler and Wessler 1980: 87–9). For example:

C.:   I get very anxious in groups.
T.:   What about groups is scary?

If that doesn't work, *leading* questions are used:

C.:   I don't know, I'm just anxious in groups.
T.:   Do you think you're afraid that they won't like you?

If the client responds in terms of a feeling rather than an idea, the therapist will continue to probe for the idea behind the feeling.

C.:   If I thought they didn't like me, I'd be depressed.
T.:   Right. But remember, how you feel is determined by what you think. You're thinking some pretty depressing thoughts. What might they be?

Challenging or *disputing* questions ask the client for evidence or proof to support the stated belief. For example (pp. 113–14):

T.: So you believe that you would be worthless if you flunked out of school. Where is the evidence that you would be worthless if that happened?

C.: I would feel like I was no good.

T.: You mean that, because you would *feel* worthless, like you were no good, that would prove you were worthless?

C.: I guess so.

T.: Does that make sense – that a feeling proves an idea correct?

C.: No, it doesn't.

T.: OK, what other evidence do you have that you'd be worthless?

The motive behind this questioning is that 'we want the client to do the work of rethinking' instead of the therapist doing it, and instead of accepting the therapist's notion that an idea is irrational. 'We want the client to *understand how* that idea is irrational' (p. 114).

Having used questions to elicit the client's idea and to show incongruities or inconsistencies in it, the therapist uses further questions to help the client to discover alternatives and consider their consequences. Here is a dialogue used to suggest how the therapist might guide a client through a self-help session (pp. 174–5):

C.: I can't go bowling because I'd feel so nervous that I wouldn't be able to roll the ball toward the pins.

T.: How do you suppose you'd be getting yourself so nervous?

C.: I know that everybody would be watching me, and I'd worry that my ball would go in the gutter or only hit one or two pins.

T.: If you were by yourself, would you worry about your performance?

C.: No. As long as there wasn't anyone on any of the lanes near me.

T.: Does it sound like you're worried about people or bowling pins?

C.: People. I know that. I worry about what they are thinking. I know they'd think me an idiot if I bowled badly.

T.: Some might; some might not. We don't know. What would *you* be thinking about you?

C.: I'd think I was an idiot.

T.: And then how would you feel?

C.: Pretty nervous.

T.: Do you see any connection between what you're thinking about yourself and what you feel?

C.: Yeah.

T.: Can you describe it?

C.: Thinking that I'd be a bloody idiot gets me nervous.

T.: Sounds right to me. Can you talk yourself out of that?

C.: Poor bowling can't make me an idiot.

T.: Right. What can?

C.: (*Pause.*) Well, nothing – when you stop to think about it.

T.: I agree. What can you do to stop and think about it?
C.: I could tie a string around my finger.
T.: As long as that helps you remember. What else can you do to thoroughly impress your insight on your memory?
C.: I guess I'd better practise. Is that what you mean?
T.: Sure. When are you going to start?
C.: I guess I'll go bowling tonight.

In a claim that is the exact opposite of claims in client-centred therapy, where questions are proscribed, here 'the frequent use of questions helped to keep the therapist from being too dominant' (p. 175). The questioning is used to promote independent thinking rather than parroting of rational ideas, and to cause the client rather than the therapist to do the work of thinking.

One problem with this use of questioning is that, as far as can be seen from the transcripts, the client is not doing the thinking; more precisely, the client is not seen to be doing the thinking. Strong indications are that he is not. The same problem plagues the use of questions in classroom recitation, which is characterized by the very same use of questioning for the very same purposes. What are its effects?

No research has examined or demonstrated the thinking processes of clients under this sort of questioning. Therefore, only the questioner and the respondent can know whether or not, and to what extent, the respondent's thinking has changed, whether he himself has changed it, and whether he is convinced of the irrationality or incorrectness of his old idea and the soundness of the new idea.

That is a fundamental problem. It attaches to the very subject-matter, purpose, process, and result of this therapy – as well as of classroom recitation. Both processes aspire to use Socratic questioning. Curiously enough, the problem does not attach to Socrates' use of questioning in the Dialogues. There the participants agree never to answer a question with anything less than that which they are personally and fully convinced is true. Only on that condition can the respondent experience the inconsistency or other illogicality of his idea, and thus be in a state that can motivate the pursuit of a sounder one. Only on that condition does the question become a question for him, a problem that he feels he needs to solve. That is the only way to use questions while at the same time avoiding verbal manoeuvres and entrapments, superficial answers and agreements, falsely claimed and refuted notions (Dillon 1979, 1980).

In that spirit, the therapist who would use a 'Socratic questioning stance' as advised in rational-emotive therapy is well advised to study the Socratic Dialogues. In addition, therapists and teachers are well advised to study the secondary analyses of Socratic questioning which set forth the complex and multiple moves of the sort, 'If answer X, then question Y' (Collins and Stevens

1982; Santas 1979). But in general, Socratic questioning cannot rightly be recommended for either teachers or therapists, on grounds that the conditions for it are likely not to be present in their circumstances. The circumstances do not support it, and the participants do not have either the character or the ability to use it. Socratic questioning is beyond the capacity of most therapists and teachers, most students and clients.

Quite apart from whether the questioning is Socratic or not, the therapist who does choose to use continuous or frequent questions is best of all advised to join it with continuous evaluation of the questioning. To what extent does this use of questioning prove to serve therapeutic purpose in this circumstance? That question is difficult to answer. No matter. Every questioner is enjoined to ask and to answer it. The very asking of it is one virtue of the practitioner regardless of the questions used, and regardless of their proven effectiveness.

To change or to help to change another person's way of thinking is difficult, too. Good practice involves making the best judgements one can as to the questions that might achieve this purpose, and, having asked them, to see how far they might actually have advanced purpose. The questioning may or may not have worked as intended, but the practice of questioning will have been well grounded in either case and better grounded in the next case. To force a paraphrase from Socrates: *the unexamined question is not worth asking*.

To be sure, there are some motives and purposes to be avoided when asking questions. Most of these are not apparent at first thought. One of them describes, in the dark terms of psychoanalysis (Olinick 1954), a scotoma in the therapist: 'to employ questioning in an unconscious effort to integrate a non-therapeutic pregenital relationship with the patient' (p. 61). The questioning should assist the patient, of course. It should not intrude on his autonomy as a result, unintentioned or not, of the analyst's counter-transference and/or unresolved anxiety. All questioning is intrusive by nature. There are no two ways about that. But there are two ways about the functions that the intrusion serves, and about the person whom it serves. Questioning readily serves the questioner's personality and can variously serve for him functions of mastering, dominating, assertive, aggressive, or sadistic (Olinick 1957: 307). The analyst may ask questions in an ostensible effort to know and understand the neurosis but actually to master the patient. 'Questioning lends itself readily to hypocritical manoeuvres that are superficially professional and ethical, but may be basically contemptuous and exploitative' (ibid.).

Less darkly rendered, the questioning should rightly have a purpose that is therapeutic, and therapeutic for the client. Hence it should not have either the purpose or the effect of making the client more dependent and less responsible, more defensive and less rational, more passive and less expressive; and the rest. Nor should the questions be put out of curiosity or intellectual and conversational whim. The very best way to tell the motives and purposes of questioning is to ask self: 'What shall I do with the *answer*?' The best way to tell the functions and effects of questioning is to ask of the exchange: 'What did I and the client *do* with the answer?' Often enough, nothing at all is done with the answer, or nothing therapeutic. One should then wonder about the use of questions.

The therapist is enjoined to discipline his/her behaviour in favour of therapeutic purposes. Hence the mere occurrence of a question to the mind is no reason for asking it. Chances are that it will be an everyday question, to everyday effect. Nor should questions be asked because authorities in some field prescribe their asking – or, worse, because skilful people in other fields use such questioning. Chances are that the authorities don't know what they are talking about when it comes to questioning, and precious little about your own circumstances; while the exemplars of questioning in some other field would only stumble around in your own.

Therapists' questions must be disciplined to serve purpose in circumstance. If the purpose is not therapeutic, the question is better not asked. If the effect is not therapeutic, the question better not be asked the next time.

Deliberate non-questioning

The client-centred therapist (transcript no. 4) asks no questions at all. In their place he uses silent pauses, fillers ('hm-mm'), and declarative statements, chiefly statements that summarize, reflect, or clarify what the client has said and seems to be feeling. For example, here is a series of such statements:

5   M-hm. Like a new discovery really.
6   As though some of the most delicate aspects of you physically almost have been crushed or hurt.
7   Just can't help but feel very deeply sorry for the person that is you.
8   Sorry to see that hurt.
9   M-mm. M-hm.
10 Feel as though that bitterness is something you'd like to be rid of because it doesn't do right by you.

These statements, fillers, and pauses are *alternatives to questioning*, treated in Chapter 12. Here the point is to observe the active *non*-use of questions and the reasons given for not using them.

In manuals of client-centred therapy, even the occasional use of questions is severely criticized as foiling the therapeutic process. At two points in one transcribed session (Rogers 1942), the therapist asks a question and the footnotes score him for it.

1 Then you've simply lived with this for quite a number of years. Why is it any worse now, or why are you trying definitely to do something about it?

This question is criticized for breaking into the client's flow of feeling, and for leading to brief client responses ending in a pause (p. 272). A little further on comes 'the second blunder of the hour' (p. 280), again a question:

2 What are these negative votes?

This question is a blunder because it draws nothing but a confused and defensive answer. The client retreats into a philosophic statement that is unspecific and unrelated to his problems. 'This whole section of the interview is much less profitable because of two directive questions' (p. 280).

What should the therapist do in place of the question? In this case he is instructed (p. 280) to make the following recommended response instead of the question actually asked:

C.:   ... and will probably occur very rapidly once the ball gets rolling. But when the negatives are in power, why, of course how can the ball begin to roll?

T. (recommended):
    You feel that someone else must start the ball rolling.

T. (actual):
    What are these negative votes?

In the second interview with this same client, the therapist again asks two questions and again the footnotes fulminate:

1 What makes you feel that [resistance]?

Instead of this 'dubious' question, the commentary advises that 'a pause would probably have elicited further attitudes from the client' (p. 289). The second question could not be more mild-mannered. Not so the criticism.

2 I wondered what were some of the experiences or feelings that raised those questions in your mind?

'The evasion continues', notes the commentary; 'note how futile it is to probe for attitudes. The only response on the client's part is to retreat into the splitting of philosophical hairs' (p. 299).

In another case, 'an unsuccessful interview' with a woman client (Curran 1952), the interview goes awry because the therapist asks an occasional question. The questions are criticized for producing blocking and resistance in the client; for inducing her to be silently co-operative by waiting for further questions; and for misleading and misdirecting the interview, keeping it on a surface informational level (pp. 236–41). The therapist himself notes at these points that the interview is going nowhere; the commentary instructs the therapist as to the better response to make – a statement.

C.: Well, we were disturbed, not exactly worried. I have been sick a lot and my sister who was living with us took care of Rita [her child].
T.: What's your husband's attitude? Is he at all concerned about Rita?

This 'unconnected and prying question' about her husband led the client to a superficial discussion of her husband's attitude. The therapist should rather have responded to her feeling of disturbance and confusion about her child and her own illness, saying something like:

Your own illness and trying to do everything you could for the child and not being able to help her, made it very difficult for you.

That statement might have permitted the woman to go into her discouragement and confusion over her child, and the conflict and resentment regarding her husband (p. 241).

Again, a bit later:

C.: Well, you know, she knows a lot of words, that is she understands a lot of words but she just doesn't want to speak or at least try very hard.
T.: How do you explain that?

Here the counsellor could have used even a 'a neutrally accepting response' such as:

She doesn't really use the words she knows.

Had he used such a response, 'he probably would have obtained much more information than he received from his direct question' (p. 240). But after the question that was actually asked, the interview was back again into the confused state where the client was staring blankly at the counsellor. 'By his directing and questioning manner the counsellor produced this resistance as well as kept the interview on a superficial conversational level. Consequently, the person did not even begin to make any penetrating analysis of herself or her problems' (p. 241).

A final case is the brief counselling session with Ben, a 15-year-old (Arbuckle 1950). Ben and his younger sister Donna are wards of the state. Donna had run away and Ben bursts into the counsellor's office to tell him that Donna has just been found. But that is not the only big news in this exciting, emotional announcement. The counsellor, though, responds ineptly with several questions. Here is the main part of the session, together with some commentary on the counsellor's responses and specific recommendations (from Arbuckle 1950: 106–9) of more therapeutic responses in place of the questions.

Ben: Gosh, I hope my sister and I can both be in the same school. It was nice before. Even though we weren't in the same house I could see her every day.

C. [Counsellor]: *Isn't your sister coming back to school?*

You like your sister. (or) *I see* [reflects feeling for sister and opens up more to express; actual question ignores feelings and restricts further expression of feeling. Or '*I see*', a filler, acknowledges receptivity and encourages further talk.]

B.: No, I guess not. Mr Jones said he wouldn't take her back. You know, this is the third time she ran away.

C.: I didn't know that.

B.: She can't stay with my father either. Mrs Ross [social worker] says she can't stay with her any more. So she'll have to go some place else. I liked it when Donna was here at school with me. Did you know I have a brother, too, Mr Anderson? I never met him until last week.

C.: No, I didn't know that, Ben.

B.: He lives in Brownville. I went to visit him on Sunday. His name isn't Dunning like mine. The people he lives with have adopted him and changed his name. He's a nice fellow and is very well dressed.

C.: *What's his first name?*

B.: John.

C.: You must have had a very nice time. *Did you take Donna with you?*

You think that this brother of yours is a pretty fine fellow. [keeps open chance for Ben to express feelings about discovery of an unknown brother, or about adoption; actual question blocks exploration, and the next question closes the topic. Nothing is served by question–answer about name, and brother is not mentioned again.]

B.: No, she was visiting my father. I have so many fathers and mothers that it's hard to keep track of. My own parents were divorced when Donna and I were very small. My father is married again and has four more children. Mr Anderson, do you believe in divorce?

C.: [*pause*]

B.: I think it's bad. Look at me. My family is scattered all over. We don't even know each other. It does awful things to kids like Donna and me. Most of the kids here have their own mothers and fathers, but we don't. We don't even have a real home. We only see our real mother once in a while and we never see my father any more. Do you think that's right?

[good move – counsellor silence for a few seconds leads to satisfying experience of client answering his own question.]

C.: *Well...*

B.: I don't know how long I can stay with Mrs Brown, either. She says when Marjorie goes back to her father she doesn't think she'll keep any more children. She says she can't afford to keep even one.

[by again holding tongue instead of answering, counsellor helps client to continue to talk freely.]

C.: *Is Marjorie going home?*

B.: Yes, her father is feeling better now. *(Continues)*

You feel worried that Mrs Brown might not keep you on. [question ignores what Ben says and feels, distracts interview into intellectual chit-chat.]

'Generally, questioning is of doubtful value in the counselling situation' (Arbuckle 1950: 106). It is intellectual distraction, leading away from the emotional and the relevant, leaving little possibility of therapy (p. 73). Hence, as these examples illustrate, client-centred therapists are advised not to ask questions at all but to substitute pauses and statements that respond to the client's expression and affect.

Selective questioning

The eclectic therapist (transcript no. 5) uses questions half or more of the time, on the view that questioning is 'a primary tool in most counselling and therapy situations' (Long *et al.* 1981: vii). The use of questions is selective, on the view that some questions at some points will facilitate therapeutic communication while others will inhibit it. 'Counselling skill lies not in avoiding questions, but in their selection and timing' (p. 10).

Inappropriate use is described as too many and wrong kinds of questions. How many? Which kinds? The wrong number is not specified but the wrong kinds are: why-questions, multiple-choice and multiple questions, rhetorical, accusative, and explanatory questions. Each of these can be rephrased into more helpful forms of questions (pp. 23–7).

The appropriate use of questions is specified as varying with the phase of the therapy process – exploration, integration, and action. Questions appropriate to the third phase are inappropriate to the second, and the second to the first.

1 Exploration

Here questions are recommended to help begin the interview, to establish a facilitative environment, and to identify the client's perceived problems. They should be phrased as open questions. For example, the therapist in transcript no. 5 begins:

(a) How are you?
(b) What is it that we can do for you?
(c) Could you tell me a little bit about the situation?

Contrary to the view in client-centred therapy, questions here are held to stimulate client self-exploration and disclosure, and to help the client elaborate a point and narrate feelings (pp. 9, 29).

2 Integration

In this phase questions are said to be useful for understanding the client's patterns of behaviour, for learning of the client's attitudes, emotions, motivations, and self-concept, for focusing a confused and rambling narrative, and for leading the client through successive learning steps to arrive at understanding (pp. 10–13). Four types or uses of questions, identified by intent or putative function, are recommended in this second phase, all in open form.

(a) *Clarifying*
    i. factual information: 'How many sisters do you have?'
    ii. specific example: 'In what ways does your brother bother you?'
    iii. definition: 'What do you mean by "leave your husband"?'
(b) *Focusing*: 'Why don't we talk about what's happening at work?'
(c) *Redirecting*: 'Could we talk a little bit about something you mentioned earlier, your reactions to his feeling?'
(d) *Confronting*: 'Earlier you stated you lost your homework. Then how could you have given it to Jane to copy when you got to school?'

These questions are not appropriate at the start of therapy, only after the therapist–client relationship is well established, and happily so.

3 Action

Here solution-oriented questions are said to help the client work through the problem-solving process, helping him to decide what he wants to do. There are six types, all phrased as suggestions in question form.

(a) *select goal*: 'What would you like things to be like?'
(b) *outline options*: 'What might you do to cope with this problem?'
(c) *suggest solutions*: 'Have you thought about X?'
(d) *evaluate solutions*: 'What are the advantages and disadvantages of X?'
(e) *select action*: 'What do you want to do about your problem?'
(f) *assess action*: 'Last week we discussed your doing X. What did you do to move toward this goal?'

These questions are held to be inappropriate earlier in therapy; they are appropriate only after the problem situation has been explored and defined.

The brief session in transcript no. 5 encapsulates these phases even within a single, initial interview. Although it is to illustrate only phase one, the interview moves quickly from exploration through integration and down to selection of action. (Numbers below refer to exchanges in transcript no. 5.)

1 *Exploration*
        (a)   How are you? (1)
        (b)   What is it that we can do for you? (2)
        (c)   Could you tell me a little bit about the situation? (3)

2 *Integration*
focusing   (d)   Could you tell me a little bit more about how you feel when you do leave the room? (5)
clarifying   (e)   How do you mean? (7)
redirecting (f)   Could we back up for a second? (9)
        (g)   Could you tell me a little bit more about that? (10)
problem-defining
        (h)   Is that what you see as the overall problem? (13)

3 *Action*
select goal (i)   Well, Sally, how would you like to see this situation resolved? (14)
outline options
        (j)   How do you think you can resolve this problem? (16)
suggest solutions
        (k)   Have you thought about X? (19)

    (l) How are things between you after Y? (20)

evaluate solutions

    (m) This may be a good approach to your problem. (22)

select action (n) Does this sound like something you would like to start working on? (22)

This scheme appears to be a reasonable use of questioning. But appearances may (or may not) be deceptive. The one great deficiency is the scheme's tautological claim that facilitative questions facilitate therapy; 'in contrast, non-facilitative questions are ineffective' (p. 30). As do manuals in many other fields, this scheme confounds the intent or purpose of the question and its actual function or effect: clarifying questions clarify; stimulating questions stimulate; and so on – facilitative questions facilitate. No research has even examined, far less demonstrated, these effects of questions in therapy. To that extent it is not known what questions do to clients, or to the purposes, processes, and products of psychotherapeutic interviewing. In that respect only the therapist (and client) can know. And just here lies one virtue of this 'eclectic' manual, for, after detailing the recommended use of questions in each phase of therapy, it provides detailed check-lists for the therapist to use in *evaluating* his/her use of questions at each stage (pp. 87–8, 145–6, 202–203).

Naturally, the details of evaluation suit the details of the recommended use of questions – and these, naturally enough, will vary among differing orientations or processes of therapy. In general, though, evaluation would consist of answering three questions about one's use of questions in a therapy session:

1 What was the purpose of each of the questions?
2 Wherein was that purpose therapeutic?
3 To what observed extent did the question achieve this purpose?

Answering these questions will be more difficult than imagined, and their answers more surprising, but the important thing is to ask the questions of self's use of questions.

The usefulness of this 'eclectic' scheme of questioning in therapy lies in specifying various question-functions and in distinguishing various uses of questions at various stages of therapy. That shows the complexity of practice in this field – sub-contexts of questioning in this one, 'eclectic', context of practice in a field of other contexts (for example, rational-emotive therapy), each with its own sub-contexts of questioning. In each case, the issue would run:

What is the apt use of questioning in this context?

– that is, the apt use in this stage or phase of this process or school of therapy. And the answer must run:

That use of questioning which serves to purpose in this circumstance.

In one process or school of therapy, the continual use of questions marks therapeutic behaviour. In another process the very use of questions denotes *un*therapeutic behaviour. In still a third process of therapy, certain kinds of questions are thought to facilitate therapy and other questions to inhibit it. In several schools of therapy, certain kinds of questions are useful in given phases of the process, or of an interview, such that the particular use of questions that is appropriate in one given phase is inappropriate in another. Questioning, then, skilfully done or not, constitutes blundering and effective communication according to process of therapy and phase within process.

It is therefore pointless to recommend uses of questioning in psychotherapy. No imaginable use can serve to purpose in the various contexts of therapy – the different orientations and processes, and the different phases and steps within each. Rather, the practitioner must devise a use of questions that will serve to particular purposes in particular circumstances. That is the use which will constitute communicative skill of questioning in this field. Any other use will still be questioning but no skill. Indeed, any other use will be *mis*-communication through questioning.

Chapter five

Clinic questioning: medicine

In medical interviews, questioning is the principal device which physicians and other health professionals use to communicate with patients. Patients in turn must communicate through answers. For example, in transcripts 6A and 6B (Appendix), the doctor speaks nothing but questions. Doctors use questions to discover the patient's problem, to obtain a medical history, to examine the patient, to determine a diagnosis, to establish a course of therapy, and later to ascertain compliance, progress, and success of treatment.

Yet next to nothing is known about how doctors actually use questions, nor which usage of questioning proves most effective to purpose. Manuals and courses for health professionals offer a variety of advice but there is little research on actual questioning practices. Moreover, physicians commonly believe that questioning skills are unnecessary (Woolliscroft 1988). That is a popular everyday belief, one shared by many practitioners in various fields. But as for doctors, the way they ask questions can clearly affect both the information-gathering and therapeutic value of the interview.

The medical interview

Contrary to appearance and widespread belief, the medical interview is 'a very complex social situation' (Woolliscroft 1988). The initial interview, especially, must accomplish a variety of tasks through a number of stages in a setting defined by a whole series of changing variables. The variables, for instance, include:

1 *type of problem:* acute vs. chronic, life-threatening, or minor, and single or multiple;
2 *setting:* in-patient vs. ambulatory;
3 *physician expertise:* generally, and particularly;
4 *physician–patient relationship:* new vs. established, 'rapport' vs. distance;
5 *patient communicativeness:* talkative vs. taciturn, rambling vs. precise;
6 *meaning of the problem to the patient.*

Moreover, the purposes and perspectives of the two participants in the interview may well differ. The doctor may be trying to elicit information from the patient in order to adjudge and treat the medical problem, while the patient may be trying to determine whether he/she can trust the doctor with this information and trust his judgement about it – whether, in short, to work with this doctor (Woolliscroft 1988). And, in fact, the patient might not even have the information being sought or be willing and able to communicate it. The patient might possess only part of that information, while that information which he does offer may be unimportant for diagnosis. The patient can ignore or minimize certain experiences; lack sufficient capacity to examine or to express self adequately; or be influenced by preconceived ideas and popular opinions about disease and medicine (Lazarescu 1988).

Since question–answer is their primary mode of communication, physician and patient may be using and viewing the same question–answer in different ways, to divergent effects. They might even be trying to accomplish two quite different purposes through the same question–answer communication. This complexity of circumstance and purpose continually complicates the apt use of questions in medical interviews. But the actual use of questions by doctors is simple and straightforward. What purposes it achieves is another question.

Use of questions

The most striking aspects of questioning in medical interviews are also the most commonplace ones. The doctor speaks primarily in questions, and the patient speaks primarily in answers. That single linguistic fact entails multiple effects on communication.

The basic structural unit of communication between physician and patient is a recurrent cycle composed of three units of discourse (Mishler 1984) – invariably these speech acts by these speakers in this order, and no other:

1 Doctor's question
2 Patient's response
3 Doctor's assessment plus next question

That is precisely the cycle of teacher–student talk in classrooms: teacher question, student response, teacher evaluation plus next question. Just as with teachers in classrooms, in medical interviews the doctor speaks in questions and the questions that are spoken are spoken by the doctor; patients, like students, speak answers but little else.

For instance, in interviews conducted by 21 doctors in family practice – whether initial interviews or long-established relationships, whether old or new problems – it was the doctors who asked the questions (West 1983):

Doctor – 91% of questions
Patient – 9%

Just like students, patients do not ask questions. Indeed, the title of the study of these interviews runs, 'Ask me no questions'. Moreover, the few questions that these patients did ask were routinely marked by speech disturbances – hitches, stutters, repairs, reiterations – all showing 'the troublesomeness of asking doctors questions' (p. 98). Patients sense that they are *not to ask* questions of the doctor; and they know that they can ask their questions more easily of other medical personnel – nurses, technicians, pharmacists, even receptionists. As a practical matter, these other health professionals in the medical clinic might dispose themselves to keep open the one medically reliable avenue available to patients for expressing their questions and getting some helpful answers.

The use of questions may vary according to the stage or portion of an interview. An initial interview can be seen to proceed through three segments – medical history, examination, and conclusion (Stiles *et al.* 1979). In the first segment, the patient tells of reasons for coming to the doctor and the doctor gathers background data. Then the doctor physically examines the patient. Lastly the doctor gives a diagnosis and a plan for therapy. On the face of it, this final segment involves explanations and instructions more than questions – and, probably, more questions from the patient. Here are the observed questions in 52 interviews with adult outpatients (Stiles *et al.* 1979):

		Doctor Q	Patient Q
1	Medical history	43%	1%
2	Physical examination	22	4
3	Conclusion	13	7

The patients never ask more than a very few questions but they do ask one or two more as the interview progresses, while the doctor's use of questions diminishes. The doctor still asks a great many questions and remains the speaker who asks the questions; the patient remains the speaker who gives answers. The answers that can be given obviously depend on the type of questions asked.

Types of questions

The types of questions asked by physicians affect the kind of information they learn from the patient, as well as affecting the therapeutic value of the interview as perceived both by patient and physician. On these points physician and patient differ. So too, apparently, do the recommended and actual practices of questioning differ.

The manuals advise, for example, the use of open-ended questions and attentive silence. These are 'good'; closed questions and interruptions are 'bad'. Yet physicians seem to ask predominantly closed questions and continually interrupt the patient. Which purposes are being served by these practices?

To illustrate, here are the questions used by 31 doctors in half-hour interviews with one of three patients, each with multiple complications (Woolliscroft *et al.* 1986):

Narrow questions	87%
Biomedical questions	84%
Attentive silence	29 seconds

The overwhelming majority of questions are narrow or closed, by contrast to broad or open; and they are biomedical by contrast to psychosocial. On average, the doctors observed half a minute of attentive silence in half an hour's interview. These are the same features found in family-practice interviews (West 1983), where doctors asked 'response-constraining' questions – chains of multiple-choice or yes/no questions, with the next question overlapping the patient's last answer.

Examples of the types of questions cited are as follows:

Broad/open: What is the chest pain like?
Narrow/closed: Is the pain sharp or dull?

These examples (but not the types) also illustrate biomedical questions. *Psychosocial* questions, by contrast, would include:

Do you have friends or family to help you get to the clinic?
How active are you in community or church groups?

Physicians and patients view these questions differently. In rating the interviews, the doctors attributed to *narrow* questions the satisfying result of eliciting critical data about the patient's problem. The patients saw things otherwise. Their satisfaction related to the *broad* questions asked; and their judgement of the thoroughness of the data collected was based not on the biomedical but on the *psychosocial* questions asked. To satisfy these different perspectives would require the use of divergent questioning techniques (Woolliscroft *et al.* 1986).

The patients were satisfied by being able to tell their own story in their own words. The doctors were satisfied by asking patients to speak explicitly about this or that detail, in narrow and biomedical terms. For the one participant, the interview's success lay in the acquisition of critical biomedical data; for the other, success lay in exposing data about lifestyle, personal and environmental support systems, and the impact of the illness on one's life. Each of the different types of question and styles of questioning satisfies some purposes and not others, both of physician and patient. In general, medical questioning appears to stress one purpose or part of purpose while dismissing the other; and in so doing, it appears to achieve that purpose only partially and uncertainly.

No one but the medical practitioner him/herself can know the extent to which a given practice of questioning achieves a given purpose in that circumstance. Unfortunately, however, no one does seem to know. The common perception of physicians is that questioning skills are unnecessary (Woolliscroft 1988), so it is unlikely that they attend to their questioning, examine the practice and seek to ascertain its effect on the patient, the process, the purpose, or the desired outcome. Few research studies have examined the medical practice of questioning, even to describe it, while the even fewer studies that have investigated its effects report equivocal and inconstant evidence (as reviewed by Woolliscroft 1988). Therefore it remains for the medical practitioner to decide upon the apt use of questioning to serve purpose in circumstance. Some ways of thinking might help to decide among the possibilities.

One possibility for practice is to give greater place to the patient. That would place the patient as an actor rather than mere reactor in the medical dialogue, and as an agent rather than an object in a co-operative or mutual rather than a directive and unilateral medical task. That is fearsomely difficult, if not certainly impossible of achievement, in face of the presently defined differential in status, knowledge, and competence of the physician and patient. Yet it does not require that the patient's scientifically woeful knowledge substitute for the physician's accomplished expertise. The physician might just ask open questions as well as closed ones, psychosocial as well as biomedical, and attend a bit more to the patient's account and questions. That would require considerable skill of questioning. But the skill is easy enough to wield once the purpose and circumstance are reconceived.

For instance, the physician might seek to understand the patient not merely as 'an organism in dysfunction' but 'as a sentient, spiritual, problematic being, in a special, dramatic moment of his life' (Lazarescu 1988). The questions might elicit not only technical scientific data but also information about the patient's biography, character, personality, recent stressful life events, interests, affective condition, attitude towards disease, wish for healing or death, the identity of his being and its originality and uniqueness (Lazarescu 1988). The doctor might listen more to the patient's scientifically deficient exposition of his problem, and take it more into account, in order to understand the patient's problem as experienced and thus to enhance not only the information acquired but also the therapeutic value of both the interview and the resulting course of treatment.

Such an adjustment in practice entails of necessity an adjustment in conception – of the task, the actors, the circumstance, and the purpose. In order to appreciate these conceptual adjustments and their possible implications for practice, we will examine in detail cases of routine vs. alternative questioning practices in medical interviews (as analysed by Mishler 1984).

Routine question–answer

The routine practice of question–answer describes the 'dialectics' of medical interviews: the conflict and struggle between two different domains of meaning, the voices of the life-world and of medicine (Mishler 1984). These voices speak through the question–answer of doctor and patient. They can clearly be heard in the routine question–answer dialectics in transcripts 6A and 6B (Appendix).

The general scheme of question–answer in medical interviews depends on a view of physicians as applied-scientific collectors and analysers of technical data elicited from patients by a particular mode of questioning. In turn, the patient is seen ideally as a passive object responding to the stimuli of the doctor's questions (Mishler 1984).

The questions bear on objective, physical features that are standardized properties of all persons:

What does it look/feel like?
Where is it?
When does it happen?
How often?
How much?
What makes it better/worse?

The answers that are appropriate to give – those that will be accepted as adequate – are brief, objective, and specific, precisely in terms of the question as posed. If an answer does not refer to objective physical signs or indicators of the medical problem in medical terms, the physician will interrupt the patient, ignore the answers, and/or ask the question again. 'Patients are pressed to speak in the one voice that will be heard' (p. 139) – that is, the voice of medicine rather than the *life-world*. The voice of medicine is made to predominate through the physician's particular use of questions.

The physician's utterances are almost exclusively *questions*, and the questions are overwhelmingly *closed*-ended. To illustrate, in transcript no. 6A, 13 out of the 13 physician utterances are questions, and 13 out of 14 in transcript 6B. In both cases the first question is open-ended ('What's the problem?', 'What do you mean?'), but from the second question on nearly all are closed ('A cold you mean what – stuffy nose?', 'Does it burn over here?'). As mentioned, in 31 interviews (Woolliscroft *et al.* 1986), fully 87 per cent of the doctors' questions were closed.

The questions function to maintain the physician's control over all significant aspects of the interview: its form, content, structure, turn-taking, flow of conversation.

The doctor controls the interview through the question–answer *turn-taking* mechanism, by:

initiating each cycle of talk with a question;
assessing the adequacy of the patient's response;
closing the cycle with his assessment; and then
immediately opening the next cycle with a next question.

Other means of control include the *form* of questions asked. They are typically closed questions, restricting response: yes/no questions, polar/disjunctive questions, restricted wh-questions.

The *sequence* of questions is disconnected, one question following another without apparent reason or relation. We faithfully *presume* reason and relation but we haplessly perceive neither one. As one result, the patient cannot maintain the flow of conversation or the coherence of his/her account of the problem. Consider, for example, this series of questions (from transcript no. 6A):

3 And a cough?
4 Any fever?
5 How about your ears?
6 Now this uh cough what are you producing anything or is it a dry cough?
7 What about the nasal discharge? Any?
8 What color is it?
9 What?
10 Do you have any pressure around your eyes?
11 How do you feel?

Only the doctor knows the rhyme or reason of this sequence. We are all familiar with such series of questions but we cannot follow it, much less explain it; all we can do is go along and answer the questions as they come. If this questioning strategy were *deliberate*, it would remind us of the hop-skip-jump approach to questioning in cross-examination (for example, the questions asked of Beverley in transcript no. 2), or the sudden switches and dead ends of questioning in classroom recitation (transcript no. 1).

The doctor controls the content of the interview by specifying the *topic* of the question and also its reference or relation to other information – whatever that might be. After the patient's response, the doctor defines the relevance and appropriateness of information through questions that are selectively *inattentive* to particular features of the patient's account. Compare, for example, this patient's rich account and the doctor's question that follows (from transcript no. 6B).

D.: How long have you been drinking that heavily? [*10 vodkas a night*]

P.: Since I've been married.

D.: How long is that?

P.: *(giggle)* Four years. *(giggle)* huh Well I started out with before then I
was   drinkin beer but um I had a job and I was ya know had more
things on   my mind and ya know I like – but since I got married I been
in and out of jobs and everything so ... I – I have ta have something to
go to sleep.

D.: Hmm.

P.: I mean I'm not gonna – It's either gonna be pills or it's gonna be alcohol
... and uh alcohol seems to satisfy me more than pills do. They don't
seem to get strong enough ... pills that I have got I had – I do have
Valium but they're two milligrams ... and that's supposed to quiet me
down during the day but it doesn't.

D.: How often do you take them?

The doctor's control of conversational *flow* is also maintained by two typical moves. Either the doctor immediately takes the next turn without pause,
or he breaks into the patient's statement before it is completed, 'thus indicating that the response is complete for his purposes' (Mishler 1984: 74). The
very same feature was also observed in the family-practice interviews (West
1983), where the doctor's question followed upon the patient's answer within
one-tenth of a second. 'Through the staccato pacing of his questions and their
incursions into the patient's turns, this doctor is demonstrating that a simple
"yes" or "no" is all that he will listen to' (p. 91).

Alternative question–answer

By contrast to routine practice, 'alternative practices' characterize a medical
interview in which the voice of the life-world figures more prominently. Transcript no. 6C (Appendix) illustrates these practices. They can be seen through
an analysis of the textual, interpersonal, and ideational functions of language
in the transcript (Mishler 1984). Table 5.1 summarizes these functions.

1   Textual function

Textual function of language refers to the coherence and continuity of discourse constructed by the speakers' exchanges. Routine or standard medical
interviews are characterized especially by the physician's overwhelming use of
response-constraining questions (for example, yes/no). The physician also
typically interrupts the patient's statements. He does not acknowledge the patient's response, does not supply transitions to introduce the next question,
and does not make references in the question to the patient's response.

Table 5.1 Routine vs. alternative practices in medical interviews

Routine practices	*Alternative practices*
Textual function	
1 response-constraining questions	1 asks open-ended questions as well, that
2 interruptions of patient's statements	tie the enquiry to patient's narrative
3 lack of acknowledgement of patient's responses	2 listens with minimum interruption to patient's account, allowing full and
4 lack of transitions to introduce next question	elaborate answers to questions
5 lack of references in question to patient's responses	3 Uses patient's own terms in next questions
	4 Explicitly acknowledges patient's life-world concerns and circumstances
	5 Explains what he is going to do and ask next
Interpersonal function	
1 affective neutrality	1 reciprocity of 'voices' (medicine and life-world)
– impersonal speech	
– lack of responsiveness to patient's feelings	2 affirms common humanity vs. stressing differences; minimizes role distance vs. emphasizing separation
2 functional specificity	3 acknowledges patient's particular
3 universalistic norms	circumstances
	4 responds to patient's feelings, and expresses own feelings
Ideational function	
1 fragmentation of meaning	1 network of meaningful relations
2 abstract and schematized list of questions on unrelated topics	2 focus on and exploration of patient's experiences

Source: Mishler 1984

By contrast, the physician in transcript no. 6C asks *open*-ended questions (in addition to closed ones). For example, he starts the interview by asking, 'Now what brings you to the clinic today?' And he ends it with: 'Is there anything that we haven't talked about that's bothering you at all? Or anything like that?'

The physician *listens* to the patient's account with minimum interruption, allowing the patient to continue giving full and elaborate answers to the questions (for example, exchanges 4–6).

The physician uses the *patient's own terms* in his next question, tying the enquiry to the patient's narrative. For example:

P.:   ... cause I felt worse. ...
D.:   How did you feel worse? What was going on?
P.:   Well I was having weak spells. ...
D.:   Hm hm. How would you describe this spell?

Such questions 'help to sustain and develop the coherent meaning of the patient's account' (Mishler 1984: 153).

In routine practice, however, the patient has difficulty developing a coherent account, chiefly by reason of answering a series of specific, closed, and unrelated questions. Patients try to add surplus information or additional comment, particularly in their life-world voice, but these are routinely either interrupted or ignored by the physician. 'The patient will have to find other ways than responses to his questions to make her account more coherent and sensible' (Mishler 1984: 103).

Other alternative practices include the physician's explicit acknowledgement of the patient's life-world concerns and circumstances (for example, the 'psychosocial' exchanges 7–9), and his provision of explanations regarding what he is going to do and to ask next (such as exchange 14).

2   Interpersonal function

Interpersonal function of language refers to the speakers' social roles and relationship. The language of routine practice consists of 'affectively neutral, functionally specific, context-stripping questions and responses by physicians' (Mishler 1984: 164). It is impersonal speech, unresponsive to the patient's feelings, and translating the patient's account into technical terms and universalistic norms.

By contrast, *reciprocity of voices* – medicine and life-world – characterizes alternative practice, which is marked especially by the doctor's greater attentiveness to the patient's account of the problem. Rather than stressing the differences in their special roles in the situation, the physician affirms common humanity with the patient; he minimizes the role distance rather than emphasizing the separation. He acknowledges the patient's particular circumstances, responds to the patient's feelings, and expresses his own feelings. For example, the physician in transcript no. 6C says to the elderly, anaemic patient:

– And I dare say that alone would make me feel a little dizzy.
– Well I guess seven kids are enough to give me a headache anyway I
   don't know.
– Oh you don't look 76 at all. You're still pretty.

We can note that none of these is in form of questions. Indeed, this interview is marked by far fewer questions overall – as well as by more open rather than closed questions – than are characteristic of routine practice. Moreover, at two points in this interview the physician politely requests permission to ask questions.

- ... but you are anemic so that we have to pursue some sort of an investigation [hm hm] right now in terms of why you are anemic.... So let me just talk with you ask you a few questions to begin with about that. You – you cook for yourself?
- So you don't have any problem there. Let me ask you a few more questions though. [*P.:* Hm hm.]

That seems the reverse of routine practice, where doctors are presumed to have the right to ask questions; where patients never reject any of the questions as inappropriate, however abrupt and disconnected they may be; where few questions are ever heard from the patient; and where it is the patient who must request permission to ask. These are precisely the features of question–answer in classroom discourse as well. For example, here are a patient and a student requesting permission to ask a question, both of them using a hesitant and deprecating manner.

Patient: Would that – Yeah. I wanna ask ya – uh (dknow) – it's nothi – it's – it might be a crazy question but (...). [*Doctor:* No, go ahead.]

Student: I was just wondering, like – I dunno, this might be kinda dumb and stuff – but, OK, like *(Continues.)*

Other alternative practices by this physician include various non-question forms of response to the patient's account. For example, he uses:

(a)   *Phatics and comments*
– Oh really.
– Sure.
– Oh good I'm glad you brought them in. [*Pills*]
– Oh you don't look 76. You don't look 76 at all. You're still pretty.

(b)   *Restatements of patient's responses*
– Two weeks ago. Okay. Yeah.
– Haven't had them for years.

(c)   *Fillers*
– Hm hm.

(d)   *Self-declarations*
– And I dare say that alone would make me feel a little dizzy.
– Well I guess seven kids are enough to give me a headache anyway I don't know.

These are *alternatives to questioning.* They are suitable for use in group discussion as well as in dyadic interview, so as to avoid the features of talk entailed by the typical cycle of question–response–evaluation plus next question. Chapters 12 and 13 give an extensive treatment of the practice and research on alternatives to questioning. Here, the alternative practices in medical interviews give greater attention to the voice of the life-world, sustaining and developing the patient's coherent and meaningful narrative of the medical problem and the physician's joining in enquiry to identify and to address it.

3 Ideational function

Ideational function of language describes referential meaning, the topics and contents of discourse. Fragmentation of meaning characterizes routine medical interviews, with their abstract and schematized series of questions on unrelated topics, and the rest.

By contrast, a network of meaningful relations is developed by alternative practices, with their focus on and exploration of the patient's experiences.

In summary: 'A physician who listens, asks open-ended questions, and translates his technical understanding into the language of the life-world contrasts sharply with other physicians' (Mishler 1984: 184). That is how questioning and answering might better be done by physicians and patients.

Chapter six

Personnel interviewing

Among various types of personnel interviews, the employment screening interview presents the most interesting case to examine here. Communication in employment interviews depends on questions asked by the job applicant as well as the company recruiter. For example, one-third of the questions in transcript no. 7 are asked by the applicant.

The interview

Employment interviews involve a company interviewer or recruiter and a job applicant or candidate who meet for the first and, probably, last time, in a half-hour exchange during which each party appears to be interviewing the other. It is a task-oriented, decision-making situation in which both parties share information, analyse and evaluate the 'match' between their respective needs and goals, and come to a decision – all in one session (McComb and Jablin 1984).

Of course the main task and key decision seem to lie on the recruiter's side. Yet, while the candidate may be 'selling self' for the job, the recruiter also has to 'sell the job' to the candidate (Arvey and Campion 1982). This reciprocity of purpose and function makes for an interesting mix of communicative behaviours.

For instance, although the recruiter asks questions to find out about the applicant, the recruiter also needs to elicit questions from the applicant. The applicant's questions give clues as to which information the recruiter can best give to sell the job. At the same time, the recruiter's questions give similar clues to the applicant. Both parties need to elicit and to give information in order to achieve their respective purposes.

But the two participants are strangers. As such they experience 'high levels of relational anxiety' (McComb and Jablin 1984). Neither is likely to disclose much of self, and both are likely to be cautious and prudent in choosing the apt information to share. In addition, the applicant may understandably be somewhat tense and anxious in the situation. Applicants would be even more tense if they knew that research has shown recruiters to be more impressed by negative information than positive, and to make their decisions early in the interview, within the first four minutes or so (Arvey and Campion 1982).

The interview proceeds over a number of specified topics and may progress through segments or stages. For example, the interview in transcript no. 7 shows clearly marked segments with different topics, as announced by the interviewer at the start (exchange 4). Moreover, the devices used to communicate vary with the segment and the topic.

1 *Opening*
  (a) weather   – small talk (exchanges 1–3)
  (b) interview process   – recruiter's statement (4–5)
2 *Applicant*   – recruiter's questions (6–36)
3 *Company*   – recruiter's statements (37–41)
4 *Job*   – applicant's questions (42–57)
5 *Closing*
  (a) selection process   – recruiter's statement (58–9)
  (b) thank you/goodbye – small talk (59–61)

The opening/closing segments are marked by the recruiter's statement defining first the interview process and last the selection process. The first part of the interview is marked by the recruiter's questions about the applicant, and the last part by the applicant's questions about the job; in between are the recruiter's statements about the company. All of the recruiter's questions appear in the first part of the interview, and all of the applicant's questions in the last part. While both recruiter and applicant ask and answer questions, the recruiter also makes statements and uses in addition other techniques for obtaining information from the applicant.

The use of questions and other techniques observed in 49 employment interviews is summarized in Table 6.1 (from Babbitt and Jablin 1985; McComb and Jablin 1984; Tengler and Jablin 1983). Here this usage will be detailed and illustrated with transcript no. 7. For instance, Table 6.1 reports that, on average, the recruiters asked 21 questions and the applicants 11; hence one-third of the questions were asked by applicants. Similarly, in transcript no. 7, both parties asked questions (19 in all), with the recruiter asking two-thirds of the questions and the applicant one-third. The recruiter also used other techniques such as statements and verbal encouragers, also reported in Table 6.1 and described here in the text.

At the outset, some general characteristics of the talk are useful to note. The interview lasts 30 minutes. Of this time recruiter talk accounts for two-thirds and applicant talk for one-third. The pace is fairly quick. Table 6.1 reports that the recruiter utters, on average, 21 questions, 32 statements, and 15 verbal encouragers. Thus there must be 2–3 exchanges per minute, within which the applicant's responses must also be fitted. Moreover, the silence or latency between the two parties' utterances is far less than one second. To wit: no sooner has the recruiter asked a question than the applicant begins to answer, and no sooner is the answer given than the next question is asked. There is a lot to accomplish in this one session, on the part of both parties; and the feeling of 'time constraint' is frequently cited. Which use of questions would best serve to elicit and to give information in this situation?

Recruiter's questions and other techniques

Any individual interviewer may well use questions predominantly or even exclusively. But that does not seem to serve well to purpose. Overall, the recruiters observed in the 40 interviews use questions less than half of the time. The average frequency of recruiter questions is 21, compared to 32 statements and 15 verbal encouragers (Table 6.1).

As to the type of questions, recruiters ask somewhat more open than closed questions, and more follow-up than primary questions. A primary question introduces a new topic, and a follow-up or probing question seeks further information about it. Examples from transcript no. 7 are:

open – How did you come across your job for mortgage banking?
    (exchange 23)
closed – How long have you been at this job? (exchange 25)
primary – What would you consider as an option [to marketing]?
    (exchange 20)
follow-up – Why do you say that? (exchange 21)

The first two questions also illustrate follow-up questions, while the latter two also illustrate open questions.

Applicants respond at many times greater length to open than to closed questions, and to follow-up compared to primary questions (Table 6.1). Perhaps the applicant is cautious or uncertain as to what and how much to say about a new topic introduced by the interviewer, while the further questions give clues as to desirable content and extent. The applicant also appears to speak more as the interview progresses, since recruiters tend to use fewer closed and primary questions in later episodes. Here are the proportions in arbitrarily divided segments of the interviews studied (Tengler and Jablin 1983):

	Closed (%)	Primary (%)
1	55	47
2	35	36
3	42	39

The distribution is not too systematic, but there clearly are more closed questions and primary questions in the early part of the interview; conversely, there are more open and follow-up questions in the later parts. That is, whereas overall there are more open than closed questions (Table 6.1), in the first part of the interview there are more closed than open questions, and far more closed questions than in the later parts, which have more open than closed questions. And although overall and in each segment there are more follow-up than primary questions, in the first part of the interview there are many fewer follow-up questions than in the later segments. Since applicants respond longer to open and to follow-up questions, they may be speaking more in the later than in the earlier parts of the interview. In the later segments as well they tend to ask their own questions. Oddly enough, the recruiter may already have reached his decision by then, one way or the other, in the very first few minutes of the interview, when the applicant has spoken less than he will later, and inevitably less in response to the closed questions – 4 seconds each, on average (Table 6.1).

Table 6.1 Use of questions in employment interviews (averages for 49 half-hour interviews)

Interviewer questions and other techniques*	Usage	Response (sec)	Applicant questions†	
Questions				
Frequency	21	15	Frequency	11
Type			Placement	
			before being asked	
open	55%	31	for questions	39%
closed	45%	4	after being asked	
			for questions	61%
primary	41%	16		
follow-up	59%	23	Structure	
			closed (vs open)	62%
Other techniques			single (vs multiple)	98%
Statements	32%	–	1st person (vs not 1st)	17%
Verbal encouragers	15	6		
('hm-mm')			Purpose	
Interruptions			1 seek new information 58%	
question	1	–	job	46%
statement	3	–	interviewer	19%
			interview	19%
Silences ('latencies')			miscellany	16%
between question				
and response	0.68 sec	–	2 seek interviewer's	
between response			opinions	16%
and next question	0.65 sec	–		
			3 seek clarification	31%
			facts	73%
			opinions	27%

Sources: *McComb and Jablin 1984; Tengler and Jablin 1983;
† Babbitt and Jablin 1985

The applicant in transcript no. 7 is in a better position since all but two of this recruiter's questions are open. Unfortunately, the very second question is a closed one. The situation at this juncture is odd and the use of the question strange – not to mention the content of the question. The recruiter had just put to the applicant the broadest, most open question possible (exchange 4), inviting a discursive response about the applicant's circumstances:

background: 'where you were born and where you've lived';
education: 'how you decided where to go to school and what you majored in';
miscellany: 'anything else that's important – work experience, travel, or hobbies or whatever.'

'Story of my life?' the applicant says; 'right.' He then launches into the story of his life but gets no further than a dozen words into it when the recruiter's question hits him:

A.:   I grew up in Omaha and I went all through high school there and I was active in high school.
R.:   How large is Omaha?

We may ask: what is the purpose served by this question – open or closed? What is done with the answer? These are good evaluative questions for the practitioner to ask about his use of questions.

Having asked this question about Omaha's size, the recruiter recovers nicely by not putting a next question but by instead making good and effective use of other, non-questioning techniques. The use is effective because the applicant begins speaking at greater and greater length, disclosing richer details relevant to his work experience, motives, and aspirations. The use is good because the recruiter systematically follows each of the questions with a series of non-question techniques in response to the developing exposition of the applicant. Each question (Q) initiates an exchange that continues through the recruiter's use of phatics (P), comments or statements (S), and fillers (F). His favourite phatics are 'really' and 'right', and his favourite filler or verbal encourager is 'um-hm, uh-huh'. Here are the types of recruiter utterances in the exchanges initiated by a question, beginning with the question about Omaha's size.

6	Q – P – S – P
10	Q – P – F
14	Q – P
16	Q – F – F – P
20	Q – P + Q – F
23	Q – F
25	Q – S – F – P – P
30	Q
31	Q
32	Q – P – F – F – P

With questions 31–2 we are back to Omaha's size, this time with some possible purpose related to the applicant's sense of real-estate marketing, which is the job position being discussed.

After developing this final answer through a series of non-question techniques, the recruiter terminates the episode of questioning about the applicant. He turns to the next episode of telling the applicant about the company (exchanges 39–41). He has done with asking questions. The remaining questions are all asked by the applicant.

In all, this recruiter asked a dozen questions and used a dozen each of non-question techniques – statements, phatics, and fillers. Overall, the recruiters in the 49 interviews studied asked an average of 21 questions and used 32 statements and 15 fillers or verbal encouragers (Table 6.1). Hence, questions accounted for about one-fourth of recruiter utterances. Recruiters used questions, and questions of different types, selectively, conjoining alternative, non-questioning techniques to obtain information from the applicant. Applicants too needed to obtain information, and they too asked questions.

Applicant questions

Applicant questions also serve purposes of the employment interview, and not only the applicant's purpose of obtaining information. Recruiters can find these questions useful for knowing just what kind of information to provide an applicant to whom they are trying to sell the job; and useful for assessing some of the applicant's motives, thinking, and personality dynamics (for example, assertiveness). Indeed, applicant questions are ranked third among twelve factors influencing a recruiter's decision. Moreover, the questions serve the general communication purpose of balancing the distribution of status and power or authority in the two-party exchange (Babbitt and Jablin 1985). Hence it is useful for the recruiter to elicit applicant questions, just as it is useful for the applicant to ask them.

The recruiter in transcript no. 7 provides for applicant questions at the start of the interview (exchange 4) while setting out the stages and topics: ' … and answer any questions you have about the company after that'. Towards the end he invites the questions: 'And have you come up with any questions?' (exchange 42). The applicant asks six questions in all, representing one-third of all questions in this interview. Two-thirds of them are asked after the recruiter specifically invites questions. That is the overall case with the 49 interviews studied (Table 6.1). Applicant questions represented one-third of all questions asked, and two-thirds of the applicants' questions were asked after the recruiter invited them. Waiting until being asked for questions, instead of asking them earlier or throughout the interview as they occur, may be one further indicator of the finding that applicants tend to play fairly passive roles, or at least play it safe (McComb and Jablin 1984).

Indeed, in transcript no. 7, the two questions asked by the applicant before being invited to ask still occur in the last third of the interview, and just before the invitation to ask (exchanges 37, 40). Moreover, they are truncated or minimal questions in response to the interviewer's extensive exposition about the company. All the substantive questions from the applicant follow the invitation to ask, and they crowd at the interview's end (exchanges 49, 53, 54–5, 57). Even when invited to ask, this applicant at first demurred: 'Yeah, well just maybe comments' (exchange 42). Not until seven exchanges later did he start to ask questions. In the meantime the recruiter wisely refrained from asking questions, and continued to use non-questioning responses. Had he recurred to questioning, the applicant would never have begun to ask questions.

Overall, applicants ask single rather than multiple questions at a time, closed in form and *not* phrased in the first person (Table 6.1). Only a very few are phrased in the first person. For example, all of the applicant's questions in transcript no. 7 are closed (and all of the recruiter's questions are open). Only one of the applicant's questions is in the first person (exchange 49), and it is given hesitant, confused expression:

> Do you like ... you know say I went out and got accounts ... is that ... would I have time to do that ... or do you advertise or...?
>
> (exchange 49)

The next question drops the first person and all personal phrasing. It appears to address relative job positions and supervisory lines, and in those terms it is answered. But this impersonal question actually is a veiled enquiry about personal advancement:

> ah this is the position of an assistant researcher. Is there just, like one, main researcher? or –
>
> (exchange 53)

Then the key question is asked, as if out of mere curiosity, phrased about 'a person' doing good work and 'that person' being promoted:

> Well just out of, like say three years a person was a good hard worker. [Um hm.] And did good, do you see that person in one of those main positions definitely or –?
>
> (exchanges 54–5)

As to the purpose of applicant questions, overall half of them in the 49 interviews (Table 6.1) sought information about a topic not previously discussed in the interview. Of these, about half concerned the job and half the interviewer or interview process – equal concerns of the applicant. For example:

What type of promotion policy is there?
What is your job title?
When will you let me know about the outcome?

The remaining questions sought to clarify some statement of the recruiter, especially about factual matters rather than matters of opinion; and some few questions sought the interviewer's opinions – 'What do *you* think of the promotion policy?'

In short, the questions stay close to the facts, especially about the job, and away from opinions, especially the interviewer's; and they are carefully phrased so as not to implicate the person who is asking them. That is indeed to play it safe: no presumption that the job will be mine or that I am involved in the things being asked about.

Effect of questions

To what extent does this use of questions achieve purposes in the employment interview? In general there seems no publicly known answer. Although the tradition of research on employment interviews dates to before the First World War, very little research has examined the communication aspects of these interviews, and barely a handful of studies have examined the questions used – there is only one study on applicant questions; while even fewer findings are available, or even looked for, on the relationship between questions and interview outcomes (see reviews of research by Arvey and Campion 1982; Jablin and McComb 1984).

One small finding is that the applicant's satisfaction with the interview is related to (1) talking more and (2) getting information from the recruiter. These two sources of satisfaction can cancel each other out in the process. Moreover, the applicant might be satisfied but the recruiter might not; while applicant satisfaction implies nothing about his being actually selected and proved as a desirable employee. In general, no distinction worth mentioning has been observed for the use of questions in interviews which result in a second interview offer or not. Clearly enough, that outcome – intermediate as it is – must depend on other factors attaching to the parties involved, the information obtained, and conditions apart from the interview itself (for example, the marketplace). For instance, information of whatever sort and extent obtained by either party by means of any kind of questioning can lead to a decision to accept or reject; and either decision can be desirable or not.

What is more, research has repeatedly shown that the entire process of employment interviewing is uncertainly related to the desirable selection and recruitment of the employee. It is used none the less. And the relation of that outcome to the questions used remains undefined as well as unexamined, save indirectly. Hence questions may serve, to the extent that they do, in facilitating (or not) processes of communication and information-sharing within the interview itself. Then, from these processes, selection, agreement, and employment of desirable candidates may uncertainly result.

Thus the interview itself has its own purposes, apart from outcome, as it were. Its purposes and functions are several and reciprocal: for recruiter and applicant to elicit and to get information that they can use to evaluate their respective needs and goals. All that the recruiter can do is to keep in mind his purposes for the interview and their reciprocity with the applicant's purposes. Bearing these purposes in mind, he must continually examine the purpose of the questions he asks (and elicits), and what he shall do with the answers. Then he will know whether – and how and when – to ask about the size of Omaha.

Chapter seven

Criminal interrogation

'Interrogation' is another word for questioning. It is also the name for a fascinating field of practice with a distinctive use of questioning. We are all familiar with this questioning from films, novels, TV, and other fantastic depictions
of interrogation. The realities are quite another thing. Nearly everything
about interrogation as it is practised surprises and instructs us about effective
uses of questioning. As we enter the setting of interrogation, we find ourselves
a long way from Hollywood.

Circumstance of interrogation

Compared to all other question–answer practices, interrogation shows the
greatest variability, if not complexity, of circumstance. For instance, the interrogation can take place anywhere – at home, at work, in a restaurant, in an
automobile, on the scene, and so on. It can last for any amount of time, short
or long. There are numerous types of respondents – witnesses and suspects
varying in co-operativeness and guilt; and multiple variables describing each
respondent – personality, informedness, communicativeness, and so forth.
But whereas the circumstance may be tricky, the use of questioning is straightforward. Through all the variability two factors are constant: the purpose of
the questioning and the qualities of the questioner.

The purpose of interrogation is *to obtain factual, truthful information* about
some criminal matter at issue. Everything follows from this purpose. The
principle runs: the respondent has the information that the interrogator
needs; therefore, the questioning must be such as to obtain that information
and to avoid inhibiting its full disclosure.

To appreciate the implications of this purpose and principle, all we need do
is to reflect for a moment on the style of questioning that would be likely to
encourage disclosure, and on those techniques of questioning that would
surely discourage and even prevent it. The best guide on this point is not to
think of self putting questions but *being questioned*. Or put yourself in the respondent's place. How does that respondent feel encouraged to co-operate by

telling, truly and fully, what he knows? What is the inducement to reveal sensitive information that implicates self or others in situations fraught with punitive consequences? Individuals who answer opinion polls regularly *lie* about voting, holding a library card, drinking beer, and donating to charity; persons under investigation are supposed to tell the truth about rape, mayhem, and murder. Which use of questions will get their full and true answer?

That is the problem of the interrogator, the same as for any practitioner: how to use questioning *to serve purpose in this circumstance?*

Interrogators are found in private, commercial, and law enforcement sectors. They may be a private investigator, an insurance examiner, corporate security officer, personnel director, police detective, or legal official. All have the same purpose – to obtain true, factual information; and all face the same practical problem – how to do it. All have come up with similar solutions, repeated in their manuals and textbooks from whatever sector: private (Buckwalter 1983), commercial (Royal and Schutt 1976), and law enforcement (Inbau and Reid 1962; Taylor 1984; Yeschke 1987).

All manuals agree on the characteristics that must be exhibited by the interrogator if the respondent is to give the needed information. These are 'winsome qualities' such as: genuineness, truthfulness, trustworthiness, concern, courtesy, tact, reasonableness, gentleness, sympathy, understanding, kindness, and considerateness (Buckwalter 1983). They include sincerity, impartiality, and empathy (Royal and Schutt 1976). They are counsellors' qualities such as congruence, positive acceptance, and empathic understanding; compassion, respect, receptivity, gratitude, warmth, and friendliness; sincere concern about the respondent as a human being (Yeschke 1987). Above all, the interrogator must be *non-judgemental*. These 'human relations' qualities need to be exhibited in the questioning even when the respondent is assuredly guilty and personally repugnant to the interrogator, and even more so when the respondent provokes, attacks, withdraws, and otherwise frustrates the interrogator.

In addition to these human relations qualities, the interrogator must be *patient and persistent* in the questioning. 'Patient and persistent' questioning characterizes, and nearly defines, interrogation.

We may wonder why on earth an interrogator should have to exhibit these qualities. The answer is easy. First, we must bear in mind the purpose: to obtain full and true information from the respondent. Then, in relation to purpose, we can rotate this question of qualities to examine its positive and negative sides.

Positive: Which qualities of questioning will win co-operation and get truthful information?
– those just cited.

Negative: What are the effects of the opposite qualities?
- not getting co-operation and information.

In short, the opposite qualities frustrate purpose. Hence interrogators are told to *avoid* rapid-fire questions, abrupt questions, trap questions, trick questions; questions that accuse, hurt, embarrass, or anger the respondent. These are self-defeating. Interrogators are to *avoid* using third-degree, threatening, Gestapo, and tough-guy tactics, whether mental or physical. These work only if the interrogator does not care about the answers to the questions; interrogators who do use them are uninformed and incompetent (Royal and Schutt 1976; Yeschke 1987). Their effect is to make the respondent resentful, fearful, anxious, defensive, reluctant, hostile; all preventing his disclosure of the information that the interrogator needs.

For the same reason the interrogator must especially be non-judgemental and non-adversarial, quite like a counsellor. His purpose is to obtain truthful information; others may later make the judgements and engage in fights. For the respondent to give that information, he must believe that the interrogator is 'neither prosecutor, judge, nor jury' (Royal and Schutt 1976). Rather, the investigator takes 'the disarming approach of a fellow human being who is only seeking the truth of the matter' (Buckwalter 1983: 195). The respondent should be able to believe that

1 the investigator's only motivation is the search for truth;
2 he/she will treat him as the respondent would like to be treated;
3 the investigator will be considerate, courteous, and understanding;
4 he will not judge, condemn, censure, ridicule, or belittle the respondent;
5 the investigator will deal fairly with the information he is given; and that
6 the investigator is a sincere, dependable person, worthy of his trust.

(Buckwalter 1983).

These are *presumptions of questioning* in interrogation. They are not social niceties; they are necessities for achieving purpose, especially in this circumstance. The circumstance of interrogation is such that, even with these presumptions in force, it is hard to obtain the information. The 'good' qualities help but are not sufficient, for most respondents are not inclined to answer the questions truthfully and fully.

Those who act as respondents in interrogations (and investigative interviews) may be witnesses, victims, litigants, complainants, informants, suspects; or accomplice, friend, accessory, associate, relative, acquaintance, or neighbour of any of these. *All* of these types – *any of these people* – may intentionally conceal or withhold information, or otherwise not provide it as desired.

Respondents may conveniently be grouped as either witnesses or suspects. A witness is anyone who has knowledge or information related to the matter under investigation. A suspect may be viewed according to the certainty (or not) of guilt. Suspects and witnesses are typed by degree of co-operation: compliant, reluctant, hostile. Whether these people are to be interviewed or interrogated depends in part upon their attitude to the questioning – the willing are interviewed, the unwilling interrogated. In any case the respondent may still withhold, distort, or conceal information, wittingly or not. How can that be?

People have very good reasons for not telling what they know. There are good reasons too why some people who do tell or who are willing to tell still do not provide the information. Dozens of reasons can be listed (Buckwalter 1983; Royal and Schutt 1976).

Let us take first the more obvious case of the suspect who is guilty. What are his reasons not to give full, truthful answers? He may be afraid of punishment, or fear the effect that his involvement may have on his family, friends, and employer. These are reasonable fears. He may be concerned about the welfare or opinion of co-conspirators or accomplices; fearful of being or being called a 'squealer' or a 'rat'; fearful of retaliation to himself or family. These too are persuasive grounds for not telling the truth. He may have deep concern to protect his reputation, to maintain his character, to get future employment, to save face. How reasonable. He may not want to surrender the fruits of the crime, to make restitution or to return goods that he has. Who would?

As for witnesses, why might the ordinary witness not tell what he knows? He too may be reluctant to get involved and reluctant to involve others. Good neighbour. He may be a co-conspirator or otherwise involved in some other, undetected crime. Best be prudent. The witness may not at all be impressed with the importance of co-operating with the investigator or his agency. Plenty of people are anti-police and anti-establishment. Lots of people cheer the robbers and not the cops. Good for them. The witness may have been threatened. Better watch out. The time or place of questioning may interfere. Too busy, too noisy. The witness may dislike inconvenience or risk, including appearing in court. What for?

Even the friendly and co-operative witness, free of all other factors, may not give desired information because:

1 He has faulty perception.
2 He does not remember.
3 He does not quite understand what is wanted.
4 He judges the information that he does possess as too irrelevant or too
   unimportant to mention, at least right now.
5 He finds the subject-matter far too distasteful, frightening, or taboo to talk
   about.
6 He is unknowingly prejudiced, or otherwise biased in selecting and
   colouring information. ('He drinks! Why, no wonder he ran over that

little girl.' He's a good/bad X, he does/doesn't do Y, he's one/not one of those Z. Of course he is guilty/innocent. What can I say/omit to prove it?)

As these items should suggest, none of the good reasons that people have for not providing the information actually causes them *not to provide information*. They may well tell you what they perceive, remember, understand, possess and know – agreeably telling you all that you ask about. None of it is true. You are better off with a tight-lipped, low-life, blood-stained gang member who fights you all the way; when he does answer he is probably giving you the rock-bottom, hard-core, god-awful facts of the matter. The other respondents, good people all, may be telling you all the non-factual misinformation they truly have. Worse still, they may agreeably be telling you what you seem to want to know. They confirm your view without your even realizing it. Then you think you have discovered the facts about this matter. But nothing has been discovered, certainly no facts.

All of these factors, for all witnesses and suspects, call into serious question our facile assumptions that all we need to do is *to ask:* that people will grant us our right to ask and accept their obligation to answer; that they have the answer, will give the answer, and will give a truthful answer. There may be a strategic fault running through our thinking about questions. We may be putting far too much emphasis on questions and on our act of putting them; much wiser to emphasize respondents and their act of answering. Attention to answers will give us good clues about questions.

For any respondent, two final good reasons not to give the information are:

1 the manner of questioning (see qualities cited earlier);
2 the failure to be asked the question.

These are tactical errors of the questioner, nothing to do with the respondent. The investigator's failure to ask is one of the surprisingly common reasons that respondents don't give the information in answer. This factor suggests the prudence of preparing the questions beforehand. The other factors suggest further good features of questioning in interrogation.

Features of questioning

Signal features of questioning in interrogation relate to the manner of asking, the importance of answering, and the essential behaviour of listening.

The most important aspects of communication in this field attach to answering. That is what the interrogator is after – to enhance answering, and answers full and true. Everything about interrogation has designs on the answering process. Consequently, on the interrogator's side, the important practices are questioning *and listening*, with listening the more important part of communication. 'Both the questioning and the listening have to be patient and persistent' (Buckwalter 1983: 193).

Oddly enough, some interrogators ask questions but do not listen to the answers. Others do not even wait for the answer, or for the full answer, but rush ahead with a further question. Still others occupy the answer time with thinking up the next question, or objections to and criticisms of the answer. These behaviours are common enough that the manuals have to put repeated emphasis on the act of listening to answers. (Such emphasis is also repeatedly given in other fields too, such as education, law, and survey interviewing.) This is due in part to the great preoccupation with questions, with little thought given to what the questions are being asked for – the answers.

On this score as on others, *patience* is the key characteristic of an effective investigator. No rush, no hurry, no pressure – no time limit.

There is in fact no time limit to an interrogation. No time limit is set for the process overall, and to some extent no limit for the individual questions. Rapid-fire questions are appropriate in courtroom cross-examination but they have no place in interrogation, even in the cross-examining phase of questioning. Questions should be asked at a moderate tempo, if not slowly. The investigator is advised to pause after every question, not bunching up the questions; and again after the answer, not rushing in with the next question (Buckwalter 1983). The proper exchange runs:

1 Question + pause.
2 Answer + pause.

The pause before and after allows the respondent *all the time it will take* to start and to finish his answer. The patient interrogator gives the respondent ample time to understand and to ponder the question, to make 'a complete and considered reply', and to make it 'as completely as he will' (Buckwalter 1983: 87, 201).

The patient interrogator is not in a hurry for any reason. He will wait –in contented expectancy we may say – until the full and true information emerges. He will allow plenty of room for free association, long and meandering answers. No matter, the respondent must disclose what he knows – which is what the interrogator does *not* know and needs to know. That is why he is asking the questions! And these answers contain valuable bits and pieces: clues as to the respondent's attitudes and openness, as well as his and others' involvement; and they may reveal unexpected details about the crime (or some other crime). The interrogator is careful not to judge as 'wandering' an answer that is not giving the *anticipated* information (Royal and Schutt 1976).

Furthermore, at any point the interrogator gladly gives the respondent every opportunity to retract or to restate any answer, to qualify and to correct it, to rethink and to clarify it, adding, subtracting, and changing whatever he will. He lets the respondent save face. He sees no point in playing the game of

'I gotcha!' (Yeschke 1987). Consequently, the interrogator patiently listens to the respondent's full answer, with no interruptions and no pouncing questions. Attending to the answer, he notes the problems with it – evasiveness, falsehood, contradiction, and so on; and later persistently questions to resolve them. For the moment, however, his behaviour is patient listening. That is to discipline behaviour in favour of purpose in this circumstance.

Patience and persistence characterize the questioning as well. The tone is conversational, as if the interrogation were a perfectly normal occurrence, with the interrogator questioning in 'a smooth, lower toned, relaxed voice' (Buckwalter 1983: 198). Loud, abusive, accusatory, third-degree questioning frustrates purpose, even in cross-examining the respondent. 'Never raise your voice' (Royal and Schutt 1976: 69).

Important questions are asked in the same manner as unimportant ones.

> Tough questions are never to be asked in a mean manner. The interrogator understands they are difficult, delicate, or distressing questions for the suspect to answer, and he asks them firmly and persistently, but also gently and with consideration for the feelings of the suspect.
>
> (Buckwalter 1983: 199–200)

The interrogator should expect a suspect to resist and moreover he should give that impression while indicating respect for the suspect's viewpoint. The correct attitude is that it is completely normal and perfectly natural for the suspect to show many forms and degrees of defensiveness and resistance. That attitude comes from considering the suspect's plight, not the interrogator's personal judgemental stance. Indeed, the contrary attitude – namely, that suspects ought not to resist – 'alone is the greatest single impediment that causes poor interrogation' (Royal and Schutt 1976: 220). Judgemental, non-accepting, and unsympathetic attitudes – not to mention hostile, accusatory, and condemnatory ones – will have as their *natural consequences* on the respondent to make it ever harder for him to open up and reveal what he knows to this questioner. And that is just what this questioner is asking questions for!

A local newspaper illustrates a case in point, under the headline: 'Detective solves old murder case by listening.' The unsuspected murderer, who was actually in gaol at the (mistakenly established) time of death, liked to chat with a particular detective during his frequent arrests for trifling matters, because this detective listened to him. The scene of the interrogation that broke the case was the neighbourhood grocery store where they often met while shopping. 'He just liked talking to me, I guess,' ventured the modest hero. 'I didn't treat him like dirt.' Indeed, it is pointless for an interrogator to treat any respondent like dirt. 'Even if dealing with so called rag bottom, puke, scum bag type interviewees, select a positive accepting attitude' (Yeschke 1987: 41). This attitude is quite easy to adopt once you put yourself in the suspect's place. That is a lousy position to be in. To whom would you reveal yourself? And why? Now retaking your rightful and comfortable place as the interrogator, you ask self: which sort of questioning behaviour will win this suspect's co-operation and full disclosure? The title of one manual puts it as *The Gentle Art of Interrogation* (Royal and Schutt 1976).

Disciplined behaviour in favour of purpose in this circumstance requires patient and persistent questioning and listening, with emphasis on the answering. These features inform the interrogator's behaviour as he enters upon the scheme of questioning, if he has any hope of getting the answers.

Scheme of questioning

Below is an outline of the questioning in investigative interviews and interrogations, with various phases and kinds of questioning to be used as the interrogator judges appropriate to the particular respondent and circumstance. Between an opening and closing phase there is (1) free narrative, (2) direct questioning, (3) cross-questioning, and (4) review questioning. After the session the interrogator asks of self evaluation questions; before the session he prepares the questions to be asked.

Preparation

Yet another surprise about interrogation is that the questions are prepared beforehand, and actually *written down on paper*. One would not guess as much by watching successful interrogators at work. Just so. Only the more experienced and successful interrogators go to such lengths as to prepare and write out their questions; the others just walk in and start asking questions as they occur to mind, then they stop asking when the questions stop occurring.

The manuals on interrogation repeatedly take care to stress the need to prepare questions beforehand. 'The interviewer must put time and effort into preparing key questions', probably spending more time in preparing them than in actually asking them (Buckwalter 1983: 13, 45). 'There is nothing hit or miss about good interviews' (p. 12). Without careful preparation the interviewer is sure to conduct a hit-and-miss session, asking everyday questions and failing to ask the important questions. So, the respondent gives everyday answers and does not give important answers. As an aside, we should realize that most people have learned far more about skilful answering than skilful questioning. For one thing, they spend most of their life, from childhood onward, *answering* questions put to them by all manner of adults, officials, and Indian chiefs everywhere. Nowhere do they learn to ask questions. Thus, the interrogator has to study and prepare his questions, otherwise they will be nothing more than everyday off-the-cuff questions put in the conceit that he knows what to ask and how to ask. 'Spontaneous inquiries that are adequate for the ordinary curiosities of life are quite inefficient for getting concealed information or for breaking down general and subjective fears. Successful interviewing and interrogation needs the support of proper planning and preparation' (Royal and Schutt 1976: 63).

As part of the preparation, the investigator asks, 'Why should I question this person?' He makes a formal outline of the matter under investigation, and then asks self some general questions that will help in preparing the specific questions to be asked. For example :

What are the elements of the crime?
What questions must be asked to cover those elements and the subject's involvement in them?
What specific information should I expect the subject to have?
What mystery still hangs over the criminal act that the subject can clear up?

(Buckwalter 1983)

Next the investigator makes a list of all the *topics* to be covered, then he makes a check-list of all the *key questions* to be asked about each topic. As an example, consider the investigator who is preparing to question the victim in a fraud case (from Buckwalter 1983). The first topic on the prepared list happens to be a description of all persons involved in the fraud with whom the victim had contact. The key questions prepared and formulated in writing on this one topic are:

1 How many persons contacted you about the alleged fraudulent transactions?
2 What names did they go by?
3 What specific identification did they show you?
4 Who else did you meet in your dealing with them?
5 Can you describe the person who seemed to be the principal operator?

'The worst fault of inexperienced interviewers is failure to ask all the important questions. This is why the pre-interview checklist of key questions is necessary' (p. 43).

As a side point, some questions must also probe the amount of fraud or money lost by the victim. Victims may lie about the amount lost. Suspects may tell the true amount. *Any* respondent may withhold, conceal, or distort information. That much, at least, the interrogator knows about the people he is questioning, so he is modest about presuming too much of the injured victim and the impartial witness, not less of the guilty suspect. 'Who cares what they are?!' describes the useful attitude of the interrogator who is trying to find out the true facts of the matter instead of busying himself apportioning blame and meting out judgements every time he meets someone who knows something. And the fact is, he doesn't know what they know. That is why he is questioning them.

Another aspect to preparation responds to the general question, 'What is unknown?' After identifying the topics, the investigator writes down all the unknown details in the form of questions arranged in some appropriate order. As an example (from Royal and Schutt 1976), here are the unknown-detail questions for an interview or interrogation of a company chauffeur who has reported the theft of the car while he was delivering mail in another building.

1   What is the identity of the driver?
2   What is the description and identification of the car?
3   When did the theft take place?
4   Where did it take place?
5   Why was he at that place?
6   How did the theft occur?
7   What precautions had been taken to prevent the theft?
8   Who else has any personal knowledge of the theft?
9   How, when, to whom was the theft reported?
10 Who can verify any parts of the driver's story?
11 Does the driver have any suspicions regarding the perpetrator of the theft?
12 What is the driver's background, driving record?
13 Was any property of value in the car when it was taken?
14 What else does the driver know of significance?

Often enough, unknown details remain unknown because the question about them is never asked.

The list of prepared questions can even be tucked into the investigator's notebook or pocket. During the questioning he may not have to ask some of them, nor in that order, because of the respondent's developing revelations. But if the information is not forthcoming he will know the questions that none the less must be asked. He will also be asking many other questions specifying, surrounding, and extending these prepared questions as the interview progresses. But he will not forget to ask the key questions about the necessary topics.

Without these prepared questions the interrogation will proceed according to what the respondent wishes or happens to say. That is, the respondent will be controlling the interrogation because the interrogator doesn't know the questions that need to be asked. Even worse, the respondent may start asking questions. Never must the interrogator permit these questions. They signal that he has lost control of the interrogation, and with it, all hope of getting answers. Now he is giving answers. The prepared questions prove essential, not just useful, in all further phases of interrogation – the free narrative, direct questioning, cross-questioning, and review questioning.

Opening

At the start no questions are asked about the crime. The point of questioning in this brief opening phase is to get the respondent talking – to get him *answering*. The questions should be easy to answer, phrased perhaps for yes/no, about anything of interest to the respondent. Only a few exchanges are needed.

If the respondent appears co-operative, the next phase of questioning begins. If he/she is unco-operative, the next phase is skipped and the interrogator begins direct questioning.

Free narrative question

The investigator names the matter and asks the respondent to tell what he knows about it, what he has seen or heard, and so forth. 'What do you know about X?' Instead of asking 'Do you know what happened?' it is better to insert something like: 'I understand you were present when the liquor was delivered, so would you please describe what happened?'

The investigator asks no further questions and makes no interruptions. He *listens*, attending to the account as the respondent freely constructs it. Of course, once the respondent has exhausted his account the investigator may ask another free narrative question if suitable, again listening without interruption and other questions. 'Hmm. And then what happened?'

Direct questioning

After the respondent has freely told, in his own words and style, what he is willing to tell about the matter, he is asked direct questions about specific items. In the other case, where no free narrative question has been asked because the respondent is unco-operative, the direct questioning begins in a particular way which will be noted later.

Direct questions bear first on items in the respondent's narrative, then on other items not mentioned but relevant to the case. Here is where the investigator makes good use of (1) his listening during the narrative answer, and (2) his prepared list of questions. By the end of this phase he should have asked *all* the key questions on his list, and all the unknown-detail questions.

In addressing these items – whether mentioned or unmentioned in the narrative – the interviewer can ask questions in two useful sequences, moving from (1) the general to the specific, and from (2) the known to the unknown. For example, transcript no. 8B (Appendix) shows a series of twelve questions used to turn the general answer 'A long way down the freeway' into the specific 'A little less than half mile away'. Transcript no. 8C shows the start of a long series of questions going from the known factor of the city where the suspect was arrested to the unknown details (how, when, with whom, and so on) lying between that faraway city and the suspect's home city.

These same uses of questioning apply also to the second case, where to begin with, no free narrative question is asked. With unco-operative respondents, whether witness or suspect, the interrogator starts with direct questioning. But the direct questioning itself starts in a somewhat different manner compared to the first case, while it further differs according to degree of unco-operativeness and certainty of guilt. In general, these are small differences in technique. Everything else remains the same – the purpose, principle, sequences, and qualities of questioning.

With suspects whose *guilt is certain*, the interrogator begins right away with a question about the crime or issue. 'Do you know', he asks:

– how the fire in the warehouse in 9th Street started?
– who robbed the bank in Vine Street?
– where the kidnap victim is buried?

With luck the arrogant suspect will answer 'I did it!' and the rest of the interrogation is just clearing up the details. If he answers, 'I didn't do it', the rest is still detail. In fact, it is more effective to question about some small detail, for respondents more easily answer to a detail than admitting the whole thing. Thus, for example (Inbau and Reid 1962), the interrogator does not ask, 'You did kill her, Joe, didn't you? Tell us all about it', but:

How did you meet her?
Where did you get the gun?
When did you do it?
What is the reason, Joe?

With one detail established, the questions merely pursue, patiently and persistently, every last one of the other details until the whole story is known.

As these examples may have suggested, interrogators find it useful *not* to use precise words in their questions: murder, confession, forger, dope addict, embezzlement. In the above examples, Joe is not asked: 'When did you kill her?' but 'When did you do it?' Interrogators do not ask about rape, assault, murder, butchery, and theft but sex, hit, shoot, cut, and take. An actual rapist will admit having sex with a woman but deny raping her. Tough guys fight somebody, not assault and batter them. Murderers don't kill, they shoot or do it. Thieves take but don't steal. As a matter of fact, in interrogation with polygraphy or lie-detector machines, a thief will probably show *no deceptive response* to the 'steal' question. 'Did you steal the shoes?' – 'No,' he mildly answers. Shown the police report to the contrary, the suspect exclaims: 'Man, that's not stealin', that's takin'!' (Taylor 1984: 218).

In general, suspects are 'involved' rather than guilty. They more readily respond to 'Tell the truth' than to 'Confess your crime.'

The questions are also phrased on the assumption that the suspect is involved. Interrogators do not ask 'did/are you?' but 'how/when did you?' Not 'Do you know Joe Jones?' but 'Where does he live?' Not 'Were you with him that night?' but 'How long did you stay with him?' A related technique uses a false assumption to test the truthfulness of an answer, or an alibi. For example, the suspect maintains that he was far from the scene of the crime – walking down by the lake, attending a concert at the Hollywood Bowl. The interrogator asks:

Did you see the excitement when they saved that kid from drowning?
How did you react when the violin player fell over from a heart attack?

A lying suspect may reply, 'Yeah, that was really something.' A truthful one will say, 'No, you must be thinking of some other time – there was no drowning/heart attack while I was there.' Note that the suspect who had lied may yet be innocent, while the truthful one may yet be guilty. 'Who cares what they are?' retorts the seasoned interrogator; 'I'm trying to figure out the true facts, not the right judgement.' Maybe he's right for this job.

Questions with false assumptions are used to probe truthfulness of answer, not to establish guilt. The interrogator rightly intends to obtain full, factual, and truthful information, not to judge the respondent. The same applies to using 'fake-evidence' questions. 'Is there any reason, Joe, why

– the dirt on your shoes matches the dirt outside the window?
– your fingerprints should be on the safe?

A guilty or otherwise involved suspect (accomplice, accessory) has worried about covering his tracks and may respond with excuses and explanations. An innocent suspect has not speculated and will respond, 'No, because I wasn't there/didn't do it.'

Great care must be taken while using any unknown, false, or fake assumptions. The interrogator must be quite sure of the subject's involvement and have a solid body of facts surrounding the detail in question, because the respondent is assuredly assessing the interrogator at the same time as the interrogator is assessing the respondent. If the respondent suspects that he is being tricked or bluffed or used, the interrogation will suffer. Rather, these assumptions 'afford the respondent an opportunity to lie if he sees fit to do so' and they are to be used only when the fact of the matter is known to the interrogator (Inbau and Reid 1962: 97). 'Why did you take twice your share of the money?' may help the respondent indignantly to reveal his truthful share; from then on the interrogation merely pursues the other details leading to a confession or admission of guilt.

With suspects whose *guilt is uncertain* – as also with witnesses who are unco-operative or hostile – the initial questions in this direct questioning phase of interrogation do *not* address the crime itself, nor any detail of it. The interrogator first asks: 'Do you know why you're here?'

Of suspect: Do you know why you're a suspect in this case?
Of witness: Do you know why you are being questioned about this crime?

The answers help to determine the further questions to ask. Also the answers may reveal details that are unknown and unsuspected on the interrogator's part – not to mention information about some other, undetected crime! 'Yeah', the respondent answers (suspect or witness) 'you think I had something to do with the jewel heist last night.' On the other hand, the interrogator must always keep in mind that even the hard-bitten career criminal in front of him may have nothing to do with the crime at issue, and may truly answer 'No' to any question about it.

As for the detailed questions, they initially bear not on details of the crime but details about the suspect.

Where were you?
What were you doing?
Have you ever thought about doing something like this before?
Why does some of the evidence point to you?

Thereafter further direct questions follow.

In both cases the respondent has been *unco-operative*, whether a witness or a suspect, and whether certainly or uncertainly guilty. He is concealing or otherwise withholding information. Accordingly, the interrogator directly asks questions about the concealing or withholding:

Is there something you know that you are reluctant to tell me?
Why should you not want to tell me about it?

Leading questions are useful for the 'why?' part of the probe. For example, instead of asking 'How do you justify withholding valuable information?', the interrogator may ask (Buckwalter 1983; Royal and Schutt 1976):

If you're not involved in this, I'm sure you would not mind discussing it with me, would you?
I'm sure you want the true facts to be known, don't you?
Surely you have no objection to discussing the truth about this occurrence, do you?
You would want to make known any information you have that would help the truth to be known [justice to be done], wouldn't you?
I need your help. You are in a position to help me get at the truth of this matter. You are going to help me, aren't you?

Direct questions are used, patiently and persistently, first to discover the reason for the withholding, next to remove or to minimize it, and then to probe the concealed item itself – just as in questioning any other item.

At any point during interrogation, when the respondent evades or refuses to answer, the interrogator repeats the question. He does not challenge the respondent, nor accuse him of lack of co-operation. Rather, he appears to overlook the answer; and he re-words, restates, tries again – patiently and persistently re-wording and re-asking the question (Yeschke 1987). As a rule, patient and persistent questioning eventuates in the answers being given. That is interrogation.

An excellent general example of questioning appears in transcript no. 8A, describing an investigation into the matter of $2,000 missing from a company safe. The example illustrates the preparing of questions that must be asked; the sequence of questions; the various types covering all aspects of the matter and the respondent's involvement; and questions that serve to indicate truthful or evasive replies. For instance, these questions are answered differently by employees (from Yeschke 1987).

Q11 – 'How about gaol for that person?' The innocent employee may answer, 'I should think so! Whatever the law says.' The deceptive or involved employee may answer, 'Well, that seems a little harsh; I can't really say, it depends.'

Q12 – 'What kind of person do you think did this thing?'
Deceptive: 'Needed money, under pressure, having problems.'
Truthful: 'A thief! Not very nice. Not caring about the rest of us going through all this.'

Q13 – 'Why do you think someone would take that money?'
Truthful: 'No reason. It's not worth it.'
Deceptive: 'The security is bad around here.'

Q14, 16 –
'Is there any reason for (a) anyone to say they think you took the money? (b) your fingerprints to be on the safe?
Truthful: 'No, I don't think so, I didn't take it.'
Deceptive: Explanations.

Cross-questioning

Here the answers to this point are checked and verified, tested against one another and the information that the interrogator knows from other sources. The questions probe the evasive and vague answers, conflicting or inconsistent ones, apparently false or inaccurate ones. The respondent is asked to repeat his statements, by means of questions asked in different ways and in no special order.

At the end, the interrogator takes care to ask: 'Anything I've missed? Any information I've not asked for?'

Review questions

These are re-examination questions. The interrogator arranges the material in some appropriate order, restates each point, and then stops, asking, 'Is that correct?'

At the end, the interrogator takes care to ask two final questions:

1 What else? (do you know)
2 Who else? (might know anything)

These are asked on the assumption that there will be more information, if only the questions are asked.

> When all questions seem to have been asked and answered, continue to believe more information is available. Ask: 'What else is there that you can tell me about what happened?' 'What else should I know about this matter?' ... Avoid using 'Is there anything else?' Always assume there is more data available. Within reason, ask: 'What else is there?' Persistence pays!
>
> (Yeschke 1987: 102–3)

In the case of a *suspect*, the interrogator asks 'what else?' in two formal ways:

1 Do you have any additional information or evidence that should be added to your statement to complete it?
2 Do you feel you have been granted ample time and fair opportunity to freely express yourself and to present all the information you have and want to present regarding the matters we have discussed?

(Buckwalter 1983)

Closing

No questioning, but alert *listening* is the interrogator's behaviour when the notebook is closed and people are leaving with their thank you/goodbye. At this time respondents feel that the questioning is over and they may be less guarded or otherwise more relaxed. Their small talk often includes a casual fact or unguarded statement that contains new or different information. For instance, the friendly and co-operative respondent may in passing remark on something that he considered too trivial or irrelevant to produce during the official situation. Or he may just remember or take thought of something. He may also answer a question that the investigator had not thought of, or prepared but forgot to ask.

Evaluation

Just as beforehand he had carefully prepared the questions for the asking, the investigator lastly reflects on the questions asked and the answers given.

About the respondent, he questions the content and manner of the answers. What did he say? How did he say it? What did he imply? What did he not say? What do his evasions and omissions imply? To what extent are the facts, if any, mixed with fancy and opinion? Did he withhold any key information that he appears to possess? If so, is that information vital to determine some fact or issue in the case?

About himself, he asks: did I ask, or otherwise check, all the questions prepared for the asking? Did the questioning achieve its purpose? How well did I use questions? Which use of questions would better serve to purpose in similar circumstance?

'Scientific' interrogation

Interrogation may also make use of technical aids such as hypnosis, polygraphy, narcoanalysis ('truth serum'), voice stress analysis, and pupillometrics (Taylor 1984). The techniques and qualities of questioning a person with these aids are generally the same as without them.

One peculiar procedure in both hypnosis and polygraphy is that all questions that are to be asked are first previewed and agreed upon by interrogator and respondent. They are *rehearsed*. There are no surprise questions, no ambiguous words, and no question that cannot be answered.

In polygraphy, eight to twelve questions are usually asked, of three types: the irrelevant or neutral question; the relevant or crime question; the control question. The control question is 'a known or assumed lie' (Taylor 1984: 229) in the same category as the crime question, yet not touching upon it. For example: 'Prior to this year, did you ever want to see anyone seriously hurt?' 'Did you ever take anything of value from an employer?' The irrelevant or neutral questions concern the respondent's age, name, and so forth. The crime question is the one critical question, such as: 'On 5 June at 8th and Vine Streets did you rob the Safeway store?' The comparison of physiological reaction to the control and crime questions serves to detect deceptiveness. The reactions spring from fear of detection in a lie, not from conscience or guilt.

Of great interest is the fact that *innocent* as well as guilty respondents feel threatened by these questions and will lie. The innocent feel most threatened by the control question, the guilty by the crime question. Both will lie in an effort to impress the examiner and to avoid admitting anti-social behaviour. As noted, in any interrogation both the innocent and the guilty suspect, and witnesses as well, will also conceal or withhold information.

Two kinds of 'tension test' are useful in particular circumstances (Taylor 1984: 223–8). In the 'peak of tension' test a graduated series of questions probes the respondent's knowledge of, say, the weapon used in a murder. The weapon in fact was a gun of .270 calibre. There are five questions, all beginning with 'Do you know whether Eugene Samuels was killed with a – ?' and the various calibres of gun are cited: .243, .357, .270, .30–.30, and .30–.06. The innocent person will respond to each question with the same level of physiological activity. But the guilty person's registered anxiety will increase with each question until reaching the .270 question, when it will peak; thereafter the stress is over and the recorded activity diminishes. For this test it is of course necessary that the investigator know the true answer beforehand; and it is necessary that the true answer not be put in first or last place in the questioning. Respondents will react to any question put in first/last place (p. 224).

The second test, 'searching peak', is used to discover an item of *unknown* information – that is, known only to the guilty person – such as the location of a missing weapon, body, or money. For example, in one case a woman had disappeared. Her husband was later arrested on an unrelated charge, and agreed to answer questions about his wife. The first test revealed that he was deceptive in denying that he had killed his wife and that he did not know where the body was. He was then given two searching-peak tests. First, he was asked five questions beginning with, 'Is your wife's body in the – ?' and citing various locations: river, railway tracks, potato field, farm buildings, house. He peaked on farm buildings. Then he was asked five questions beginning with, 'Is your wife buried by the – ?' and citing: house, barn, shed, shop, silo. He peaked on shed, where police did then go and find the body.

All other aspects of scientific interrogation are similar to those in any other circumstance. For instance, the 'scientific' interrogator also must be honest, equal, objective, and non-judgemental in attitude. The questions ask about 'kill' and 'sex' instead of 'murder' and 'rape' and about one detail at a time – rob, shoot, instead of rob and shoot. The pace of questioning is slow. Interrogating hypnotists allow lag time for the response to occur; polygraphers wait 15–20 seconds after the response before putting the next question. Otherwise, 'significant data may be lost' (Taylor 1984: 42, 212). Respondents attempt to discern the interrogator's beliefs and adapt their answers accordingly, whether truthfully or no. They give distorted answers about behaviours seen as socially desirable. The questioning threatens the innocent, the guilty, and ordinary people alike. The interrogator has to discriminate between guilt and deception, as when it is the victim who lies about the large sum of money that the guilty suspect truthfully denies having stolen.

Finally, even in an interrogation using polygraphy, most results depend on the skill of the interrogator, just as they do in any other interrogation. As one expert testified in court, regarding even pathological liars: 'They couldn't beat the machine, but they could beat the examiner' (Taylor 1984: 286).

Chapter eight

Journalistic interviewing

Journalists are renowned for asking questions, and public officials are renowned for evading them. Journalists are also known to keep on asking until they get the answers, which they then tell to the rest of us who presumably want to know. For example, the journalist in transcript no. 9 (Appendix) keeps asking the same question while the politician keeps answering some other question.

Whether for print or broadcast, 'media' interviews, especially news interviews, constitute a peculiar case with peculiar uses of question–answer as a communicative device. For instance, journalists ask questions to elicit information on behalf of an audience outside of the interview. Respondents give answers to that same audience. They are asking and answering questions but they are not exchanging information, at least with one another, while neither seems even to be communicating with the other.

Circumstance of the interview

The circumstance of the interview varies with the journalistic medium that reports it. A newspaper reporter preparing a news article, for example, may conduct multiple interviews with the same respondent, or with many respondents, each of which may last up to an hour or two. The information thereby obtained is then composed and edited to appear as a narrative; the questions do not appear, nor do the answers in their character as answer. By contrast, a TV news reporter conducts a single interview with one (or two or three) respondents. Even if composed and edited for later broadcast, the report does not constitute a narrative, for both the questions and the answers are seen/heard. Moreover, there are not many of them.

Broadcast news interviews are short. The average duration of 111 BBC Radio 4 interviews studied (Jucker 1986) is four minutes, with five or six question–answer exchanges. The pace is quick, with less than half a second elapsing between speaker turns: 0.46 sec between question and answer; 0.41 sec between answer and next question (Jucker 1986: 42). Despite the press of time and the quickness of response on both sides, the respondent speaks 3–4 times more than the interviewer. (By contrast, for example, in classroom recitation the students speak less than the teacher.)

Partly because of the time factor, and partly because of the medium, with its overhearing audience, public figures can control the exchange with deliberate effect. Because there is time for only a few questions, the respondent can give the answers he wants or even sets out to give, no matter what the questions (Metzler 1977). Experienced respondents know the timing of the news segment and try to maintain the floor at the end, in the minute before the next segment must begin; in that way they prevent further questions and can instead make a speech, in the guise of a last answer, favouring their viewpoint (Jucker 1986).

The main difference between print and broadcast interviews is a theatrical feature. The broadcast interview 'is not merely a matter of getting information. It is, rather, a *performance*' (Metzler 1977: 100). The speakers appear to be playing well-defined roles, and playing to the audience. To all appearances journalist and respondent are not, themselves, asking and answering questions, and thus not communicating, at least with each other.

Although they are exchanging question and answer, journalist and respondent may readily appear (especially in broadcast interviews) not to be talking to each other. They do not make evaluative or even receptive comments about the other's speech. Journalists are advised to *avoid* even the minimal 'uh-huh' and 'hmmm' (Metzler 1977). The questions seem to be asked on behalf of some party other than the questioner, and the answers seem to be given by some party other than the respondent, and to some party other than the questioner.

Even in the case where the journalist does not know the information in question, he does not appear to be asking questions of his own self, out of his own cognition as it were. The standard of 'objectivity' applies to such an extent that the journalist not only does not express agreement or disagreement with the answer, but seemingly no opinion at all of his own. As if the question were not something that he himself is asking but passing along from someone else, he raises points from various sources, poses disputable propositions, and quotes criticisms from other people, such that the question appears to represent their viewpoint rather than his. Whatever his own view, the journalist poses questions that are routinely 'sceptical' or counter to the respondent's position. He asks in favour of 'the public's right to know'. The public is never presumed to want to know anything agreeable to the respondent.

In answering, the respondent seems to address that public – for example, the audience of a broadcast interview. But he, no more than the journalist, appears to be speaking of and for himself. Rather he represents some point of view, and on that very score he has been selected or proffered as respondent in this interview. Whatever his own opinion, he speaks in a role: political or governmental official, union leader, corporate executive, topical expert, social commentator, or other public figure. Ordinarily, that role enjoins the respondent to present and to maintain and defend an action, programme, message, image, or other 'information' which the public presumably wants to know through the questions put by the journalist presumably on its behalf.

In short, the news interview dissociates question and questioner, answer and respondent, speaker and hearer, knowledge and knower. Through this strange exchange information passes, with question and answer making their curious way around each other. For, on the whole, the responses do not answer the questions. Which purposes, then, and whose, are served by the questions and answers?

Use of questions and answers

The interview begins with a question. In one characteristic sequence, the second question presses the first again, in a move following an answer found inadequate. In another sequence, the second question develops the first, extending the topic and answer. In a third sequence, the second question raises another aspect of the topic, or another topic. (News interviews typically bear on one topic only.) The latter two sequences indicate either that the original answer is found adequate or not worth following up.

The first sequence is most characteristic, partly because of journalists' preference for probing questions, and partly because of public figures' habit of giving evasive answers. But it all goes back to the first question asked.

On the whole, the question can probably not be answered with any satisfaction, at least not by the respondent and not in the terms asked. Hence there inevitably follows a 'follow-up' question. Likely enough, the answer will again be inadequate, and another follow-up question will be asked, with sharper pointedness of questioning and correspondingly wider vagueness of answering. Journalists may well like, and be expected, to ask sceptical and challenging, even adversarial, questions. But as the questions get harder, the answers only get softer.

One characteristic use of questions which sustains such a sequence is to 'threaten the face' of the respondent or that which he is representing. The phrase connotes nothing malicious, nor passionate. It refers to a common concept in analysis of conversations, interactions, and other face-to-face behaviour wherein people are thought to make efforts to present themselves in a positive light (for any number of social and psychological reasons, including their own image of self). Respondents in news interviews are public figures. They represent other public actors and agencies, such as a business or political party. 'For many interviewees it can be a matter of political or financial survival that their positive face is sustained or enhanced throughout the interview' (Jucker 1986: 71). Thus the candidate who yet again places fifth with

3 per cent of the vote smilingly proclaims a great win because last time he only got 2 per cent.

In that spirit, public figures respond to the questions put, even if they are unwilling actually to answer them. In a similar spirit, the journalist poses questions that threaten the public face they are putting on. It is indeed a performance, before a large and live audience.

Analysis of BBC radio news interviews (Jucker 1986: 77–94) reveals 13 ways in which the questions can threaten the respondents' face. These 13 are listed in a hierarchy of threat, such that successive items presuppose the prior ones, making the threat more serious or pronounced. That is, a later-listed question does not even ask about, but *presupposes*, the earlier items. Hence in answering the question the respondent might, to save face, also have to dispute the answers that he did *not* give (to questions that were not asked) but which are assumed in the question. Moreover, the questions are put in such a way as to conduce to a 'yes' answer (a 'no' will strike oddly), while a 'yes' will always damage the respondent's face.

1 *Commit yourself to do something*
Q. Is it in your mind to invite Mr Tchernenko to come to Britain?
A. Well no no don't jump too quickly, one of the things if you're doing diplomacy is you must go stage by stage. *(Continues.)*

2 *State your opinion*
Q. Well do you think we might get better value for money out of the coal industry if it were in private hands or partly in private hands?
A. Well I'm not talking, I'm not talking about denationalizing the coal industry. *(Continues.)*

3 *Confirm your [demeaning] opinion*
Q. You're surely not suggesting as you've seemed to in the course of that answer, that strikes and unions are responsible for three million plus unemployed in this country?
A. No, Mr C., I am *not* suggesting ... *(Continues.)*

4 *Accept discrepancy between your opinion and your actions*
Q. Is there not a certain irony though in the fact that you'll be talking with Mr Botha on the very day when the England rugby team will be playing in South Africa contrary to the provisions of the agreement and very much against the wishes of this Government?
A. I see no irony about it at all. *(Continues.)*

5 *Accept discrepancy between your opinion and reality*
Q. If we were to tie a polygraph on to you you wouldn't, it wouldn't go 'ping' when you were saying things like that?

A. No I'm happy to be able to refute that proposition, there is absolutely nothing that I'm hiding. *(Continues.)*

6 *Accept that the reason for performing the action is demeaning*

Q. ... the point that Mr Q. made, that this is all politically motivated, that the idea is merely to save money. *(Continues.)*

A. No I can't accept that because ... and money is by no means the objective.

Q. But it does save money, does it not?

A. No it doesn't indeed, *no*, because in fact ... *(Continues.)*

7 *State that the action is demeaning*

Q. But you say you wished you destroyed the document, that is virtually thwarting the law, is it not? – which is almost as bad.

A. No it's, that's – that's something that happens before the legal process begins and that's what I'm talking about. *(Continues.)*

8 *Confirm the demeaning action*

Q. Now, first of all that criticism I quoted from Mr Q. that these patients had actually had to be readmitted to hospital because they weren't being treated properly, what do you say to that?

A. These patients are being discharged as part of an overall national, and regional policy, which says, on the best, expert advice ... *(Continues.)*

9 *Take responsibility for the demeaning action*

Q. But don't you accept, Mr J., that it's the duty of your prison school to make sure that pupils don't stray and commit robberies or thefts?

A. I admit it totally and we have this as our duty number one. *(Continues.)*

10 *Justify the demeaning action*

Q. Well then why did you go about it in this, some people have said 1984 way, suddenly people find that they are being denied what they thought until now was a freedom – on their desk a piece of paper saying, from now on you can't join the trade union, full stop.

A. I think when you actually take a decision of this kind... *(Continues.)*

11 *Take action against something [the demeaning]*

Q. What are you going to do about the canker of long-term youth unemployment that is the unemployment is the thing that bothers more people in this country than anything else, all the excitement set to one side.

A. But Mr C. that's exactly what I've been saying. *(Continues.)*

12 *State that the other's face is demeaning*

Q. But the Government hired Mr M. at a considerable salary in order to put the industry right. If they're now rejecting his advice, is that not foolish?

A. I think they've taken a lot of his advice and I think he's done a very good job ... I think to some extent the Government just simply has a regional policy to consider as well and I suppose it's doing that at the moment.

13 *State that your face is demeaning*

Q. Prime Minister, you say that Britain is historically and by inclination pro-American but do you accept that there is a majority of people in this country which is opposed to this deployment of cruise missiles here?

A. I see a number of polls but, I do not think, when it comes to the majority of people, that the issues have ever been fully and properly explained before the thing is put in polls.

Two-thirds of the 111 interviews studied (Jucker 1986) contained no questions more serious in threat than nos. 1 and 2. Of the remaining threats, the more serious strategies are less frequent: 30 per cent were nos. 9–13, 70 per cent were nos. 3–8. Thus these interviews are not aggressively hostile or mean-spirited, and in any event the 'threats' are commonplace to this interview situation. None the less, the frequencies are such that, since the average interview has only five questions, two-thirds of the questions must count as threats to the respondent's face. That is one characteristic feature of questioning in broadcast news interviews. Note then the answers.

In the 13 examples listed, only one respondent answers 'yes'. Four respondents answer 'no'. Eight answer neither yes/no but something else that is a response but is *not an answer* to the question (including response no. 1). For instance, they answer another question than the question asked (nos. 8, 11). The respondent in no. 12 will neither say 'yes' and thereby criticise the Government, nor will he say 'no' and thereby criticise the expert cited. Rather than answering 'yes' or 'no', and *instead of answering* at all, he denies the assumption stated in the question. That reveals to us another use of questions – to *tell* something rather than to ask after it.

Any question contains and supplies information, at the same time as eliciting and requesting information. For instance, a question assumes something in the asking. That is a presupposition of the question. But in news interviews, the questions are weighted down with information *in addition* to the silent or implicit 'pre-' suppositions: any number of assertions, attributions, and propositions are stated in the question itself. That suggests that the questions are used to express opinions, to give new information, to put forward ideas, and generally to convey messages to the overhearing audience (Harris 1989).

Moreover, the information stated in the question is either disputable or it is counter to the respondent's point of view. Never is it agreeable. The journalist inserts that information in order to make the exchange interesting and challenging – one thinks of saying, entertaining – as well as 'informative'. He also phrases the question for a yes/no answer, not some other phrasing for some other possible answers. In twelve BBC radio interviews studied (Harris

1989), fully 75 per cent of the questions are polar or disjunctive – yes/no, either/or. The effect of inserting the disputable information combined with the yes/no phrasing is that the respondent cannot, first of all, answer 'yes' and second can hardly answer at all. That is because he must also dispute and/or deny the various assertions and presuppositions, while accepting certain others that are indisputable or undeniable, at least in the eyes of those who count – the audience. That is, the respondent cannot with finesse both challenge and answer the question. No wonder the respondent commonly answers another question than the one posed. If he challenges the question he will be heard to evade the question, by force of not giving a direct answer, yes/no; and he may well lose credibility or 'face'. If he answers it yes/no he is accepting the disputable or even hostile presupposition, and thus loses credibility and face (Harris 1989). (Any answer, whether yes *or* no, confirms the presupposition of a question.) From the features that are *built into the question by the journalist*, there ensue a predictably inadequate answer and an inevitable follow-up question pressing the point and demonstrating the respondent's evasiveness or other inadequacy.

All of these points can be seen clearly in this single question put to a cabinet minister:

> Well now – when Mr Heseltine protested at the cabinet meeting on December the 12th – over the fact that Mrs Thatcher had cancelled this meeting on December 13th – he raised a protest – which as you know – in his resignation statement he said – he said wasn't recorded in the cabinet minutes – and now he's gone back and said that he wants that protest recorded – can you say – as – as a bit of an expert on the constitution – probably more than a bit of an expert – can you honestly say – as a member of the cabinet – that you were happy that Mrs Thatcher had allowed proper discussion by all the cabinet in detail of this very very important decision for the defence?
>
> (Harris 1989)

This yes/no question conveys a great deal of information to the audience, by means of presuppositions, assertions, attributions, propositions which the respondent, in answering yes or no, must accept or deny and, in answering, also 'save face' for self and others for whom he is speaking in this interview. The question contains these statements, which an answer will either accept or reject.

Presuppositions (P) – for validity of question:
1 A decision on defence was taken.
2 The decision is very important.
3 The cabinet did not properly discuss the decision.

Assertions (Q) – about others:
1 Thatcher cancelled the cabinet discussion.
2 Heseltine protested against the cancellation.
3 Somebody omitted the protest from the record.
4 Heseltine resigned over the cancellation.
5 Heseltine is demanding his protest be entered into the record.

Attributions (R) – about respondent:
1 You know that assertions Q are true.
2 You are an expert on the constitution.
3 You are a member of the cabinet.

Propositions (X) – in question:
1 Thatcher allowed discussion.
2 Thatcher allowed proper discussion.
3 Thatcher allowed discussion by all the cabinet.
4 Thatcher allowed discussion in detail.
[T allowed proper discussion by all the cabinet in detail.]

Questions (Y) – for answer:
1 Do you agree that X? [Is proposition X true?]
2 Can you say: 'I agree that X'?
3 Can you say 'I agree that X' and be honest? [Is your alternative answer
  'Proposition X is true' true? – that is, given truly.]

Answers (Z) – for respondent's choice:
1 Yes.
2 No.

In terms of its 'threat to face', this single question poses a series of increasingly serious threats to the face of the respondent and those for whom he is speaking in the interview. Of thirteen graded threats (Jucker 1986), the question presents these four, including the two most serious threats:

5 Accept the discrepancy between your opinion and reality.
7 State that the action is demeaning.
12 State that the other's face is demeaning.
13 State that your face is demeaning.

For example: If the respondent confirms assertions Q 1 and 3, he states that his Prime Minister's action is demeaning; yet if he rejects Q 2, 4, and 5, he states that his cabinet colleague's action is demeaning.

If the respondent denies attribution R 1 ('You know that assertions Q are true'), he accepts a discrepancy between his opinion and reality – and may be taken as incompetent or lying. If he denies R 2 and 3, he states that his own face is demeaning. On the other hand, if he affirms R 1 (and/or 2 and 3), he is affirming Q1–5 and therefore denying either his confirmation of Q 1 and 3 or his rejection of Q 2, 4, 5 – wherefore he is stating that either he was lying or that his action was demeaning or that his face is demeaning, and he is further stating that either his colleague's or his Prime Minister's face is demeaning.

If the respondent affirms proposition X, the proposition in question, he is denying presupposition P 3, assertions Q 1–5, and attributions R 1–3, which he has otherwise affirmed. On the other hand, if he denies X he consistently affirms all that is asserted in the question and all of those assertions which he has affirmed, at the same time also stating that the Prime Minister's action and face are demeaning while the action and face of the minister who protested and resigned are not demeaning, and consequently that his own action and face as a sitting cabinet member supporting the Prime Minister are demeaning.

All of this is stated to the overhearing public as the respondent gives his answer to the interviewer. Shall the answer be 'yes' or shall it be 'no'? In most cases *neither* answer is given, and the politician appears evasive because he does not answer the question. Equally so if he gives *both* answers, saying 'yes' to this and 'no' to that as he picks his way through parts of the question. Then he will be heard as hemming and hawing, either indecisive or incompetent – or worse, 'picky' and uncooperative. In any case he still appears evasive because he is still not answering the question.

In transcript no. 9B (Appendix) the question runs, 'Why don't you support?' In its first form, the question makes two political assertions about support deserved, and further states, by presupposition, that the politician is not giving the deserved support. Why not? That is to threaten face by asking the politician to justify his demeaning action (threat no. 10 in Jucker 1986).

The long speech that follows the question is not clear but evidently does not answer the question. Near the end the politician makes the claim that anything he might say in support cannot help at this time.

The long question that follows asks, 'Why can't you support?' The question is made more insistent by its repetition and intensifying form (why on earth). The question is pressed not by the journalist himself, as it were, but by attribution to a wider audience, a 'they' who look, see, think, and then *ask* the question (why on earth they say ...).

The long non-answer that follows attacks the media for helping people look on and misperceive the situation. Pretending that the questioner is rightly concerned about the public's perceptions, the politician expresses confidence that the public will rightly perceive the situation despite the media's misrepresenting it to them.

The next question is again put as if by the public. It presupposes that the public does not know, and it pretends that even unassisted by the media, the public might like to know, whether ...

The long speech that follows is an ambiguous non-answer, beginning with the politician's claim that his answer to that question is clear. He does not say either 'yes'or 'no' to the proposition in question but denies its presupposition while upholding with a flourish the democratic constitution.

In the final round, the journalist takes up the point about the constitution and proposes it as an answer to the first and second questions. It is a proposition for yes/no; accept or reject the stated reason for not speaking out in support. It is also a threat to the politician's face, asking him to accept that the reason for his action is demeaning (threat no. 6 in Jucker 1986). As if hiding, the politician is nevertheless making use of constitutional duties as a questionable reason for not speaking out.

The final non-answer forcefully denies not the proposition in question but the presupposition of the question, addressing not the reason for not speaking out but the act of speaking out. Now in his final response the politician affirms that which he has denied in his first response; and he affirms it by appealing to the use of media which he has attacked in his second response. He *is* speaking out, everywhere and directly, not in hiding – media, interviews, speeches, TV cameras. The form of this non-answer effectively turns the questioning on to the journalist. To the journalist's question, 'Why are you not speaking out?' the politician counters with 'Why are you talking about not speaking out?' Then the politician effectively answers his own question by rejecting the journalist's question – I *am* speaking out; and he threatens the journalist's face while sustaining his own – I am only not saying what you want me to say. The fillip at the end whips round with the marvellous ' – now of course that's something entirely different'. But none of that was in question! All of it was set up by the respondent's question and answer.

Small sense can be made out of this exchange of repeated question and repeated non-answer, ending in the respondent's own question and answer. No information has been revealed, far less exchanged. But the politician obviously shows force of rhetoric, manoeuvre of question–answer, and mastery of the interview. All the journalist can show is repetition of the same clumsy 'why?' question until a why-question is turned back upon him and then answered for him. Thus the question–answer exchange, sustained throughout by repeated questions and non-answers, ends in a single response that both poses and answers the respondent's own question. The effect is a final impression that the politician has conclusively answered the journalist's question.

From the use of such questions, and from their answers, there follows a third characteristic use of questions in news interviews – the supplementary or follow-up question. These are not questions that initiate a new topical line, even if the question does relate to the preceding response. Rather, they move along the topical line of the response, or they take up some aspect of it. On that definition, supplementary or follow-up questions are used to *probe*, to *counter*, and to *pursue* the previous answer (Greatbatch 1986). (Examples below are from BBC TV and radio interviews of public figures.)

Used *to probe*, follow-up questions solicit supportive detail regarding the previous response. They ask the respondent to:

1 *elaborate* – 'Well let me press you again, but what does "consent" really mean?'
2 *substantive* – 'You say countries are falling at the rate of one a year. What other countries and for how many years?'
3 *account* – 'Now why are you so reluctant to do that?'
4 *hypothesize* – 'Now if there is disagreement, ... what do you think should be done?'

Used *to counter*, follow-up questions call the adequacy of the response into question, or undermine it.

1 *doubt* – 'Is that *really* a realistic posture?'
2 *challenge*
   (a) by interviewer – 'That is if I may say so quite different, isn't it?'
   (b) by attribution – 'There will be quite a lot of Social Democrats watching who will say that you are not "the only alternative government." '

Used *to pursue*, follow-up questions reject a non-answer in the previous response and restate the previous question. When the interviewer does accept the non-answer, he asks a question on a new topic. If not, instead of shifting the topic he pursues it.

1 *Restate question* In this example, the interviewer states the question four times in a row, with non-answers intervening, until the Prime Minister gives an account of not-answering. Ordinarily, such an account is accepted and a new question is then asked.
   Q1 How long will you give Argentina to respond before you have to take the next military step?
   Q2 So how long now?
   Q3 So how long will you give Argentina?
   Q4 So you can't say at the moment how long you will give Argentina?
   A4 No of course I can't. And I should be very remiss if I were to give *any* hint because it would put the lives of some of our people at risk, and that I would never do.
2 *Recall question* 'Would it help you if you had to address your mind to the question which you put off for one moment as to whether you would ... ?'
3 *Restate and recall questions* 'Well, can I ask you again, would you compare the economic approach with ... .?'

4 *Reject question answered and restate question* 'But I didn't ask you what *advice* you were giving them, do you *think* that they will in fact come back to work?'

In transcript no. 9A (Appendix), the journalist three times asks the same question, and three times the respondent gives a non-answer.

Question: 'Do you accept responsibility for the mass picketing?' This question threatens face by asking the union leader to take responsibility for a demeaning action (threat no. 9 from Jucker 1986). In the second round the threat is made more explicit by calling the action a criminal matter, and by attributing that view not to the journalist but to high authority (Home Secretary) and wide public (everybody) – an attribution that is also used to give an account of why the question is being asked, again. In the third round the question is made more insistent not just by its repetition but by its form, which not only marks more insistence but also conduces more to a yes than a no answer ('So, ... are you not?').

Non-answer. At last the respondent answers 'No' – but not to the question. He never answers that question. In the first non-answer he responds with what he accepts responsibility for, 'to demonstrate solidarity' with six little workers – an action that enhances rather than demeans face. He strengthens his non-answer action and face by attributing it not to himself but to a wider and higher authority (my National Council) which the union leader, as respondent, represents. In the second non-answer the respondent repeats 'to demonstrate support' just as the journalist has repeated 'to accept responsibility'. The union leader also repeats the attribution, telling what 'we' (not I) *want* rather than accept responsibility for. In the final round, the respondent utters a clear 'no' which does not answer to the question of responsibility. As if by error, he begins to answer the question by attaching the 'no' to 'accept responsibility' ('No I'm not ac – uh endorsing') but then recovers. He tells of what he endorses, strengthening his good face and action by again attributing it, this time to a request from trade union members, again to demonstrate support for their fellows. He is doing a good thing by endorsing their request to do a good thing.

To the repeated question, 'Are you doing the bad act X?' the respondent never answers. He does *not* answer, 'No, I am not doing X.' Instead he responds, 'We are doing the good act Y.'

Purposes and practices

We can construct a useful scheme for practice by selecting among traditional stages of journalistic interviews and pairing them with typical faults of interviewers (cited in Metzler 1977). Practice consists of asking questions and listening to answers, followed by a phase of evaluation and preceded by preparation.

To prepare for an interview, the journalist first *defines purpose*, so as to know what questions to ask and why to ask them. Later, at the start of the interview, he states its purpose so that both parties, and any audience, will be in the know. The typical failure to define and state purpose led half of the respondents in some 50 interviews (Metzler 1977) to misperceive the purpose or simply left them not knowing why they had been asked those questions.

Next the journalist *prepares the questions*, according to purpose. The common complaint of 150 public officials runs that the journalists did not know what they were talking about; the common complaint of novice journalists runs, 'I never know what to ask' (Metzler 1977: 4–5). The ignorance can be redressed by study of the topics and formulation of topical questions – in advance.

According to an experienced magazine journalist, 'The perfect interview is a perfect set of questions. The older I get, the more time I spend in advance on that list' (quoted in Metzler 1977: 51). The list sets out not only the *specific questions* but also the *anticipated answers*, so that the journalist can prepare follow-up questions as well. That is, the journalist can sketch out the various answers to the first question, then set down a follow-up question for each answer. To begin with, the journalist can ask self: if I could ask only one question of this respondent, what would it be? One useful question starts at the beginning: 'How did it all begin – how did you get involved in … ?' (p. 36). If there is time for any more questions than the lone desert-island type, the remaining questions can be vetted to move from the beginning to the present (What has happened since then? What's the situation at present?) through to the future (What will happen next? What will you do about it?) and then back again (Is there some lesson that others can learn from your experience?). Because of the need to rely on the actual answers that will be given, some of the prepared questions may not turn out to be asked in that form nor in the prepared order. But thorough preparation of questions helps the journalist to know the questions to ask and even to improvise new ones. Here is a lovely example (from Metzler 1977) of a probe asked in seeming spontaneity but possibly figuring, in some form, on a prepared list of questions. A princess has been asked whether the reason she has never married might be her lack of interest in men.

A. Not interested? Young man, I'll have you know that I've had no fewer than 33 lovers in the past 20 years!
Q. Who do you have in mind for No. 34?

Once in the interview, the journalist discovers that knowing the questions is only half of the task. Asking *and listening* are the two complementary practices, both necessary to purpose. Having put the question the journalist listens to the answer for (1) the desired information and (2) the desirable next question. Amazing to recount, manuals cite failure to listen to answers as a typical fault of interviewers. After a TV interview, one journalist reflected: 'I forgot to listen to the answers to my questions. It's hard to ask follow-up questions when you have no idea what you're following up' (quoted in Metzler 1977: 95). The one essential attitude and behaviour of listening is non-judgemental: 'The interviewer must listen in a *non-judgemental* way', so that the respondent feels free to speak regardless of the interviewer's agreement (p. 28). Even veteran public figures, experienced as respondents and more than willing to talk, feel constrained by the adversarial questioning and judgemental listening. On the other hand, the journalists' *non*-listening lets them discourse as they will, changing the character of their talk into a non-*answer* and rendering pointless the journalist's use of questions – thus dissolving the whole rationale for establishing the situation as an interview to begin with. Ask and listen.

The final practice is to evaluate the interview, comparing question–answer against purposes. One interesting twist might be to ask self these same questions that are put to *respondents*, in a training exercise after an interview:

1 purpose of the interview made clear?
2 questions relevant to stated purpose?
3 interviewer a good listener?
4 you felt free to be honest and candid?

(Metzler 1977: 145)

Lastly, a good way to learn how to ask questions is by having to answer questions in an interview. 'Nothing is more revealing than to *be* interviewed, especially by someone equally inexperienced. Chances are you'll learn more from a bad interview than a good' (Metzler 1977: 139).

Yet the grand question of practice in relation to purpose arises most pointedly not for the novice but for the accomplished journalist in broadcast news interviews. To what end are the questions put? How do they function in the interview? Which purposes are being served, and which not, by the questions and answers?

The questions that are put clearly do not serve to obtain information, whether for the journalist or for the audience. The questions rarely get the expected or intended answer but typically a non-answer. They do not function to elicit the respondent's views, nor to discuss issues, positions, and alternatives. Their polar form casts everything into a yes/no, either/or frame. Their weight of loaded assertions makes them difficult to answer directly, yes or no; scarcely possible to answer at all; and impossible to respond to agreeably and coherently. The answers, such as they are, must be evasive and disagreeable. The repeated, follow-up questions only make things worse.

The questions cannot serve the lofty purposes of the public's right to know, nor the enlightenment of the citizenry. For, from the question–answer the public gleans little intelligence and that knowledge is not enlightening. Question and answer routinely pass one another by without touching, while each proposes to counter the other. All is black and white, for and against, either/or, yes/no. There is no room for shade and middle ground. Third and fourth alternatives cannot emerge and may never even be thought of. Disputable propositions are unquestioned, while adversarial ones are unanswered. The questions forward only those assertions that counter the respondent's view, while presuming that the respondent has accepted them in answers that he has not given to questions that have not been asked. So much, and that kind, of information does the elaborated and weighted question convey that the asking is minimal and the answering diffuse. The exchange may be interesting and lively, but no information is being exchanged.

Better to ask simple, straightforward questions one at a time. Better to avoid yes/no questions altogether. Better to question first the multiple presuppositions before going on to the big question that assumes their truth. Better too to forward propositions that are agreeable or conducive to the respondent's position. Better to collaborate in the developing expression and discussion of views on the matter. Of course, broadcast time will not permit any of that, and journalistic standards may forbid it, in the rush to ask the big, main question. Journalists do not shy from asking the tough questions; they are afraid of asking the easy ones.

All of these practices serve to some purposes and not others. The routine practices provoke confrontation and no discussion but a mismatch between questions and non-answers. The 'better' practices will provoke exposition and discussion of viewpoints on important public issues. The exchange is likely to be less entertaining but far more informative. Otherwise, we must ask: why ask questions to elicit information that the public has a right to know? Something else may be going on instead.

Chapter nine

Survey questioning

In surveys, polls, and censuses of commercial, social, political, and demographic types, interviewers do nothing but ask people of all kinds questions about their attitudes, behaviours, knowledge, and personal characteristics. For instance, the demographic survey in transcript no. 10 (Appendix) asks an entire populace about name, age, occupation, and the like.

Nothing would seem easier than to ask people about their attitudes or behaviours, not to mention their name and age. It is indeed easy enough to ask; to get reliable answers, though, is surprisingly hard. The great distinction of this field of practice, compared to most others, is its unremitting attention to *answers*. Answers almost seem more important than questions, and the questions seem to be a result of the answers rather than vice versa. That is, the artfulness of the questioning is a product of intense study of the answers that people give.

There are more books in this field than articles in most other fields. A single book on survey questions can report more research studies than are found in all sources combined in other fields. For instance, the authors of one book (Schuman and Presser 1981) have conducted 200 experimental studies of questions in national attitude surveys. Another book (Sudman and Bradburn 1974) summarizes 500 studies and lists nearly 1,000 in its bibliography. Survey researchers put such effort into studying their question–answer practice because the whole point of surveys is to get reliable information in answer, and because people routinely give the most unexpected responses to the simplest questions imaginable, and different responses to the same question asked in two similar ways. The results are intriguing, and often amusing. For examples from demographic surveys in 'undeveloped' countries :

Year of birth?
– Year of the tiger.
Length of residence?
– 20 metres.
Do you use sterilization?

– For the baby's bottle.

(Lucas 1985)

Because of these unexpected twists in the answers, people who conduct survey interviews take unusual precautions to formulate the questions correctly long before beginning the interview.

The interview

By contrast to other fields of interviewing, survey interviews (or opinion poll, census, marketing survey, and so on) involve numerous interviewers all asking the identically same questions, in precisely the same way, to a large number of respondents – say a minimum of 1,000. The responses are then collocated to answer one or two grand questions put not by the interviewer but by someone else – the party who commissioned the survey, say the researcher. The purpose is 'to collect information to be used in the answering of a research question' (Sudman and Bradburn 1974: 5).

Among other peculiar features, the survey interview is a task-oriented question–answer exchange between an interviewer and respondent who are strangers to begin with and who remain anonymous throughout. Indeed, the very answers remain confidential. None the less, the questions do not bear directly on the respondent's needs or interests but on someone else's. That someone else is not the interviewer, for the questions that the interviewer asks do not come from him; they are not products of his own cognition or motivation but were thought up and written down by someone else. The interviewer puts them as if by rote. Hence neither the question nor the answer serves the interest of either the interviewer or the respondent. They are strangers asking and answering questions for some unknown purpose on behalf of some unknown party.

Everything depends on the answers. Despite being asked questions that do not serve their own needs and interests, by a questioner who obviously does not ask in his own interest or out of his own need, respondents willingly give answers, often unreliable ones. They guess, distort, and even lie in answering the most factual and innocent questions, while giving truthful and factual answers to some question other than the simple one put to them. On that account, the greatest possible effort must be made to formulate the questions beforehand in order to have the best possible chance of getting reliable answers. In this field, the questioning begins long before the interview and the answers are counted long afterwards.

Preparation of questions

The first step is not to write questions but to define the purpose for asking. In this case, purpose is defined in terms of the grand question (or questions) which the information from the survey can be used to answer. When well conceived, and precisely formulated in writing, that question will reveal what information the survey needs to collect. The next step is to start formulating the specific questions to ask, such that the responses will provide the desired information.

The first big mistake in practice, accordingly, is to rush ahead with listing the individual questions without first defining and formulating the research question. The mistake becomes plain only after the survey, when the expensively collected responses do not provide the desired information – or, worse, do not even make sense. No one can know what to do with these data, since no one knows what question they are supposed to answer.

The second preparatory step is to *start* formulating the individual questions to appear on the questionnaire or interview schedule. For each question, the researcher (opinion pollster, survey interviewer, etc.) must ask two analytic questions.

First, *Why am I asking this question*? (Sudman and Bradburn 1982). In each instance the researcher must 'be able to explain how this particular question is closely related to the research question that underlies the survey' (p. 13). Failing that, the questions look as if the surveyors don't know what they are trying to find out. 'If you do not know what you want to know, respondents cannot help' (p. 123).

Second, *What am I taking for granted in this question*? (Payne 1951). In each instance, the researcher must be able to specify everything possible about the question, asking of it the familiar string of who? what? when? where? how? and why? (pp. 26–7). That helps to reveal how non-specific the question probably is, and how it can well mean two or three different things to the respondent other than the one thing it means to the questioner. Survey questions, as with most questions, easily take far too much for granted, leaving the specific unspecified. Most people do not think through just what it is that they are asking, and how someone else might take the question. That is due in part to our common over-emphasis on the question and the questioner. Preparing the questions beforehand, in light of an eventual respondent, helps make the questions more specific and hence more reliably answerable.

The rule of practice is to make each question as specific as possible. That turns out unexpectedly hard to do, even for the experts. Consider this simple question (Sudman and Bradburn 1982: 39):

What brand of soft drink do you usually buy?

Every part of this question is problematic for taking too much for granted, and for not being specific enough. Many people buy several and various brands, not one; they will respond, however, with the first brand name that comes to mind, and that name is likely to be the most widely known or advertised brand (such as Coca-Cola). In that way an advertising survey will discover the brand already advertised. 'Soft drink' may be crystal clear to the questioner but the respondent may wonder if it includes lemonade, iced tea, punch, and mineral water. What time period and frequency does 'usually' refer to? No one can know. Much better to specify the time period, asking about dates such as yesterday. Under which conditions does 'buy' apply? – purchases for home use, or also purchases at work, in restaurants, outdoor places, and so on. Finally, who is 'you'? Is it the respondent him/herself, or the respondent and spouse, or household? And what of the purchases that the respondent makes for others, as for family and household? If the first meaning, the useful word is 'you, yourself'.

This is to be picky. And that is what practice in this field must be if purposes are to be achieved. The pickiness is a corrective, redressing the questioner's remedial assumptions that he understands what he is asking and that everyone else understands it too, and in the same way that he understands the question. Advance analysis of the question to be asked in a survey is essential to getting reliable information in response.

It will take many second thoughts and at least as many reformulations before the question is written with specificity enough. As a humorous example, compare the initial and final versions of this question from a past master of survey questions.

Initial: Which do you prefer, dichotomous or open questions?
Final: Which type of question do you like best to be asked in opinion surveys – those stating two answers to decide between, those stating more than two answers, or those leaving the answer for you to state?

(Payne 1951: 214–23)

The final version is the *fortieth* reformulation of the first question. (Of course, smarter people will get it right on the first or second try. Only the old-timers take as long as four or forty tries.) A useful exercise for the reader is to pick apart either version, trying to capture the second thoughts and the reformulations that they led to, say in four of the forty cases. The example also implicitly illustrates most of the major problems with writing survey questions. Clues to these problems, and hints for solution, can be found by peeking ahead to the tables in this section.

Testing and revision of questions

The next phase of practice is still not to ask the questions that have been so well and arduously formulated. It is to pilot-test and revise the questions, repeatedly. The manuals insist on an indispensable minimum of two (Converse and Presser 1986), four (Sudman and Bradburn 1982), or even eight (Oppenheim 1966) tests and revisions.

For instance, the practitioner should subject his carefully wrought questions to this series (Sudman and Bradburn 1982):

1 criticism from experienced peers;
2 revision and testing on friends, relatives, co-workers;
3 revision and testing on about 50 people resembling the eventual respondents in the survey – an absolute minimum is to interview strangers by knocking on doors close to home (Converse and Presser 1986);
4 revision and testing again;
5 revision.

Revisions must be tested too, for they are new formulations that may embed new problems. Now, all of this pilot-testing takes time, effort, money, and patience just when the researcher is pressing to get on with the field survey. At this point the emphatic advice runs: *'If you do not have the resources to pilot-test your questionnaire, don't do the study'* (Sudman and Bradburn 1982: 283).

A good lesson on this point is taught us by a study of survey questions about television watching at home (Belson 1981). All questions in this survey were knowingly defective in typical ways. Nearly all respondents *mis*understood the questions in major ways, without themselves *or* the interviewer being aware of the misunderstanding. Much of the problem lay in varying interpretation of words, even common ones: usually, advertising, programme, watch, weekday, you, and so on. Only 29 per cent of responses fell within 'permissible limits' of what the question was meant to ask. All but six of the questions fell below the 50 per cent mark. The highest score for any question was only 58 per cent; and for one question, *not a single response* came within range. We can imagine the results of this survey being used to report some conclusion about people's habits or attitudes regarding television. Or we can construe this study as a *pilot-test* of the questions, revealing serious problems leading to the reformulation and retesting of the trial questions before going on to ask them in the survey.

One useful way to pilot-test is first to ask the questions in an interview, just as eventually will be done, and next to check question and answer after the interview, by asking the respondent to explain the answers (Belson 1981). After reading question and answer back to the respondent, the interviewer might ask these questions (Converse and Presser 1986: 52):

1 How would *you* say the question?

2 What did (*word*) mean to you?
3 Consider the same question this way: '_____.' How would you answer it now?
4 You said '_____.' Would you feel different if I said '_____'?

Finally, one useful component of the pilot-test is to collect and treat the responses just as eventually will be done. The responses are coded, collated, distributed in tables or whatever, and analysed for the information they contain. This procedure will reveal what will and what *can* be done with the answers that will come to the questions. That in turn will suggest either new forms of the questions or new questions altogether. It is impractical not to test the answers. For, imagine that all of the questions prove clear to the respondents, while none of the answers proves useful for answering the question of the survey. A test would show that reliable but useless answers were being given to wrong questions asked the right way.

More practical, because more serviceable to purpose, is to ask the right questions in the right way. But how to tell right from wrong? The way to tell is by looking fixedly at the answers that people give to questions put now this way and now that.

Response to question words

Survey researchers spend most of their effort on the wording of questions. 'Wording' may refer to everything about the question-sentence, such as its form, structure, phrasing. One part of this omnibus wording is the vocabulary or *words*, chosen over other *words*, in particular slots of the question.

The principle here is simple, yet hard to follow in practice.

> Use words that everyone in the sample understands and that have only the meaning you intend. Writing questions that satisfy this principle is a difficult art that requires experience and judgement. You must expect to engage in a good deal of trial and error as well as pilot testing before all the words are satisfactory.
>
> (Sudman and Bradburn 1982: 48)

As noted, even the word 'you' is easily but variously understood, meaning to respondents more than the one, unspecified meaning intended by the questioner.

Other words misunderstood or variously construed by respondents in the survey of TV watching (Belson 1981) are, in addition to 'you': 'usually', 'proportion', 'weekday', 'household', 'impartial', 'appropriate', 'efficient', 'advertising', 'programme', and 'watch'. A long list of common but problematic words (Payne 1951) begins with 'about', 'all', 'always', 'any'; and ends with 'warm', 'way', 'wide', 'work' – and, of course, 'you.'

Table 9.1 Responses to different words in question

Positive vs negative words			Positive vs neutral words		
	Yes (%)	No (%)		Yes (%)	No (%)
1 speeches against democracy[1]			1 atheists against religion[1]		
forbid	21	79	allowed to speak	69	31
allow	48	52	allowed freedom to speak	80	20
2 speeches for communism[1]			2 proposed policy[4]		
forbid	40	60	the idea	17	–
allow	56	44	the President's idea	21	–
3 presidential term of office[2]			3 policy mistake[5]		
add law to Constitution	36	50	to defend Korea	49	38
change the Constitution	26	65	to stop communist invasion of S. Korea	36	55
4 balance government budget[3]			4 another Vietnam situation[1]		
desirable	61	15	send troops	18	82
undesirable	25	37	send troops to stop communist takeover	37	63

Sources: [1]Schuman and Presser 1981; [2]Payne 1951; [3]Blankenship 1940; [4]Roslow et al., 1940; [5] Sudman and Bradburn 1982

One especially intriguing aspect of question words (as also of question wording in general) is the positive/negative 'load', tone, or slant of a word. The same question can be taken two different ways when a single word is varied with another seemingly synonymous word that is more positive/negative. Table 9.1 gives examples of these paired words.

For instance (Table 9.1), 25 per cent more Americans will 'allow' public speeches against democracy than will 'forbid' them, and 25 per cent more will 'not forbid' than will 'not allow'. Similarly for speeches favouring communism: more people will allow than forbid them, and more will not forbid than not allow. More people are also willing to add a law to the Constitution than to change the Constitution, and more think it desirable to balance the government budget than not think it undesirable.

Positive/negative words further present the respondent with a confusing choice over the negative, while the very dichotomy of choice presents another problem. People tend to shy away from negativeness (forbid, control, ban, and un-, non-, and so on) and towards positiveness, yet without quite knowing in certain cases what favour/oppose, agree/disagree, yes/no responses entail. Apart from all considerations of the issue or proposition in question, many respondents wish to avoid the negative, whatever it is; but they trip over it in the process of responding. They're against the negative, all right, and for the positive, but which response will express that? As for the dichotomy of choice, 'not allow' may well connote weaker opposition than 'forbid', and 'not forbid' weaker support than 'allow'; the observed asymmetry of yes/no responses might vanish if the questions were to take account of people who are weakly inclined or indifferent, by explicitly offering them a 'don't care' or 'leave as is' option for response (Molenaar 1989). That is good practice in general, since providing a middle term proves to make a great deal of difference in the responses.

Just as with positive/negative words, responses differ to positive vs. neutral words. For example (Table 9.1), more people will allow atheists the *freedom* to speak in public against religion, compared to (merely) allowing them to speak in public against religion; and more favour the *President's* policy than the policy mere. Fewer people at the time regarded it as a mistake to stop the communist invasion of Korea than to defend Korea; and, given 'another Vietnam situation', far fewer people will agree to send troops than to send troops to stop a communist takeover. In other words, the other word increases or decreases public support.

Even more interesting is the problem of finding the right words for common concepts. Demographers carefully avoid using the common word for the concept, since people continually take these words to refer to various things, differing on whom or what to include/exclude, on which basis and for which purpose. These include vexing items like nuptuality but also simple things like household, occupation, and even name.

Typical demographic questions for fourteen concepts are listed in transcript no. 10. A good exercise for the reader is to think first of the way in which he/she would naturally ask the question, then to compare the way in which demographers typically word it. In general, there are good reasons for the particular words in the question as asked. In a number of cases, though, demographers have found no satisfying way to cast the question, or no way to choose between two alternative wordings. Each serves some purposes but not others, and every one has some problems with getting the desired information in response.

For example, take the question about nuptuality (no. 5 in transcript 10) (all examples are from Lucas 1985). Demographers have found it impossible to frame a question that will embody a universally acceptable definition of marriage, and to find a word that will capture both legal and *de facto* marital status; a series of no fewer than nine questions is recommended. A survey in Guyana used questions that allowed for separate relationships with up to six different partners, each relationship taking on one of three distinct forms – legal marriage, common law marriage, or visiting union. Everyone knows there are problems with marriage! But few would have thought it difficult to find out whether someone is married.

The problems with names (question no. 2) are surprising to anyone who has never tried to ask for them. One problem is, Which names to ask for? Other problems are that not all respondents, or respondents in certain locales, have family names or even individually distinguishing names. Some people have changing names, others are known by names other than their name, while in some societies respondents cannot use or speak their name, if they are named after a deceased.

Age and sex (nos. 3 and 4) are problematic too. In an Indonesian survey, 6 per cent of the cases misreported the sex of one or more children. 'Ask, do not guess!' runs the instruction for this question. Also, cultural preferences may work not to count girls accurately. In some societies dates count for little and people do not know either when they were born or how old they are. Yet when pressed they may feel they have to state some number. One tendency is 'digit preference', reporting one's age with a 0 or 5.

Similarly, demographers have trouble finding out fertility and birth intervals (nos. 6 and 7). Even when the questions simply ask 'how many births?' and 'in what year?', people do not give the correct number. One problem is to count *all* the births – births of still-born, short-lived, and female children, and children given away. 'Recall lapse' describes the fact that respondents cannot recall (or do not count in recalling) certain births, especially those earlier in life or those just cited. 'Event displacement' describes the tendency of respondents to advance recent events towards the present and to refer distant events towards the past, 'leaving a trough in the interval some time to 20 years before the survey' (Lucas 1985: 119). 'Period preference' describes the tendency to heap responses in certain durations such as 6 months and its multiples.

Questions about migration, occupation, and ancestry (nos. 11, 13, 14) show the difficulty of defining simple things. Migration is not an obviously recognizable phenomenon, and there is no single definition of it. Concepts of space, time, move, residence vary from culture to culture. Furthermore, people rarely move for simple reasons; and they themselves may be unclear about why they migrate. Respondents tend to give industry answers to occupation questions, and to answer less frequently to the industry/occupation question when they have already answered to the occupation/industry question. Other problems are which work to count, when, and whose. Some respondents have good reasons not to answer the question about ethnicity or ancestry, while others find the question meaningless or impossible to answer. In an Australian census, one-third of respondents said that they had no ethnic origin! In a repeat American census, more than a third of respondents gave a different ethnic origin for themselves between one survey year and the next. Moreover, few people know much about their family's origin; many have multiple origins or descents; while others regard themselves simply as 'New Zealanders' or 'Americans' regardless of the panoply of origins listed for choice in the question. At any rate, people are offended not to see their origin listed.

Response to question form

The major preoccupation is whether to cast the question in open or closed form. Open/closed refers rather more to form of answers, however, whether the answer is to be stated in the respondent's own words or selected from a list of answers (categories, options, alternatives, and so on). As can be expected, answers to these two forms of question differ. But as might not be expected, people give systematically different answers about the same things, in responding to an open or closed form of the same question. In a series of experimental studies, every open/closed comparison revealed 'statistically significant and substantively important differences' (Schuman and Presser 1981: 107). Table 9.2 gives examples.

For instance, here are open and closed forms of the same question.

Open: What do you think is the most important problem facing this country at present?

Closed: Which of these is the most important problem facing this country at present?

In response to the open form, the respondent *volunteers* or identifies an item; for the closed form he *selects* one of the listed items, or checks it off. To this question, twice as many people *selected* 'crime' in the closed form as volunteered it in the open form (Table 9.2). How important, then, is crime?

Asked about their work values, more people selected as the most preferred thing in a job 'opportunity for advancement' and 'feeling of accomplishment' than they *volunteered* either of these in response to the open question. And they ranked (by frequency of mention) 'good pay' first in the open form and last in the closed. How salient is pay as a work value?

Asked about the most important thing for children to learn in life, many times more people selected 'to think for themselves' and 'to obey' than volunteered either of these. Fully two-thirds of the respondents answered 'to think for themselves' on the closed form, compared to a minimal 5 per cent on the

Table 9.2 Responses to open and closed questions

Attitude questions*	Open (%)	Closed (%)	Behavior questions†	open long and familiar	closed short and standard
1 most important problem			1 Alcohol consumption		
crime	16	35	cans of beer	286	147
2 most important for children to learn			glasses of wine	108	55
to obey	2	19	2 Sexual activity		
to think for self	5	61	intercourse	137	91
3 most prefer in job			masturbation	182	49
opportunity for advancement	2	17			
feeling of accomplishment	14	31			
good pay	most	least			

Sources: * Schuman and Presser 1981; †Bradburn and Sudman 1979

open form. Imagine, then, a survey concluding that the majority of people hold 'to think for themselves' as the most important thing for children to learn. Survey researchers know better (or ought now to know better). They must take careful note of the form of the question. Their careful note must be taken first, before asking the question in a survey.

Both open and closed forms of question are useful, yet each yields different responses. The recommended practice (Schuman and Presser 1981) is obviously to use both forms of question, but at different stages. In preparing the questions for a survey, open questions are well used to discover and develop the categories of response items to be put into the closed form of the question for the survey. (Closed questions are also preferred for reasons of no interest here, such as relative cost, ease of coding, and statistical manipulation of responses.) Otherwise, the items specified for answer in a closed question will with certainty *not* represent the respondents' attitudes – which is most unsuitable to purpose in an attitude survey. The respondents will merely reconfirm the surveyor's own frame of reference, without his even realizing it (Schuman and Presser 1981: 108, 110). For instance, in the question about work values, no less than 60 per cent of responses to the open question fell *outside* of the five pre-fixed choices in the closed question (p. 90).

There is a further, troublesome corollary: people respond to the question *anyway*. In other words, they respond in terms of the question. That means that the terms of answer are not determined by the respondent but are predetermined by the questioner.

Even if none of their values appears on the list of possible answers, respondents will none the less tell you which is their most important value, of those values which you think are their most important. Hence the questioner substitutes his categories, frame of reference, or even values, for those of the respondents whose values he is asking to find out. Then he unwittingly reports, with statistical significance, that the majority of people reliably think what he thought they think in the first place: that the most important thing for children to learn is to think for themselves.

Response to question topic

A different use of open questions is appropriate for topics that are sensitive or threatening to respondents. For example, Table 9.2 shows that, in response to open compared to closed questions, people reported drinking twice as many cans of beer. That response turns out to be more reliable than the half-as-many in the closed question. For, perceiving the topic as threatening, and wishing to appear socially desirable, respondents typically under-report such behaviour. By contrast, they *over*-report behaviour which they perceive as socially desirable. Questions about both types of behaviour are threatening to respondents.

A question is threatening if a respondent can feel that there is a right or wrong answer, or that the interviewer will approve/disapprove of him for the response. For instance, questions are threatening that ask about behaviours perceived as socially desirable and undesirable. Respondents tend to distort their responses to these questions, but in reverse ways (Bradburn and Sudman 1979; Sudman and Bradburn 1982).

Socially desirable behaviours describe the good citizen, the well-informed and cultured person, and the individual who fulfils moral and social responsibilities. These behaviours include registering to vote, voting, and knowing the issues; reading, using libraries, going to cultural and educational events; giving to charity, being employed, and even wearing seat belts while driving. All of these are over-reported. For example, one-third of respondents who reported giving to charity did not in fact give; one-third more of respondents reported having voted, and for the winner, than did actually vote.

Socially undesirable behaviours describe illness and disability, illegal or counternormative behaviour. These include cancer, venereal disease, and mental illness; crime, use of drugs and alcohol, ownership of guns, and sexual activity. All of these are under-reported. Also under-reported are items related to financial status, such as income, savings, assets, and bankruptcy. For example, half of respondents charged with drunken driving deny ever being so charged.

How can survey researchers know that people over- or under-report these behaviours? In many cases they cannot. In some cases they can find out from informants in the household or friendship group. In other cases the responses can be validated by inspecting records, documents, and other sources, or even just by looking around the house during the interview. Validation is a procedure used for other, common behaviours. For example, consider the innocent question about the amount of coffee purchased in the past week. The responses can be validated against records of coffee shipments and retail sales that week. Such comparisons typically show that the amount reportedly purchased is more than twice the amount manufactured and sold. (The responses are distorted not because of perceived threat but for other reasons involving both the formulation of the question and the memory of the respondent. For instance, coffee purchased ten days ago is unwittingly reported for 'last week'.)

Another research approach first inspects the records, next asks the questions, then compares responses with the foreknown record. Such studies (Bradburn and Sudman 1979) have found the following distorted responses:

1 voter registration   15%
2 holding library card 19%
3 bankruptcy   32%
4 voting   39%
5 drunken driving   47%

That is, 15 per cent of respondents who claimed to be registered voters were not registered on the rolls; and 47 per cent who claimed never to have been charged with drunken driving were listed in court records. The distortion is always in one direction only – over-reporting the positive, under-reporting the negative. Respondents never report not voting when they have indeed voted, for example, nor do they report a drunken driving charge when they have never been so charged.

Why should people lie about holding a library card? Part of the reason lies in the interesting mix of decisions that respondents have to make in their attempt to be a good respondent while at the same time appearing to be socially desirable. These are problems of self-presentation and response acquiescence, and they are common in all kinds of surveys (Sudman and Bradburn 1974).

The respondent may face a conflict between telling the truth and appearing to be socially desirable. Hence he may over-report the desirable and under-report the undesirable behaviour. For questions about attitudes or knowledge, the respondent who does not know the answer or has no opinion on the issue faces a conflict between telling the truth (don't know) and being a good respondent (give answer). To avoid embarrassment, respondents commonly give answers to questions they know nothing about, giving opinions they do not have. A third conflict arises between the social norms of politeness and agreeableness, and the respondent's true answer or no-answer. The respondent may follow the social norms and just agree with the interviewer's statement. Rather than being impolite or disagreeable, the good respondent answers 'yes'.

Agreeableness is particularly intriguing. It suggests that respondents are trying to figure out the interviewer's opinion so as to agree with that. Or they are trying to figure out the answer that the interviewer or the question seems to expect, from the way the question is formulated and put. (These manoeuvres may have been learned from long experiences with teacher questioning.) Especially if the issue is controversial or the question ambiguous or difficult to understand, respondents simply agree – whether they in fact agree or disagree, and even when they know nothing about it or have no opinion either way. Respondents will agreeably say yes even to two contrary statements. For example, 10 per cent of respondents agreed to both of these statements :

1 It is hardly fair to bring children into the world, the way things look for them.
2 Children born today have a wonderful future to look forward to.

(Converse and Presser 1986)

Another factor supporting agreeableness is the sociolinguistic fact that a 'yes' answer is treated as sufficient, whereas a 'no' must be explained (Stenstroem 1984). A simple 'yes' will with one stroke avoid the need to elaborate and justify; cover the embarrassment of not-knowing or not having an opinion; forestall impolite and disagreeable behaviour towards the interviewer; and resolve assorted conflicts that threaten peace of mind and co-operativeness of communication. So respondents just say 'yes' and let it go at that.

The result is unreliable responses. To get more reliable responses the surveyor has to put the questions in certain careful ways.

With threatening questions (Sudman and Bradburn 1982), the most important thing, because the most serviceable to purpose, is for the interviewer to ask and listen in a plainly accepting and *non-judgemental* way. An alternative is to put the questions to someone else, such as a household informant. Another is to formulate the question in open rather than closed form, longer rather than short (by adding an introduction of 15 words or so), and in familiar rather than standard vocabulary (the interviewer describes the behaviour and asks the respondent for the familiar term). These formulations of the question increase the reporting of undesirable behaviour by some 30 per cent. For example, Table 9.2 shows that respondents reported twice as much alcohol use and sexual activity when asked the open, long, familiar question.

Other techniques to increase the reliability of responses vary with the behaviour in question, whether desirable or undesirable (Sudman and Bradburn 1982). One specifies the time period involved. For an undesirable behaviour, the questions first ask about 'ever, even once', then ask about current behaviour. For desirable behaviours the questions first ask about current behaviour, then past or usual behaviour. A second technique deliberately loads the question, providing a special introduction (cf. 'long' question, above) for each case. For desirable behaviour the phrasing can be casual ('Did you happen to ... ') or it can state reasons for not performing the behaviour ('Did things come up that kept you from voting?'). These will help to reduce over-reporting. They must not be used to ask about undesirable behaviour, however, for fear of increasing the under-reporting. Similarly, the techniques suitable for undesirable behaviour are inappropriate for desirable behaviour. The question formulates, by attribution, reasons for doing the behaviour: authority justifies it ('Many doctors/scientists now think ... '); everybody does it ('Even the calmest parents get angry with their children some of the time').

The more general problem of respondent acquiescence – agreeably giving distorted responses – is addressed by reformulating the structure of the question, as seen next.

Response to question structure

Structure here refers to the specification of alternatives in the question – or the alternatives provided for answer. People give systematically different responses to variously structured questions. Examples for eight aspects of structure appear in Table 9.3 (all examples are from Schuman and Presser 1981).

Consider first the common question about a certain proposition X: 'Do you agree that X?' The structure of this question also structures the possible answers: Yes (agree/favour), or No (disagree/oppose). As noted, respondents tend to acquiesce by agreeably answering 'yes' to whatever is in question. Two other ways of structuring the question change these responses.

Table 9.3 Responses to different structures of question (percentages)

1	ALTERNATIVE STATED	*Russian leaders trying*		
		(a)	to get along with US	59
		(b)	to get along	49
			or to dominate	–
2	'DON'T KNOW' ANSWER OPTION	*Russian leaders trying*		
			to get along	28
			or you have no opinion	43
3	'DON'T KNOW' FILTER QUESTION	*Russian leaders get along*		
		(a)	any opinion? (no opinion)	56
		(b)	(if opinion) agree?	23
4	COUNTER ARGUMENT ADDED	*workers to join union*		
		(a)	require to join	32
		(b)	require to join	20
			or leave to individual	80
5	MIDDLE TERM ADDED	*your politics*		
		(a)	liberal	30
			conservative	58
		(b)	liberal	20
			conservative	33
			middle of road	42
6	ORDER OF ALTERNATIVES	*divorce should be*		
		(a)	easier to get	40
			harder to get	50
		(b)	easier	21
			harder	34
			stay as is	45
		(c)	easier	23
			stay as is	35
			harder	41
7	ORDER OF QUESTIONS	*let reporters in*		
		(a)	Communists here	55
			Americans there	64
		(b)	Americans there	82
			Communists here	75
		rated 'very happy'		
		(a)	things altogether	52
			my marriage	70
		(b)	my marriage	63
			things altogether	38
8	ACQUIESCENCE OF RESPONSE	*blame for crime*		
		(a)	individuals more than	60
			social conditions	
		(b)	social conditions more	57
			than individuals	
		(c)	individuals	46
			or social conditions	54

Source: Schuman and Presser 1981

1 *State an alternative proposition.* 'Do you agree that X, or do you agree that Y?'
2 *Provide a 'don't know' option.* (a) 'Do you agree that X, do you disagree that X, or do you have no opinion?' (b) 'Do you agree that X, do you agree that Y, or do you have no opinion?'

For examples, let us examine the different ways of structuring one question about Russian leaders (examples nos. 1, 2, and 3 in Table 9.3). The first case contrasts structuring a question with and without a stated alternative to the proposition X in question.

(a) Do you agree or disagree with this statement? The Russian leaders are basically trying to get along with America.
(b) Would you say that the Russian leaders are basically trying to get along with America, or that they are basically trying to dominate America?

Without an alternative stated, 59 per cent of respondents agreed with the proposition X in question. Only 49 per cent agreed with X when the question offered an alternative proposition Y.

In the next case, the question is structured to offer an alternative response to the bipolar yes/no, agree/disagree.

Here is a statement about another country: The Russian leaders are basically trying to get along with America. Do you agree, disagree, or do you not have an opinion on that?

In this case, only 28 per cent of respondents agreed with proposition X – half the proportion that agreed to X in the first example; while 43 per cent stated they had *no opinion* about X. The responses shift even further when the 'don't know' is offered first, then the 'agree/disagree' is offered to those who *do* know or do have an opinion.

Here is a statement about another country. Not everyone has an opinion on this. If you do not have an opinion, just say so. Here's the statement: The Russian leaders are basically trying to get along with America. Do you have an opinion on that? (If so:) Do you agree or disagree?

To this 'filter' question, 56 per cent of respondents stated they had no opinion, while only 23 per cent agreed with proposition X. Hence, according to the structure of the question, public opinion that Russian leaders are trying to get along with America diminishes from 59 per cent to 49 per cent to 28 per cent and 23 per cent, while the public holding no opinion on the matter grows from nothing to 43 per cent to 56 per cent. In the first question, well over half the public agreed; in the last question, well over half had no opinion at all.

Numerous experimental studies (Schuman and Presser 1981) have demonstrated that providing a 'don't know' option shifts an average of 22 per cent of responses away from agree/disagree towards no opinion; and using a filter question shifts even more. These people actually have little or no knowledge or opinion on the issue in question. They none the less *agreeably answer* the question, since an answer is being called for and they are good respondents. If the question is structured to provide an alternative to X or an alternative to agree/disagree, a large proportion of respondents will choose the alternative. Then those responses that do agree with X are more reliable.

A further way of structuring a question provides some balance to the affirmative side of the issue. 'Do you agree that X?' speaks only to the affirmative, and, as noted, favours responses that agreeably acquiesce. 'Do you agree that X or do you agree that Y?' provides some formal balance. A more effective balance structures the question by adding some consideration for the negative side of the issue, making formally explicit that negative responses are as legitimate as affirmative ones. For instance, the question could state the fact of opposition: 'Some people favour X, some people oppose X. Do you favour X or oppose X?' Or it could state grounds for the negative. ' ... or oppose X because of Y?' For example (no. 4 in Table 9.3), here is a question with and without a counter-argument added.

(a) If there is a union at a particular company or business, do you think that all workers there should be required to be union members?

(b) ... or should it be left to the individual to decide whether or not he wants to be in the union?

Far fewer respondents agree to require joining the union when the question provides a counter-argument. Experimental studies (Schuman and Presser 1981) demonstrate a shift of 8 per cent in responses when the question adds some consideration for the other side of an issue.

A similar shift – but twice as large, 15 per cent – occurs when the question adds a middle term or category for response. This is something like adding 'in between' to the choice of 'up or down?'. For example (no. 5 in Table 9.3), when the question adds 'middle of the road', 42 per cent of respondents describe their politics as neither 'liberal' nor 'conservative.' These 42 per cent desert that political dichotomy, leaving both liberal and conservative parties much impoverished by contrast to the first question structure (namely, 'liberal or conservative?').

Yet another shift in responses occurs when the question varies the placement of the alternatives. The last-mentioned alternative attracts, on average, 10 per cent additional responses than when mentioned in first or second place. Quite irrespective of content, any alternative Z will be chosen more in last position – 'X, Y, or Z?' It will be chosen more than when it places as 'X, Z, or Y?'; and more than when 'Z, X, or Y?' In these other two versions, it is *Y* that will benefit from being in last place. For example, consider this question about divorce (no. 6 in Table 9.3):

Should divorce be easier or more difficult to obtain than it is now?

More people think it should be harder to get. But that question is structured as a dichotomy, 'X or Y?' Add the middle term, 'stay as it is now'. Given the three alternatives, half of the respondents (45 per cent) no longer think that divorce should be *either* easier or harder to get, but that it should 'stay as is'. Furthermore, 'stay as is' is chosen by more respondents when it is in last place. And so is 'harder' when in last place. More respondents chose either one in last place than they chose either of the other alternatives in the other places. Moreover, both alternatives are chosen by more respondents when in last place than when they are in second place. When last, 'stay as is' gets 45 per cent of the responses, compared to 35 per cent in second place. 'Harder' gets 34 per cent in second place but 41 per cent when last. In short, by virtue of its position alone, the last-mentioned of two or three alternatives tends to be the response of choice.

The order in which questions are asked also may affect responses. For example (no. 7 in Table 9.3), consider the questions about letting communist reporters into the US and American reporters into the USSR. More people – 20 per cent more – are willing to let the communists in here when they are first asked about letting Americans in there. Fewer people – 18 per cent fewer – want American reporters to go there after they have answered about communist reporters coming here. The same with happiness. More people are happy with their marriage when first asked about their happiness with things generally, and far fewer are happy generally when first answering about their marriage.

Acquiescence of response continues to show up everywhere. Consider the question about blame for crime (no. 8 in Table 9.3). The majority of respondents blame individuals more than social conditions, when the interviewer asks if they agree with that statement; and the majority blame social conditions more than individuals, when the interviewer asks that. Asked which is more to blame, half blame the one, half the other. But more blame social conditions, because it's in last place!

Assumptions about questions and answers

The artful practice and sophisticated research in this field chase away all thought of easily asking and answering questions.

Ease of asking is countered by the labour and uncertainty of masterful survey researchers who for decades have done little else than try to ask clear and simple questions. It is 'hard-won, heavy duty work' (Converse and Presser 1986: 10). The guru in this field (Payne 1951: 228–37) presents a check-list of no fewer than 100 considerations to observe when wording a question. 'How difficult it is to write good questions' runs the recurrent theme of modern authorities (Sudman and Bradburn 1982); it requires great skill and judgement, much time and experience; and yet, 'even after years of experience, no one can write a perfect question' (pp. 3, 283). Two accomplished researchers who have conducted 200 experiments on survey questions state: 'We despaired of being able to construct questions immune from serious criticism' (Schuman and Presser 1981: 13). Ease of asking is belied by their laborious formulation, tedious testing, and repeated revision of the simplest questions they can think of, then by the unintended and unexpected ways that respondents take the questions.

Ease of answering is countered by the observed facts. Respondents regularly fail to exhibit the attention, interest, understanding, knowledge, memory, motive, ability, and willingness to answer as asked. They do indeed respond to the questions, quite easily. But easy responses are not reliable answers.

If we are not careful about asking, respondents might well just agree with us. And if we are not attentive to their responses, we might well just conclude that they gave the right answer.

Part two

Elements of Questioning

Chapter ten

Notions of questioning

Viewed simply, questioning is comprised of (a) putting (b) a question – or, an act and a sentence. It also entails sentences just before, so to speak, and sentences just after – assumptions and answers. On this view, questioning has three ordered elements, each comprised of an act and a sentence:

1 assumptions,
2 question,
3 answers.

A theoretical understanding of these three elements, above all the third one, is the best possible way to know how to manipulate them in practice.

Assumptions

Questioning entails two kinds of assumptions which, prior or preceding, are called *pre*suppositions and *pre*sumptions. The first is a logical property of the question-sentence; the second is a pragmatic property of the act of uttering that sentence. Thus, when a person asks a question, he is communicating something in addition to the very question he asks. He communicates also what he assumes by (1) the question and (2) the asking of it – his presuppositions and presumptions.

In order to understand what we are doing and to know how to do it better, we are obliged to understand what assumptions are and to know which assumptions we are making when we ask questions. For one thing, all answers depend on them. Another practical reason is that some respondents know our assumptions better than we do and use them to better advantage in the exchange. If the respondents can figure these out on the spot, we should not have too much trouble coming to understand them ourselves. We have much more time to consider these matters.

Presuppositions

Informally put, presuppositions are those sentences which (express propositions that) are entailed by the question-sentence. For a question to be valid, its presuppositions must be true. Then it can be validly answered. If the presuppositions are not true the question cannot be truly answered, because an answer affirms the presupposition of the question. Any answer, then, to a question with not-true presuppositions – whether false or indeterminate, or not known to be true or false – itself re-assumes the not-true suppositions that the question pre-assumes. The question will be answered either way, and the presuppositions affirmed. We have to know whether our question is being validly answered and our presuppositions truly affirmed. Hence we need to know our presuppositions.

Linguists and logicians are the ones who can tell us what presuppositions are. Although their analyses are formidable, for some reason their examples are funny. Here are two favourite examples. 'Is the King of France bald?' This question presupposes that:

1 there is a present king of France;
2 the king is either bald or not-bald.

'Have you stopped beating your wife?' presupposes that:

1 you have a wife;
2 you used to beat her;
3 either you have stopped beating her or you are still beating her.

Logicians also supply sprightly names for questions that fail on various presuppositional grounds. Consider these three types (from Belnap 1969; Belnap and Steel 1976):

1 *trivial* – the answer is already known (to the questioner). 'Does 2 + 2 equal 4?'; 'Are these words written in English?'
2 *foolish* – the question is known to have no true answer. 'Which of the following exist: unicorns or chimeras?'; 'Are these words printed in red or in green ink?'
3 *dumb* – the question has no direct answers whatsoever. 'What are at least three truths from among the following: A and B?'

And these two types (Keenan and Hull 1973):

4 *vacuous* – of zero truth-value; the presupposition is neither true nor false. 'Did the students who failed get drunk?' (when all students passed).
5 *pathological* – no answer is false. 'Which man likes the girl he likes?'; 'Which students came early and didn't come early?'

And these four (Rescher 1982):

6 *trivial* – the presuppositions of the question afford an answer to it. 'Does this question have an answer?'
7 *premature* – the truth-status of the presuppositions is unknown or indeterminate (but none is known to be false). 'What is the reason or the cause for the existence of the world?'; 'What are the learning processes of extra-terrestrial inhabitants of our galaxy?'
8 *inappropriate* – every answer is false, since some presupposition is false. 'How long is a novel?'; 'Why is the moon made of green cheese?'
9 *absurd* – there is no answer at all, every answer is self-inconsistent. 'Why is that tree inorganic?' 'Is "no" the correct answer to this question?'
10 By contrast, a *legitimate* or proper question is 'one whose presuppositions are all (known to be) true' (Rescher 1982: 136–7).

The implication for practice is that the questioner should know the presuppositions and their truth. We should be able to answer clearly to ourselves these two analytic questions:

1 What does the question presuppose?
2 Is that which it presupposes known to be true?

If we cannot answer these, then we cannot know the meaning and worth of the respondent's answer.

The implication is not that we ask questions that are true, only that we know the truth of the questions we ask. Most questioners do neither. Some knowingly ask questions with false presuppositions, or with indeterminate ones. These might be called trick questions, used as a tactic in some cases, most notoriously in such cases as 'Have you stopped beating your wife?' Whether the answer is yes *or* no, and whether the answer is true *or* false, the answer communicates 'I did beat my wife'.

What the practitioner must do is to know the content and the truth of the presuppositions and then elect to ask the question or not, according to purpose. Some purposes are served only by questions with true presuppositions; other purposes are also served by false and indeterminate ones. It is part of the skill of questioning to use this presupposition and not another for this purpose and not another. Not to know which is which is already by definition lack of skill.

An example of a deliberately false and serviceable presupposition is as follows. An interrogator who believes that a criminal suspect is lying that he was at a concert at the crucial hour in question, may make up a fictitious event and then ask a question that presupposes the truth of this falsity: 'How did you react when the tuba player had a heart attack?' (Buckwalter 1983). Whatever the answer, it will prove to be false because it affirms the truth of the false presupposition.

Cross-examiners, by contrast, may try to insert a *true* or indeterminate presupposition into a question in order that, whatever the answer, it may be affirmed as true. 'Did you ever get those brakes fixed on that truck?' In that way the adversarial witness unwittingly testifies to something that damages his case, for the presupposition is now admitted into evidence. For that reason opposing counsel must be alert to the presuppositions of every question being asked by his counterpart, and speedily object to the question before *any* answer is given, that is, before the presupposition of the question is affirmed.

With suspects whose guilt is reasonably known, the investigator's questions presuppose certain facts rather than question them. The questions are not 'Did you?' or 'Are you?', for these presuppose that *either* yes or no is true. The investigator does not believe in the truth of that presupposition, so he uses questions that presuppose the truth of 'you did' and the falsity of 'you didn't'. The questions are 'How did you?' and 'Why did you?' and so on (Buckwalter 1983).

Presumptions

This second kind of prior assumption (again, in our informal terms) attaches not to the question-sentence but to the act of uttering it. For a question to be valid, its presuppositions must be true. For the questioning to be genuine or sincere, its presumptions must be true – that is, they must accurately describe the conditions that hold in the question-situation.

When a person asks a question, he communicates his belief in certain conditions that obtain. These conditions describe such states as knowing the answer, desiring the answer, believing that there is an answer and one true answer, and estimating that the respondent can and will supply the answer. The respondent is invited to presume likewise or, at least, to believe that the questioner so presumes. For example, here are the presumptions describing what is called the *standard* question-situation. These are not standard in any field of question–answer practice, but every field will show some variation of each of these presumptions.

The first or primary presumption is that the questioner believes that the presupposition(s) to the question is/are true. It may be false, but no matter; asking the question presumes its truth, that is, commits the speaker to it as true, or expresses the speaker's belief that it is true. The analytic question for us and our respondent to answer here is, does the questioner believe that the question's presuppositions are true?

The other 'standard' presumptions may be variously enumerated and formulated. One formulation (Dillon 1986) holds that the person who asks a question asseverates and communicates these eight attitudes:

1 *Ignorance*. I am in a state of not-knowing, and I realize that I do not know.
2 *Perplexity*. I am experiencing perplexity (puzzlement, uncertainty, and so on) as a consequence of not-knowing.
3 *Need*. I feel a necessity to know.
4 *Desire*. I aspire to know.
5 *Belief*. I commit myself to the truth of the question (I believe its presuppositions are true, its words are as I intend them, and so forth).
6 *Faith*. I am confident that the unknown is knowable.
7 *Courage*. I venture to face the unknown and its consequences both within myself and the world.
8 *Will*. I resolve to undertake to know.

These are the presumptions for standard enquiry, as when a student or scientist raises a question about the subject-matter being studied. But hardly any questioner in fields of practice holds to *these* particular presumptions, and few respondents would believe it if they pretended to. These presumptions make the clearest distinction between two sorts of questioning: the raising or asking of questions; and the putting of questions to others for answer. This book is concerned only with the second sort of questioning.

To understand the role of presumptions, all we need do is to go down the list of 'standard-enquiry' presumptions and formulate each one in terms of our field of practice. We hold presumptions in our questioning; what are they?

For example, cross-examiners know the answers to the questions they ask. Their practice positively requires them not to ask a question to which they do not know the answer. The rule of thumb runs, 'Never ask a question unless you already know the answer.' Examiners in any field already know the answer, whereas the candidates are not presumed to know it. Media interviewers may not care what the answer is, nor whether it be true or not, rather that *an* answer be given that is of a certain quality – revealing, quotable, and so on.

In other cases the presumptions may vary according to context. Teachers might be viewed as already knowing the answers to their questions, but in practice teachers and students participate in a complex of shifting presumptions. Sociolinguistic research (Johnson 1979) has identified nine possible sets of teacher/student assumptions regarding knowledge of the matter in question, and belief in the truth of the question's presuppositions. Here are the presumptions in the three most common types of questioning observed in classrooms.

1. *Request for demonstration of information*. The teacher (T) knows the answer and does not assume that the student (S) does not know it. Similarly, T believes what the question presupposes, and does not believe that S disbelieves it. Note that the presumption is not 'T believes that S knows the answer'. This test-like kind of question is insincere only when T assumes that S does not know the answer.

2 *Request for factual information*. T does not know the answer and thinks that S at least may know it; T at least does not disbelieve the presupposition, and believes that S does believe it.
3 *Request for opinion information*. Same as (2), save that here S does know the answer.

This analysis describes shared beliefs. T believes, and S believes, and each believes the other believes. Yet it should be evident that the beliefs can in practice be held by one party but not another. This introduces a further complexity in theory, and one that in certain fields is deliberately introduced into practice.

For example, interrogators of criminal suspects and reluctant witnesses or informants will at times communicate by their questioning that they already know the answer, whereas in truth they are trying to find it out. The suspect is to believe in a condition that the interrogator believes not to hold in the question–answer situation. Thus the suspect comes to believe, 'He already knows more than I thought, I might as well confess.' The interrogator who asks a question with a deliberately false presupposition ('How did you react when the tuba player had a heart attack?'), is involved in a situation with these presumptions:

1 The suspect might believe in the truth of the question's presupposition, and the interrogator knows it to be false.
2 The interrogator does not believe that there exists any true answer, and the suspect presumes that some answer must be true (but which one?).
3 The suspect wants to give the true (correct, right) answer, but the interrogator does not want any true answer at all, rather he wants a false one.
4 The investigator doesn't care what the answer is, any answer will do because all answers will be false.

The implications for practice are that the questioner know just which conditions are being presumed, both by himself and by the respondent, and how accurately these presumptions describe the situation. Then the questioning can be pursued with skill – whether the situation is such as to require that the presumptions be accurate or that they be not, or that this or that presumption hold to such or such a degree, or be held by such or such a party to the exchange. Not to know these things is already to blunder.

Question

This second element too has two parts, the question-sentence and the act of uttering it. Of all the aspects under which these may be considered, we will treat only the formulation of the question and the manner of its expression.

Formulation

Formulation refers to the verbal form in which the question in mind is couched. As is the case in general with language, most questioners find it difficult to put into words just what it is they want to know or to find out from the respondent. Apart from this enduring problem, the major point about the formulation of a question is that it defines the kind of answer possible and it affects several characteristics of the eventual answer given. We will examine selected semantic and syntactic aspects of the question's formulation – its vocabulary and structure.

1 Vocabulary

It is obvious that the wording of a question affects the answer. Here we note that the *choice* of words can influence the answer, as survey researchers have demonstrated long ago in a number of classic experiments. For example, more than twice as many American respondents will not 'allow' speeches against democracy as will 'forbid' them (Schuman and Presser 1981). Similarly, in trying to get reliable answers about the respondent's socially undesirable behaviour (for example, intoxication, drug addiction), survey researchers discover that by using familiar rather than formally correct words in the question, people report having consumed twice as many cans of beer and masturbated thrice as often (Bradburn and Sudman 1979).

For their part, investigators find that their choice of words affects the readiness of suspects to reveal information. The questioners *avoid* correct, precise terms like 'kill', 'steal', 'rape', and ask about 'shoot', 'take', 'sex'. In assault-and-battery cases, the question 'Why did you hit him?' will be evaded, but 'Did you fight him?' affirmed. In a case of murder, motives are revealed in answer to 'Why did you do it?' more than to 'Why did you murder the man?'.

The choice of words also affects answers about ordinary things that people have just seen. An observed person is reported to be 10 inches taller in answer to 'How tall?' than to 'How short?', and a movie 30 minutes longer for 'How long?' than for 'How short?' Eyewitnesses to traffic collisions give systematically higher estimates of speed when asked 'How fast were the cars going when they contacted/hit/smashed?' – 31/34/41 mph (Loftus 1979).

What is more, the wording of the question can influence people not only to over-under-report but also to give, truly, answers about non-existent things. A tradition of psychological experiments since Muscio (1916) has amply shown that people will witness to events that never took place, and aver having seen objects that were not present in the scene before them. They do so unwittingly by way of answering questions that assert that event or object in the wording of the question.

The classic case, and the simplest, is for the questioner to denote by 'the' instead of 'an' an object that was not present in the observed scene. Where there was no X, more people will say 'yes' to 'Did you see the X?' than will say 'no' to 'Did you see an X?' For example, three times as many college students answered 'yes' as 'no' to questions about their instructor's non-existent moustache, eyeglasses, accent, and lisp. 'Did you detect his/a southern accent?' (Davis and Schiffman 1985). In our view, we attribute this result not to words alone but to the *presuppositions* marked by the wording. The first question presupposes the existence of X, while the second does not (that is, it presupposes that X either did or did not exist). Here we see again that answers affirm the presuppositions and we see that respondents tend to agree with the presuppositions in the course of answering in terms of the question.

In general, respondents find it easier – even more desirable – to go along with the question as posed rather than to dispute it and complicate the exchange. For, where the X in question did not exist, a respondent would first have to reject the question, 'Did you see the X?'; deny and then correct the false presupposition ('There was an X'); next negotiate a new understanding with the questioner who, although the more authoritative speaker in the exchange, now stands awkwardly corrected; and last await yet further questions about that one point. It is easier to say yes and let it go at that.

We note further that people say 'yes' but *not* 'no' in such cases. 'No' would reveal their ignorance or uncertainty about a commonplace event to which they were supposedly a witness and the occurrence of which the questioner has just affirmed. Hence a 'no' would call into question for the respondents themselves their own competence as an ordinary observer and knower. 'Be agreeable and say yes' seems to be the pragmatic motto.

Once having been so agreeably incorrect in their answer, respondents base their answers to subsequent questions upon the truth of the false presupposition that they had affirmed in their previous answer. In that way their 'eyewitness' testimony can build fiction upon fiction, without either the questioner or the answerer recognizing it as fiction. Or, otherwise viewed, this is a case where the non-existent event, once heard in the question, passes into the respondent's memory and is retrieved therefrom in answer to subsequent questions. For example, witnesses who agreeably answer to 'How fast was the car going when it passed the barn?', at a scene where no barn stood, tend subsequently to answer 'yes' to 'Did you see the barn?' (Loftus 1982). Eyewitnesses asked the 'smashed' version of the question, 'How fast were the cars going when they – ?' tend to answer 'yes' to the subsequent question, 'Did you see any broken glass?', when no broken glass existed at the scene they had witnessed (Loftus 1979).

We note that these witnesses are not making up answers. They are searching their memory for information that is indeed truly remembered. But it is false information. It is traceable to the false presupposition the truth of which they had affirmed in agreeably answering the prior question. It is a false answer truly given.

In that way we return to the usefulness for the questioner of knowing the presuppositions to his questions, and then of choosing, rightly *or* wrongly, to ask these questions, false *or* true. On that will depend the content and the worth of the answer, irrespective of whether the answer in turn be X or not-X, and valuable or not. The value of question–answer does not turn on its truth/falsity but on its suitableness to purpose in a particular circumstance of practice. True answers can be worthless, as also false answers truly given.

2 Structure

As a matter of logic, the syntactic structure of a question circumscribes the set of possible answers. And, as a matter of pragmatics, it influences the answers actually given. Of the multiple aspects of structure, we shall examine only the working of alternative-questions and compare them to questions without alternatives.

Alternative-questions One class of questions is structured so as to specify the alternatives in answer. For our purpose, the two most useful points about alternatives are that questioners rarely specify them correctly (for example, the wrong ones or too few), and that the number and kind of alternatives in the question affect the content and worth of the answer.

Questions may frequently be structured for a yes/no, either/or answer when the case in fact is not one of yes or no, either X or Y, or even Z. In general, it is difficult to structure a question with correctly dichotomous alternatives or with mutually exclusive and jointly exhaustive ones. This difficulty describes a common intellectual deficiency that is exhibited in but is not specific to the formulation of questions. Of course, false-dichotomous questions can also be used as a deliberate ploy, as in asking a loaded question ('Would you rather be Red or dead?').

Both the number and the content of alternatives affect the answers. For example, shoppers report having tried more new products, and having suffered more headaches, when asked 'How many – one? five? ten?' than for 'one? two? three?' (Loftus 1982). A series of experiments (Schuman and Presser 1981) has demonstrated particularly interesting effects of changing the alternatives in four different ways. The results are useful for showing how to formulate such questions in practice.

1 *Don't-know.* As a result of explicitly adding a don't-know or no-opinion alternative to the basic agree–disagree question, an average of 22 per cent more respondents (in 19 experiments) shifted from agree–disagree to don't-know. Thus a questioner might take care to provide in an explicit and permissive way for the alternative case that the respondent does not know the answer or has no answer to give. As noted earlier, people may tend to respond agreeably in terms of the question and/or avoid displaying ignorance or uncer-

tainty. Where our purposes benefit, we should explicitly make 'don't-know' OK.

2   *Counter-argument*. Adding a consideration for the negative or opposite view in question resulted in a shift of 8 per cent to the negative (nine experiments). Without such a consideration, the respondent is faced with such a choice as 'X, or anti-X?'. As noted, respondents may tend to agree with the proposition in question, especially when no balancing terms are provided for the opposite view: indeed, the opposite view may even remain unidentified in the question. A general way to provide balance is 'Some people think X, some people think not-X, which do you think?' or 'X because of A, and not-X because of B; X or not-X?'.

3   *Middle term*. Adding a logical middle term resulted in a shift of 15 per cent more respondents to the middle alternative (16 experiments). For example, 'strict, lenient, or about right?'.

4   *Placement*. Whatever its content, the last-listed of two or three alternatives was chosen by 10 per cent more respondents than when this same alternative was in first or second place. For example, 14 per cent more respondents answered 'plenty' when asked if America is running out of oil or has plenty, than for plenty or running out. When asked if divorce should be made easier to obtain, more difficult, or stay as it is, 10 per cent more respondents chose 'more difficult' when that was the last alternative (vs. when it was the second), and 12 per cent more chose 'as is' when that was last (vs. second).

The implication for practice is to appreciate the workings of alternatives and then manipulate them according to purpose. Far from benefiting from added alternatives, some purposes may require avoiding them altogether. For example, lawyers are advised to avoid questions that offer alternatives (Kestler 1982). In discovery proceedings, the witness might choose one of the two proffered alternatives instead of giving yet a third which would be more damaging; and on cross-examination there is no point to giving a choice: 'Pin the witness down to the answer you want' (p. 75).

Open/closed questions   Questions can be structured without specified alternatives. These are sometimes called 'open/free' questions, in contrast to 'closed/fixed' ones, but it is important to adopt the notion and not these terms, for the terms uselessly refer to multiple divergent things in various fields and books.

The notion being described here is that one generic form of question permits respondents to bespeak their own ideas in their own words, whereas the other generic form specifies ideas and words for them to choose. Both types constrain the response, but in differing ways. For example, asked about what they most prefer in a job, only half as many people volunteered 'a feeling of accomplishment' as selected it from the alternatives. Good pay was mentioned by as many respondents in both cases, but it was the least frequently chosen alternative and the most frequently volunteered answer. Fully 60 per cent of the responses to the open question fell outside of the five alternatives in the closed question (Schuman and Presser 1981).

What is to be made of these differences? The implication for practice is altogether conceptual. It is to recognize that different answers are given to the two forms of question, and that the answers given to the one form may not even be given *at all* to the other form. The conceptual significance is that the questioner who asks closed questions may be specifying categories of thought that are unrepresentative of what respondents think, with the result that respondents confirm our own frame of reference without our even realizing it.

Narrative/directive questions Here too the terms vary. And here again we shall attend to the notion, regardless of the terms. The notion runs that the one structure permits the respondent to speak at some length about his knowledge of a topic, the other directs him to answer point for point. For example, a witness might be asked, 'And then what happened?' and, after retailing the events, be asked any kind of question about specific points mentioned or omitted. The difference in the answers has long been known.

For example, one of the oldest experiments (Yamada 1913) had students read a geographical description of South America, and then asked a free-narrative question ('What do you know about the surface of South America?') followed by a series of 24 specific questions from the reading. On average, the students made three times more errors in answering the specific questions, even incorrectly answering about points that they had correctly reported during their narrative answer.

Apart from the accuracy of answer, there is its completeness or the exhaustiveness of detail. A number of studies have examined these two characteristics as they vary by three types of question (Loftus 1979):

1 Answers to the free-narrative or open question are the most accurate but least complete,
2 Answers to the controlled-narrative or specific questions are less accurate and more complete,
3 Answers to multiple-choice or alternative questions are the least accurate and the most complete.

The implication for practice is obviously that each of the different types of question has advantages and disadvantages. In some fields the implication is to use these types in a particular order. Investigators, for example, are advised to interview co-operative witnesses by first asking a free-narrative question, then a series of specific questions about the points mentioned, going from general to specific information and from known to unknown; next to ask some cross-questions to re-examine, test, verify, or probe selected points; and lastly to ask some open, summary questions such as to see if anything important has been left out or remains to be clarified. But that is not the case when faced with a reluctant witness; then the interrogator is to use patient, persistent, probing questions (Buckwalter 1983).

Finally, one practical implication is to prepare our questions with care, to formulate them in writing, and to arrange them in some order – all beforehand. This advice is given to interviewers and interrogators, survey-takers, lawyers, journalists, and teachers. What is more, practitioners in some fields are advised to test the formulation of their questions before using them in practice. Lawyers are urged to rehearse the questions with their own witnesses, to proceed to a mock cross-examination, and to video-record the whole so that they and the witness can evaluate the question–answer – all before the trial (Kestler 1982).

Nothing looks as effortless and spontaneous as the facile questioning by lawyers, journalists, teachers, and the like seen on TV or experienced in real life. They ask an impressive number of questions. Are the questions effective to purpose? Is the questioning skilful? One wonders, not knowing. That depends not only on the formulation of the question but also on the manner of expressing it.

Expression

Formulation refers to the question-sentence; expression refers to the act of putting the question. Here too there are multiple aspects to consider, and divergent ways in which any one manner of questioning can affect responses. We shall note only two aspects – the flow of questions, and the attitude expressed in the questioning. These seem useful enough to show the variety of manner and the necessity of adopting a manner suited to particular purpose.

1 Flow

Flow of questioning refers to such things as the frequency, rate, and sequence of questions asked. The most useful generalization is that people don't like to be asked numbers of questions, especially at a fast pace. At minimum the experience is vaguely comfortable; from there it can become actively stressful. According to purpose, then, the practitioner would adjust the flow of questioning.

One would think, for example, that where purposes include the stimulation of respondents' expressivity or enhancement of understanding, the questioning would be deliberate, measured, and calm. And, where the purpose is to get respondents to disclose information that they do not wish to give, the questioning would be fast, urgent, and hectic. Yet that is not the case, at least not in classrooms and interrogations.

Ever since the very start of research into classroom questioning (Stevens 1912), observers have noted regularly and with some astonishment that teachers ask a great number of questions at a markedly high rate – too fast for pupils to think, let alone to express their thought. The average lapse of time between the pupil's answer and the teacher's next question has been measured at less than one second (Rowe 1974). It has proved to take arduous training for teachers to increase their pausing or 'wait-time' even to two seconds (Swift and Gooding 1983).

What purposes are served by this fast, continuous questioning? One of the purposes seems to be to maintain control over social and verbal behaviour in the classroom, whence the understandably great difficulty of persuading teachers to reduce the number or rate of questions asked – that is, seemingly to reduce their control over the classroom. This manner of questioning is manifestly effective for that purpose. On the other hand, it cannot be demonstrated to advance other purposes such as the enhancement of pupils' cognitive, affective, and expressive processes.

Interrogators too can be seen to use this manner of questioning – in police dramas and Second World War movies. But in practice, as far as is known, their manner of questioning is advisedly measured and calm. According to the manuals, the questions should be asked in a conversational tone, in a smooth, lower, relaxed voice (Buckwalter 1983). The interrogator is to *avoid* all rapid-fire questions and rushing any answers; he is to wait for the full answer, as complete as the respondent wishes, and to give the respondent the opportunity to qualify it. What purpose is served? The intended purpose is to obtain true, factual information from someone who is reluctant to disclose it. Rapid, rough questioning seems to frustrate this purpose; it is better to use persistent yet patient questioning, with a pause before and after the question.

For some reason, physicians use a manner of questioning similar to that popularly thought to be used by interrogators but not actually used by them, and identical to that actually used by teachers but seemingly not expected to be used by them. In doctor–patient interviews, the doctor speaks almost nothing but questions, asks numerous, response-constraining questions (yes/no, multiple-choice), at a staccato pace with incursions into patient turns, and with scarcely a pause between the patient's answer and the doctor's next question – as little as one-tenth of a second (West 1983). What purposes are being served, and which ones frustrated, by this questioning?

Cross-examiners also use rapid-fire questioning, but advisedly so. It is relentless and intimidating, keeping pressure on the witness and keeping him off-balance, while enforcing his subordinate status (Kestler 1982). The purpose is to give the witness no time to think, and no opportunity to formulate the answer carefully. 'There should be no gap between questions which would allow the witness time to think' (p. 46). As the classic manual put it, 'He cannot invent answers as fast as you can invent questions' (Wellman 1936: 68). The sequencing of the questions is also according to purpose. In carefully preparing the questions, the examiner arranges them in logical order but he must not ask them in logical order (Wellman 1936), rather eliminating any semblance of order at all, using 'the hop, skip, and jump' approach (Kestler 1982). The trick is not in using chaotic questioning but in creating order from it for the jury, not to mention for the examiner himself.

As these four cases – teachers, interrogators, physicians, cross-examiners – show, the flow of questioning differs in various practices, as do the purposes that are served *and* that are not served by the manner of questioning in a given practice.

2 Attitude

Here too the practitioner may ask self, 'Just what am I questioning *for*?', and then adopt an attitude of questioning which achieves that purpose. There is no one attitude to adopt, and no point in adopting the attitude of successful questioners in other circumstances.

Again, the only generalization that appears to hold is that people find it threatening or somehow diminishing to be asked questions, even when the questioner does not set out to be threatening. Great care must therefore be taken to see that the attitude which is received is the attitude that the questioner wishes to convey, and that both be suitable to purpose. A threatening manner is conducive to some purposes but not others, even in the same situation.

The questioner must be clear both as to what his purpose is, and which purposes are being served by his manner of questioning. The case is complicated because there are multiple purposes that can be held in any one situation, such that one purpose but not another may be served by the questioning.

For instance, one purpose in a classroom might be to stimulate student thought, and in a personnel interview, to get the applicant to talk about self; yet the teacher's questioning may serve rather the purpose of social and verbal control, and the interviewer's may cause the respondent to talk less and less with each successive question. There is a therapeutic purpose in psychoanalysis that the analyst's questioning might not only not serve but actually contravene, both by reinforcing such things as dependency and defensiveness in the patient and by serving the therapist's pregenital desire to master and dominate in the relationship (Olinick 1954).

Such are the purposes that are exactly appropriate, on the other hand, in cross-examination. But they are quite inappropriate to interrogation and they are ruinous to survey interviewing. Interrogators and interviewers must deliberately adopt a non-judgemental manner of questioning, the first because they need all true information, the second because they need all reliable responses. The two cases form a surprising pair, for respondents in an opinion poll are not coerced into answering the questions and seemingly stand to lose nothing by answering them correctly, whereas suspects are in a coercive situation where they can lose a great deal by giving truthful answers. Yet survey respondents give distorted answers to innocuous questions about everyday matters. To avoid such distortion to the extent possible, interviewers must not only formulate their questions in a certain way but also ask them in a non-judgemental way, conveying neither approval nor disapproval to the respondent.

Interrogators too, oddly enough, must ask questions in a non-judgemental manner. As the manuals repeatedly point out, what the interrogator needs is truthful information; others, later, will make the judgements. Far from being judgemental, here are the attitudes and qualities to be exhibited by the interrogator: understanding, consideration, sympathy, empathy, concern, gentleness, kindness, courtesy, tact, reasonableness, fairness, honesty, warmth, respect, friendliness. One manual is even entitled, *The Gentle Art of Interrogation* (Royal and Schutt 1976).

It is this manner of questioning, rather than the Hollywoodish opposite, that more likely induces a person who is deeply implicated in a bad situation to tell the truth. We may think that the pragmatics of this question–answer situation are that the suspect or otherwise involved person comes to believe something like, 'The truth is the best solution to my predicament; I can trust him, he will understand, I can explain'. By contrast, a judgemental, superior, threatening or intimidating style of questioning seems to confirm the person's initial reluctance to disclose what he knows. If individuals in an opinion poll have trouble averring that they do not hold a library card or that they prefer this opinion over that, we can imagine the difficulty of confessing to murder, rapine, and mayhem.

The case of teachers is all the more complicated because they too need to know what the students truly think (for example, in a discussion) and know (for instance, in a recitation) at the same time as they are required to be judgemental. In classroom question–answer situations, whether for questions of fact or opinion, it is obligatory that the teacher follow the answer with a judgement as to its quality (such as, accept/reject and/or modify). The role of teaching by definition entails judgement and correction of pupils' thought processes.

Finally, as noted, the case of counsellors and therapists – as well as of others, such as personnel interviewers – is not only complicated but variegated. According to therapeutic purpose and process as variously and divergently conceived, one form of question and one manner of questioning, as well as their contraries, might serve to purpose and either be required or prohibited in practice. It is odd to think that some counsellors can appear to be inquisitors, whereas interrogators adopt the attitude of counsellors.

In sum, there is no one form of question and no one manner of asking questions that is reliably known to have one given effect, even in given situations.

In a field where the most extensive research has been carried on for half a century, one conclusion still runs that 'knowledge of questioning effects of all kinds is likely to be a slow and uphill struggle' (Schuman and Presser 1981).

What, then, are the types of questions that should be used? What strategies of questioning should be pursued? These are pressing questions in practice and they are perplexing ones for theoretical and empirical research. To both questions the fairest answer for the practitioner is, 'No one but you can really know.' That is, the answer is better found by the practitioner in a particular circumstance. And the best way to look for it is to attend not so much to questions and questioning as to answers and answering.

Answers

Of the three elements of questioning, this last is as complex, more interesting, and the most important both theoretically and practically. Understanding what answers are is a good way to understand what questions are, while a theoretical knowledge of answers is the best practical guide to formulating and putting questions – and then seeing what the answer is and whether it is an answer at all.

Like the other elements of questioning, this one consists of a sentence and an act, or answer and answering. We will speak rather of response and responding. For it turns out that, of all the things that people may say and do when asked a question, the very *least* is to give an answer. We will examine types of responses and styles of responding.

Types of responses

It may help to appreciate at the outset that most responses are not answers and that the defining characteristic of an answer is not 'something said in response to a question'. For, although answers are indeed responses to a question, so also are all manner of other things.

In conceptual terms, we will say that 'answer' is not a thing but a *notion*, and in large part a pragmatic one. It describes a certain character that we attribute to a given sentence such that we conceive of that sentence as being of the kind labelled 'answer', when following upon a given question, and that same sentence as 'non-answer' when following upon some other question or no question at all.

What, then, makes a sentence an answer? That is not an easy question, and so far no one has a good answer to it. We can approach this question by considering the variety of responses that can be given to a sentence.

Unfortunately, the available terminology is unclear and the typologies are ill-founded. We will have to accept for the moment that there are multiple terms used in divergent senses for the variety of things that have to be described and distinguished. Some of the terms will refer to the response-sentence, others to the act of responding, and yet others to the respondent; still other terms will confound these three. We will proceed by paying attention to the notions. First, there are things that follow a question but are non-responses; second, there are responses that are non-answers; and third, there are answer-responses.

1 Non-responses

Nothing at all may follow upon a question, or nothing remotely connected with it, or nothing appropriately connected. An instance of each would be: silence, wild talk, change of topic (although any of these could also represent a deliberate mode of responding).

Speech wildly unrelated to the preceding question is a non-response. Speech that is somehow related is a response. There are multiplicitous relations that a piece of speech can have with a preceding question. For example, response may be an utterance coherently related to a preceding question by grammatical and lexical cohesion, such as reference, substitution, ellipsis; and/or by prosodic, semantic, and pragmatic agreement (Stenstroem 1984). There are also delayed responses such as requests for repetition and clarification (Stenstroem 1984) or other procedural problems (Churchill 1978), such as 'Huh?'

2 Non-answer responses

Most responses are non-answers. The questioner may fancy that the other person is required to give an answer, and he may expect, want, or intend an answer of some particular type, but all that seems to be required in most question–answer situations is that the person give a response. All manner of non-answer responses can be given, most of which must be politely treated as acceptable in address to the question or to the act of asking it.

Completion of invitation, ellipsis, interruption, emotion, and *clarification* are among the types of non-answer responses found in conversations of a married couple (Churchill 1978). Only half of the response were answers, whether direct or indirect. Not only were the non-answers given by the respondent, but they were also accepted or tolerated by the questioner. The questioner apparently applies two tests to what follows upon the question:

1 Is it recognizable as a response?
2 If not, can the non-compliance be explained away?

Some types of responses supply or constitute explanations.

Excuses are any responses that explicitly indicate either inability or unwillingness to answer (Johnson 1979). 'I don't know' indicates inability, as also does a denial of the question's presupposition – 'the best possible excuse for not answering' (p. 31). But respondents rarely indicate, in a direct or serious way, an unwillingness to answer. For example, students will camouflage unwillingness as inability ('I don't know'), while teachers choose to infer inability rather than face what both parties suspect is an unwillingness to answer.

Evade and *disclaim* are appropriate responses, although not answers, because they relate coherently to the questioning act, although not to the question-sentence (Stenstroem 1984). As the terms suggest, these are interactional moves rather than sentences. A respondent may evade with 'You know that' or 'What a stupid question'; disclaim by 'I don't know' or 'I don't want to tell you'; and do either by saying 'How should I know?'

These examples are taken from everyday conversations, where evade and disclaim together accounted for only 4 per cent of all responses studied (Stenstroem 1984). Yet in certain circumstances of practice they account for the near totality of responses.

Non-answers characterize the responses of public officials in broadcast news interviews. These respondents are practised and skilled at giving not only evasive answers but outright non-answers. Analysis of interviews (Greatbatch 1986) reveals a variety of non-answers of four types.

First, the respondent can *claim inability*, or make an excuse. The most common claim is to assert lack of information, saying 'I don't know' in some form or other. For example:

Well, I can't deny or confirm it until I receive the evidence that you tell me I'm going to get tomorrow.

Or: 'until I see the report, study the case', and so on. Another claim is to assert privilege or prevention from answering. Pressed four times in a row to answer, the Prime Minister finally responded:

No of course I can't say. And I should be very remiss if I were to give *any* hint because it would put the lives of some of our people at risk, and that I would never do.

Variations include: 'That's classified'; 'I'm not at liberty to say'.

Second, the non-answering respondent can *reject the question*. One way is to deny its relevance or to deny the question itself.

Q. Do you quite like Mr Wilson?
A. Well, I think in politics you see, it's not a question of going about *liking* people or not, it's a question of *dealing* with people. And I've always been able to deal perfectly well with Mr Wilson and indeed he has with me.

Another way is to deny the presupposition of the question:

Q. Should local authorities be forced to sell?
A. Well they're not being forced to sell.

Or, third, the respondent can *repeat the question*, by reasserting the presupposition or by repeating the question utterance.

Q. What job do you see for Tony Benn?
A. Of course, if Tony Benn is elected he will be offered some job in the
Cabinet, and I'd be very happy to do that, and I hope that that will occur.

The presupposition of that question states, 'There will be a job for Tony Benn', and the non-answer states, 'There will be a job for Tony Benn'. Actually repeating the question ('What job do I see for Tony Benn?') is nearly always an effective non-answer response, since all but the most obdurate questioners will reply with 'Yes' plus some commentary ending in a different question:

Finally, the respondent may *refuse to answer*. This is a move which most everyday respondents will not risk, but which practised respondents accomplish with finesse. Most of the time the refusal is covert. The respondent talks on the topic but not to the question:

A. The advice to our members is ... That is the advice to our members.
Q. But mhm I didn't ask you what advice you were giving, do you think
that ...

An excellent example of this strategy is detailed in Chapter 8, where the journalist four times presses the question about support for illegal strikers, and four times the politician gives non-answers, covertly refusing to answer (see page 105 and transcript no. 9A). Less common is an overt refusal, especially a direct one:

I will not answer that question, I'm not deliberately answering that question.

If the refusal is to be overt, it is more commonly polite:

Well, that's a matter I wouldn't want to comment on.

A favourite way of refusing is merely to talk about something else: 'Well, let me say first that ... ' The long response continues without ever finishing the preface and getting 'secondly' to the answer.

3   Answer-responses

There remains the class of responses which are answers. A variety of definitions have been proposed and a variety of types distinguished. All of these exhibit a degree of confusion among three criterial aspects: the cognition of the questioner, the form of the question, and the act of questioning. To which one, and in which respect, is the character of answer being attributed?

Sociolinguists, for example, have defined 'answer' as those responses that fulfil the logical or substantive expectations of the question (Johnson 1979). Logicians, on the other hand, have viewed answers as those responses that are appropriate from the questioner's point of view (Harrah 1985). Sociolinguists have distinguished 'direct answer' as a response that gives exactly the information required, and an indirect answer as giving information from which a direct answer may be deduced (Stenstroem 1984). Logicians distinguish a direct answer as giving exactly what the question calls for, while an indirect answer gives some of that (Harrah 1985).

Who and what is requiring, expecting, calling for? We shall have to bear in mind that answers are imperfectly understood as relating now to the questioner, now to the question, and now to the questioning.

As expected, most manuals of practice give confused and useless typologies of answers, as they do of questions. And, as expected, logicians provide helpful ones.

To the question, 'Is glass a liquid at 70° F?' logicians (Belnap and Steel 1976) say that:

– a *just-complete* (or direct) answer is, 'Glass is a liquid at 70° F'; and
– a *complete* answer (implies direct answer) is 'Glass is a liquid at 70° F, and China is populous'.

To the question, 'Was she wearing the green dress, the emerald bracelet, or both?',

– an *eliminative* answer (negation of partial answer, implies denial of some direct answer) is 'She wasn't wearing green' or 'emeralds', and
– a *corrective* answer (implies denial of every direct answer) is, 'She was naked'.

More generally, logicians (Harrah 1985) distinguish replies that are *sufficient*, comprised of the set of indicated replies plus wanted replies (a subset of indicated) plus corrective replies (negate the presupposition or core assertion of the question); and *relevant*, comprised of full replies (imply the sufficient) and partial replies (implied by the sufficient).

With these lists in hand we can ask ourselves, what are the kinds of answer that I am after, and what kinds am I actually getting? For, answers relate not only to the logic and syntax of the question but also to the knowledge and purposes of the questioner.

Conclusive answer A reply to a question constitutes a conclusive answer to it if and only if it brings about the truth of the desideratum in question, making it the case that the questioner conclusively knows the X in question–answer (Hintikka 1983). 'Who killed Julius Caesar?' The answer is 'Cassius', and it is a direct and true answer. But it is a conclusive answer only if the questioner can say not only, 'I know that Cassius killed Caesar' but also essentially, 'I know who Cassius is'. Similarly, 'Charles Dodgson' is no conclusive answer to 'Who wrote *Alice in Wonderland*?' unless the questioner also knows Lewis

Carroll. The criterion of conclusiveness describes answers in relation to the knowledge-state of the questioner.

Significant answer Both the purposes and the knowledge of the questioner are described by the concept of a 'pragmatically significant answer' (Grewendorf 1983). An answer is significant when it is both informative and useful to the questioner in that situation in which the question is asked. For a simple example, consider how informative and useful 'Paris' is as an answer to the question 'Where is the Eiffel Tower?' asked on the streets of Paris.

To be both informative and useful, the answer must take into account the knowledge and the purposes of the questioner in the question-situation. For example, here is one question (Q) with five different answers according to situation (S): 'Where is Lutter and Wegner?' (Grewendorf 1983).

S1 In Munich two friends are conversing about taverns and another friend joins in, realizes that L & W is a tavern, and asks Q. *Answer:* In Berlin.

S2 In Berlin someone gets into a taxi and says 'Take me to L & W'. The driver asks Q. *Answer:* Schlueterstrasse 55.

S3 At the Wittenbergplatz in Berlin a pedestrian asks Q. *Answer:* Take the Underground to the stop BU and then ask again.

S4 On the corner of Kant and Leibniz streets in Berlin a pedestrian asks Q. *Answer:* Go straight ahead, take the first left as far as the second traffic light and it's right there.

S5 From a point where one can see L & W a pedestrian asks Q. Answer: Over there.

The range of significant answers is different in each of these situations, to the point that in no case does the given answer in any one situation belong to the range of alternative answers available for any of the other situations. All five of the answers given to this question are correct answers, and any one of them may be informative. Yet only one of them is in addition useful, helpful, valuable – and that one is a different one in each of the five cases. That one is the pragmatically significant answer.

We may put it that the answer provides that which the questioner needs to know in order to complement his situational ignorance and to accomplish his situational purpose. The respondent is charged with finding these things out before finding out the answer. He/she must, then, make assumptions and estimates about:

(a) the credulity of the questioner (the questioner believes what the answerer says to be true);

(b) the questioner's state of knowledge, in this situation;

(c) given (b), the questioner's purpose, in this situation;

(d) given (abc), the value for the questioner, of a given possible answer in this situation (Grewendorf 1983).

The respondent therefore makes estimates about the questioner's knowledge and purposes in this situation; assesses the value to the questioner of the various answers possible in this situation; and then gives an answer according to this pragmatic postulate:

Choose among the answers which you think are true that one for which the assumed/expected pragmatic significance is greatest.

Here we see a demonstration that answerhood is a *pragmatic notion*. Answer is a character attributed to a response that exhibits certain qualities in relation to the question that is asked, the knowledge and the purposes of the questioner, and the situation wherein question and answer transpire. These can make the answer not only informative and useful but also interesting or obvious.

Interesting answer An interesting answer denies the truth of some part of the routinely but weakly held assumption-ground of the audience that hears it. The answer is interesting not because it tells us some truth that we did not already know, but that some truth which we already know is wrong (Davis 1971). Interesting answers or propositions have the form, *What seems to be X is in reality non-X*, where X represents a characteristic of the phenomenon in question. Twelve categories of propositions have been identified as an 'index of the interesting' (Davis 1971). For example, here are three categories, each illustrated by a proposition from Sigmund Freud:

1 *Composition*. The X, non-X proposition runs: What seem to be assorted, heterogeneous phenomena are in reality composed of a single element. Freud proposed that the behaviours of children, primitives, neurotics, and adults in crowds, as well as dreams, jokes, and slips of the tongue and pen, are various manifestations of the same instinctual drives.
2 *Generalization*. What seems to be a local phenomenon is in reality a general phenomenon. Freud proposed that sexual impulses are a major influence on the behaviour not only of adults (which was fairly obvious) but also of children (not so obvious).
3 *Coexistence*. What seem to be phenomena which cannot exist together are in reality phenomena which can exist together. Freud proposed that love and hate are compatible.

To give an interesting answer is a matter apart from giving a correct answer. The audience can reject the answer's value while affirming its truth. Much depends on who will hear or receive and eventually use the answer, such as advocates and opponents on an issue, experts and lay persons. Their relevant beliefs and hopes are mutually contradictory. The assumptions of the one already constitute a denial of the assumptions of the other. Which answer, then, is interesting to whom?

Experts will find interesting an answer that strikes lay persons as obvious. The answer denies expert assumptions while affirming lay ones. It says: What everybody, except experts on the subject, think is true is in fact true. That's interesting! A boring answer tells experts that what they think is true is true. That's obvious!

In general, the answer relates to the audience's assumption-grounds. When an answer is not interesting, it is obvious, absurd, or irrelevant (Davis 1971).

Obvious. Instead of denying, the answer affirms some aspect of the audience's assumption-ground. 'Husbands often influence their wives' political behaviour.' Such an answer says: What seems to be the case is in fact the case; what you always thought was true is really true. The reaction to this answer is: That's obvious!

Absurd. Instead of denying some aspect, the answer denies the whole assumption-ground. 'Social factors have no effect on a person's behaviour.' Such an answer says: Everything that seems to be the case is not the case at all; everything that you always thought was true is really false. That's absurd!

Irrelevant. Instead of denying or affirming, the answer does not speak to any aspect of this assumption-ground at all. 'Eskimos are more likely than Jews to … ' Such an answer says: What is really true has no connection with what you always thought was true. That's irrelevant!

These unwelcome reactions signal that the answer is not interesting. They reveal not that the answer is wrong but that the question was the wrong one to begin with. It may have been, logically speaking, a dumb question (Belnap 1969). Pragmatically speaking, it was a dumb question to have to answer.

Influential answers The related concept of influential answers turns on how much influence each of the conceivable answers to a question can be expected to have (Cronbach 1982). The valence of the answer is related to the values of the audience. For instance, on the issue of using Laetrile for cancer treatment, a positive answer will have great effect on unbelievers but a negative one will leave enthusiasts unmoved. As a general principle, answers may be assessed by the degree to which they promise to reduce uncertainty *and* to exert leverage. An influential answer would rate strongly on these evaluative questions:

1 Will each fraction of the audience
   (a) attend to the answer,
   (b) understand it, and
   (c) find it credible?
2 Will the answer alter the preconceptions of the audience?
3 Will the answer enrich and elevate the dialogue leading to decisions?

On these counts, we might discover and weigh the sociopolitical as well as cognitive positions of those who will receive the answer. Otherwise our great effort to obtain reliable results, meaningful and true and good ones, will eventuate in the frustrated offer of a useless answer.

Fallible answers We have to concede and cope with the many respects in which answers are commonly deficient. Direct, complete answers can be incorrect. Think of student answers! The answer may be a lie. The answer may be incorrect and/or non-veridical even when the respondent is answering truly and genuinely. Medical patients may give full and forthcoming answers that are only partly informative and important, while otherwise deficient because of the patient's neglect, incapacity, ignorance, or preconceptions related to medical events and information. Survey respondents give distorted answers to commonplace questions. Informants in investigations and interrogations answer from their faulty perception, memory, understanding, and knowledge in addition to blinding prejudice. Eyewitnesses testify to events that never transpired, and they are sure of having seen them. Witnesses in courtrooms may be perjured, mistaken, incompetent, partisan, or otherwise prejudiced. With the exception of the outright liar, *all* of these respondents may be answering as best they can, giving woefully deficient answers.

We have no reason to expect that an answer sound on all other counts – logic, linguistics, conclusiveness, significance, interest, influence, directness, completeness, forthcomingness, genuineness, or even truthfulness – must for all of that also be an answer good and true. It can still fail on a dozen counts.

These are the types of responses. What are the different ways that people may use in responding to questions?

Strategies of responding

Just as was the case with responses and answers, so too there are many ways of responding without answering the question. Practitioners have to know these responding strategies in theory in order to spot and outmanoeuvre them in practice.

1 Evading

Evading is a routine strategy for responding to a question without answering it. There are any number of ways to evade or otherwise not to answer a question. For instance, seven purposive devices have been identified for a woman to avoid answering a man's question, 'How old are you?' (Weiser 1975).

One device is to be pointedly non-responsive. 'Nice weather we're having.' Another is a masquerade over something unconnected with the question. You have a sudden thought – 'Oh, no! I think I left my headlights on'. Something is happening – 'Look at the sunset, quick, before it changes'. You didn't hear the question – 'What are you writing your dissertation on?'

A further device is to respond with a question that is semantically connected with the question asked. 'How old do you think I am?' The respondent might also maintain silence, or yet directly refuse to answer. 'I'd rather not answer that.'

Finally, the respondent can use selective ambiguity in a pretence of co-operativeness, answering as if the questioner wants to know that one term of ambiguity in the question rather than the other. You take the question another way. 'Don't worry, they'll let me into that bar.'

These examples come from everyday conversation. Far more practised evading can be seen and heard in broadcast news interviews. Politicians and other public figures are renowned for giving evasive answers. Despite the great variety of non-answering strategies which they use (see Chapter 8 and the previous section in this chapter on 'refusal to answer', page 149) they also give out two simple linguistic signals whereby we can tell their vague and evasive answers. As revealed by analysis of their answers (Jucker 1986), these devices are routinely used to avoid or to reduce explicitness and commitment of answer.

The first device is the parenthetic verb, especially 'think, mean, suppose, imagine'. Apart from appearing throughout an answer, these four verbs mark the start alone of 20 per cent of the answers studied. The following example begins with 'I think' and shows 'I think' twice more and one 'I suppose'.

> I think they've taken a lot of his advice and I think he's done a very good job. I think to some extent the Government has a regional policy to consider and I suppose it's doing that at the moment.

Having been asked to criticize either the Government or the expert in question, the respondent manages to praise both.

The other common device is the particle or qualifier 'well'. It signals a lack of direct cohesion or relevance between answer and question, and it signals a forthcoming lack of information in response. In this example, both question and answer are prefaced by 'well':

> *Q.* Well do you think we might get better value for money out of the coal industry if it were in private hands or partly in private hands?
> *A.* Well I'm not talking, I'm not talking about denationalizing the coal industry ...

The Prime Minister talks on without giving a statement of opinion as asked on the matter in question.

Answers that state clearly affirming/negating, yes/no positions are rarely marked by 'well', whereas the hedged or less direct answers tend to be prefaced by 'well' (Jucker 1986). The same applies to answers to wh-questions. Fully 85 per cent of those which did not give the requested information were prefaced by 'well'; by contrast, 63 per cent of answers that did give the information were not prefaced by 'well'. All the examples given in the previous section herein on 'refusal to answer' begin with 'well'.

Two popular American Presidents in recent decades used 'well' so routinely in answering to press questions that their style of evasiveness passed into comic mimicry. One would start: 'Well, let me say this about that'. In other words, let me not answer that question. The other would just say 'well', shaking his head and pausing – a clear signal that the sequel would be no answer. He might just as well have ended there, for 'well' was all the answer he would be giving.

2 Lying

Lying is the most satisfying strategy for the unwilling respondent. It is not an evasive strategy, for it directly answers the question. 'Lying is the only way of "not answering" a question that will work when the questioner is absolutely determined to get an answer' (Weiser 1975: 653).

People routinely lie in answer to questions. Lying is even regarded as a right or norm, especially in situations where the questions are asked by those of superior authority or social status. 'People in power have the "right" to ask questions; people of less power feel they have the right to lie or to evade in answering' (Reisman and Benney 1956).

Those who would not lie can routinely be induced to lie. A long tradition of psychological experiments proves the point, as does a more recent line of communication research on deception. The most ordinary people in the most ordinary situations will lie; and when they are lying they usually get away with it, save in the experimental research situations where they are foreknown to be lying. One finding that is useful to the questioner is that *negative* probing makes liars appear to be more truthful (Stiff and Miller 1986). Positive probes may relax the deceiver's effort. To illustrate, here are the positive/negative probes put to experimental subjects who had cheated on a task of identifying dots on cards (Stiff and Miller 1986). After the first question about their successful strategy, the probes run:

2 That seems quite plausible. Could you go into more detail about ... ? (vs. negative, 'That doesn't seem very plausible'.)
3 It is pretty clear and convincing how you made such a notable improvement. What strategy caused the improvement? (vs. 'It is hard for me to grasp how anyone could have improved this much'.)
4 Now that you've given me a good explanation for your success, ... Did you think up the strategy, did your partner think it up, or was it something that evolved from your discussion? (vs. 'Frankly, I'm a little sceptical about your explanation'.)

Negative probes only increase the incentive to create an impression of truthfulness – to lie more effectively. Positive probes are more useful to the questioner's purposes. On the other hand, with people who appear to be telling the truth, negative probes create incentive to make it more plainly apparent that the answers are truthful.

3 Stonewalling

Far from evading or lying, stonewalling is giving direct, correct answers to questions when and as asked. But the answers may be meaningless. A witness, for example, might answer just exactly as required but, if not asked or if not asked rightly, he will not answer with the crucial knowledge that he has.

The problem for the questioner is to ask *all* the right questions, each in *just* the right way. Yet he might not know enough to ask and what he does know might be mistaken. Thus the questions may be based on false presuppositions and mistaken presumptions which the stonewalling witness affirms to be true in the course of giving a perfectly direct and correct answer that only confounds or misleads the questioner. If the questioner is lucky enough to catch on, he must press against the stone wall with a series of little, corrective questions pointed this way and that. Each will yield just one more tiny bit of information.

For example, suppose an administrative official is called to a hearing about racial discrimination in his department's hiring practices, and suppose that no employment tests happened to be given during October.

How many minority candidates failed the test in October?
– None.
They all passed?
– No.
Well, how many passed, then?
– Zero.
Did any minorities even take the test?
– No.
Why not? How many candidates were there in all?
– Zero.
You mean, nobody even took the test?
– Right.
What – You do have a test, don't you?
– Yes.
And you give it regularly?
– Yes.
Did you give it in October?
– No.
All right, how about November? (and so on)

By contrast, a co-operative witness would have answered to the very first question, 'There wasn't any test in October'.

4 Co-operating

Co-operative responding consists of giving a corrective, indirect response rather than a correct, direct answer. It corrects the false presuppositions and mistaken presumptions entailed in the questioning, and it goes on to provide the supportive and/or suggestive information at issue.

Giving a direct, correct answer is sometimes not helpful; co-operative answers are called for. They are called for in the frequent case of discrepancy in the mutual beliefs of questioner and answerer regarding the structure and content of the information. A co-operative answer is defined as 'both giving a truthful and informative response and 'squaring away' the discrepancies in mutual beliefs discerned during the interaction' (Joshi 1983: 237). For example, in the case where no linguistics courses had been offered:

Q. Which students got an F in linguistics in Autumn 1989?
A1. None.
A2. I don't know of any linguistics course in Autumn 1989.

The first answer is correct and direct but it is misleading. The second is corrective and indirect, co-operative and informative.

The principle of co-operative responding holds that not only must the respondent not give a false answer, but also he must not permit the questioner to infer from the true answer something that the respondent knows to be false (Joshi 1982). The respondent not only must correct the questioner's assumptions but also supply additional information, supportive and suggestive, to make the answer *helpful* – both truthful and informative (Joshi 1983).

Wonders never cease in the world of questioning, for machines have been designed to give co-operative responses. These are computerized query systems, such as the aptly named CO-OP (Kaplan 1981). Some are natural-language question–answering systems such as PLIDIS (Berry-Rogghe *et al.* 1980). PLIDIS has actually been used in the control of industrial water pollution in Germany. It is designed to give 'communicatively adequate answers' to busy officials who are expert about pollution but naïve about question-answering systems. They put their questions in German language. PLIDIS checks their questions and corrects their assumptions instead of mindlessly producing a correct but meaningless answer.

For example, the question 'Did Brecht check the samples from Lauxmann in Stuttgart in 1986?' presumes that Brecht is entitled to collect samples. And it presupposes the existence of the person Brecht, the firm Lauxmann, the location Stuttgart, the time 1986. It further presupposes samples from 1986, firms in Stuttgart, a firm Lauxmann in Stuttgart, and samples from the firm Lauxmann in Stuttgart in 1986. Should any of these be mistaken, PLIDIS will refrain from answering with a brute 'no' and will kindly rectify the question. PLIDIS even engages in a preliminary dialogue with the questioner, enquiring into the meaning of the question and clarifying any vagueness about it, as in this example:

Q. Was there any cyanide in the Lutz sample?
A. Lutz unknown, what syntactic class does the word belong to? – noun, adjective ...
Q. It's a name.
A. Name of what kind of thing? – company, person, place ...
Q. Person.
A. Lutz is not entitled to collect samples.

We might say that, before giving an answer, PLIDIS takes care to discover what the questioner is asking, what he understands and means by the question, and what sort of answer will satisfy not just the question but especially the questioner. Whatever the question, what is it that the questioner knows? – presumes and presupposes. And what is it that he wishes to know? – an informative answer.

How nice of PLIDIS and the other machines. But also how smart of them. Many of our respondents may be nice, but few of them will be so nice and smart. Unlike machines, respondents cannot be programmed to give co-operative answers. Some respondents know the presuppositions and presumptions better than the questioner does, and use them to better advantage.

Co-operative responding seems the best strategy of all from the questioner's point of view. But by now we should be sophisticated enough to realize that it is only desirable according to purpose in circumstance. In some cases it is not desirable at all, rather counter to purpose. In courtrooms, for instance, co-operative responses are the great fear of the questioner. The witness best answers only if and as asked, precisely in terms of the question and not a syllable more. He must not impose his additional or better knowledge upon the court. He must not give an opinion. He must not be asked a question that he wishes to answer. He must not offer to correct a falsehood that the court does not ask to be corrected. He must not volunteer answers to questions that have been objected to. He is there only to answer precisely as asked (Tierney 1971).

In these terms, a 'co-operative' witness – one using a strategy of co-operative responding – suffers complete frustration. And then it is the questioner who is satisfied. The questioner wants to prevent co-operative responding at all costs, seeking instead delimited answers in terms of the questions put. Anything more in response may frustrate purpose in circumstance. Of course, the opposing lawyer has a contrary purpose and may put the precise question for the feared response. The witness who would be co-operative must await the solicitous question from lawyer or judge. Even then he must only give answers to those questions he is asked and he must only give short, direct, and pointed answers. Otherwise the witness must remain silent – as if 'uncooperative', even stonewalling. That is the best way of responding in this circumstance – best for the questioner, not the respondent – and vice versa in other circumstances to other purposes.

5   Withholding and concealing

These are by definition uncooperative strategies of responding. Many respondents do not disclose what they know, either intentionally concealing it or withholding it wittingly or not. It is a commonplace way to respond to questions.

To give only one example, in various types of investigations (criminal, insurance, industrial), both the innocent as well as the guilty may withhold or conceal information intentionally and unintentionally.

Investigators question not only the tight-lipped criminal but also all manner of other people who for one reason or another may be hostile, reluctant, uncooperative, or just prejudiced about things. *Any* of these respondents may withhold or conceal information. Even friendly and co-operative witnesses still may not give information, for a dozen good reasons (cited in Chapter 7, page 78) – such as protection of self or others and fear of becoming involved. The respondent may not even be aware of withholding information, by reason of ignorance of the legalities or other failure to recognize that what he knows is relevant.

People who are deliberately withholding or concealing what they know give off a dozen signals which help the questioner to perceive their strategy (Buckwalter 1983).

Verbal signals include vagueness, evasion, contradiction, and inconsistency of answers. For instance, if the respondent has answered to certain things then he is aware of other, closely related matters which he has not disclosed.

Circumstantial signals place the respondent in a position to know information that he is withholding. Other circumstances include information from other sources, such as an accomplice or co-worker, indicating that the respondent does in fact know certain matters he is not disclosing.

Body signals include extreme restlessness, avoidance of eye contact, continued tenseness, and physiological reactions such as dryness of mouth, excessive sweating and swallowing, and marked carotid pulsation.

Body signals are not foolproof. Related research on deception suggests that many visual cues taken to indicate lying are not reliable indicators; moreover, people have been demonstrated to be unable to detect deception at greater than chance levels (Stiff and Miller 1986). Withholding and concealing are not lying, of course. They are indirect strategies of non-answering, whereas lying is giving direct but false answers. Withholding and concealing are probably best detected by assessing the situation as a whole, the set of answers to this point, and the verbal and circumstantial signals cited.

Criminals and other duplicitous types are not the only ones to use these strategies. Nice people, too – and children and other subordinates – will withhold and conceal while responding. To appreciate these commonplace strategies, all we need do is to think of spouses and neighbours living side by side their life long while withholding and concealing; death and tragedy finally reveal the answers.

Indeed, for nice people these may be the preferred strategies, for they permit nice people to avoid lying while still not telling what they know. Just because we are asking the questions is no good reason for people to give us the answers. They know how to use plenty of other ways to respond.

6   Distorting

Distorting is the common strategy of giving inaccurate answers. Quite ordinary people give distorted answers to quite ordinary questions. They say more, or less, or differently from what they know. They are not lying. Often enough they distort unwittingly. It is up to the questioner to perceive the distortion.

Everyone can be considered prejudiced to some extent about some things and people. Wittingly or no, prejudice readily leads people to distort their responses, such as to questions asked in investigations of various kinds. Witnesses in courtroom examinations are known to be partisan in addition to being commonly prejudiced, showing bias for or against one side and version of events or the other. Even witnesses with no other interest in the case whatsoever are partisan to 'their' side (Wellman 1936). They exaggerate or minimize the facts; they colour, slant, and edit their answers.

Distorting is not limited to dramatic situations like courtrooms. Even in market surveys and opinion polls respondents commonly give distorted responses, even to questions about everyday things – including their own opinion. For instance, people over-report socially desirable behaviour such as holding a library card and going to concerts; and they under-report socially undesirable behaviour such as being sick and out of work (Bradburn and Sudman 1979). The general factors are whether the question is perceived to have a 'right/wrong' answer, and whether the questioner is anticipated to give approval/disapproval of the response or the respondent. These factors describe many survey questions other than behaviour questions, and multiple other situations beyond the opinion-poll. For instance, in answering teacher questions, students may distort their knowledge, understanding, and opinion about the matters in question.

Used wilfully or not, these apparently negative strategies of responding need not signify malicious or negative motives. They present a problem to the questioner but they solve a problem for the respondent. This becomes clear in the case of acquiescent responding, an apparently positive but equally troublesome strategy of responding.

7 Acquiescing

Acquiescing is to give an agreeable response, going along with what the questioner seems to be saying and demanding. It is not the same as co-operative responding; rather, it is closer to stonewalling. A co-operative response will not always be agreeable but will correct the question and questioner if they are mistaken. Stonewalling is to answer precisely in terms of the question as posed, be they correct or incorrect. Acquiescent responding agreeably goes along with the demands of the question-situation, the formulation of the question, and the perceived view of the questioner.

For instance, respondents in survey interviews tend to agree with what they think the interviewer is stating or thinking. They may say 'yes' to any statement whatsoever, even to two contradictory statements. People will agree that social conditions are more to blame than individuals for crime, and they will agree that individuals are more to blame than social conditions. They will readily respond in terms of the structure and form of the question regardless of their own opinion, knowledge, behaviour, or lack thereof. In that case, the answer tells nothing about the respondent but only confirms the questioner's frame of reference.

Acquiescence is a wonderful way for the respondent to solve several problems in the situation. The primary problem is being *a good respondent* (Sudman and Bradburn 1974). Good respondents give answers as requested. If the respondents do not understand the question, if they have no knowledge of the matter or no opinion on it, a simple 'yes' will show them to be a good respondent while avoiding all the embarrassment of having to state 'I don't know' or 'I don't understand' and thus appearing uncooperative for not giving an answer. If the issue is controversial or if their stance on it seems different from that which they perceive the questioner or other informed people to hold, respondents can avoid being impolite and argumentative as well as misinformed by answering 'yes' or any other agreeable response. Finally, everyone knows that if they say 'no' or give some negative response they will be obliged by social convention to elaborate and to explain their disagreement. All of these entanglements can be avoided by answering agreeably. So respondents agreeably say 'yes' and let it go at that.

Acquiescing is all the more troublesome for the social fact that most questioners enjoy higher status, power, and authority in the situation than do respondents. The social situation conduces to respondent acquiescence. Therefore this seemingly positive and desirable strategy of responding might actually be the most negative one of all and the one most to be feared by the questioner. Much better to be faced with disagreeable respondents who will not go along with your questions but will give their own good answers.

Surprisingly enough, the implication for practice is not some questioning strategy to counter the strategies of responding. Rather, it is simply to *listen to the answers*. A basic communication problem in question–answer situations is to get the respondent to give an answer and to get the questioner to listen to it.

The overall implication is that questioning skill is not a matter of asking a specifiable set of questions in a specifiable set of ways. No type of question is a good or effective question to ask; no technique of questioning is a good or effective technique to use. Rather, good practice is an attribute of behaviour in context. Practice depends on knowing the elements of questioning and then manipulating them to purpose in circumstance. For that we need not a set of techniques but a scheme of action.

Chapter eleven

Actions of questioning

By contrast to everyday uses, the practice of questioning requires effortful thought and disciplined behaviour. We discipline our questioning behaviour in favour of purpose in circumstance.

Practice enjoins us to take thoughtful and disciplined action before, during, and after asking questions. That gives us only three major steps to take:

1 prepare the questions,
2 put the questions, and
3 ponder the question–answers.

Preparation begins the action and reflection completes it. With questions situated between forethought and afterthought, practice moves us to act with twice the thought.

At each step any number of specific acts are involved, all of them comprehended in the generic scheme of questioning outlined here. The generic scheme identifies the kinds of acts involved in using questions. In its character as generic, the scheme rightly lacks all specifics, particulars, details. These appear in practice and they are decided by the practitioner.

The way to derive specifics for practice is to answer the generic question that attaches to each count of action in the scheme. The scheme outlines the categories of action. These are the kinds of things done in using questions. For each category the scheme also identifies a generic question. That question is answered in action, in the specific doing of the kind of thing that is done. By answering these questions, each practitioner discovers the suitably specific way to enact those behaviours which together constitute the use of questioning.

Although practice is always particular and detailed, a scheme of questioning is best general and sparse. No alternative scheme will work, for two good reasons.

For one thing, there are at least a dozen fields of practice where questioning is used regularly. Each field further exhibits a number of different contexts and sub-contexts for different uses of questioning. Each concrete instance of

any context will vary in purpose and circumstance of questioning. As a consequence, practice can entail hundreds of questioning techniques, not one of
which is serviceable in general. We would have to list out the hundreds of
techniques for every conceivable purpose and circumstance, then append the
dozen exceptions and contrary recommendations for each case. Such a panoply of questions, purposes, and circumstances would be no scheme. No one
could follow it, let alone apply it in practice.

The other reason is that practice is the province of the practitioner. It consists of enacted choices, actions which are informed by a disciplined manipulation of the elements of questioning in order to serve purpose in circumstance. The practitioner is the one to decide which questioning behaviours
promise to serve, and then prove to serve, purpose in circumstance. It is the
practitioner who makes the informed choice, next enacts it, then assesses the
consequences of enacted choice. That is the scheme of questioning.

The scheme moves us to take action by preparing, putting, and pondering
questions. The action consists of our enacted answers to six generic questions,
one each for the six kinds of acts entailed in using questions. At the middle
step there is question and answer. First there is forethought, bearing on purposes and formulation of questions to ask. Last there is afterthought, bearing
on evaluation and redesign of questions. A dozen other questions might be
entertained at each step, all of which are comprehended in the generic questions listed. The scheme is summarized in Table 11.1.

These generic questions are answered in action as we prepare, put, and
ponder the many specific questions in our situation. The generic questions in
the scheme can be answered one at a time, step by step, and all at once.

The questions can be addressed all by themselves, as it were, apart from any
given case of practice. That is what we will do here, and it is what a practitioner
might do in face of the general use of questioning in his practice. For instance,
physicians and psychotherapists, salespersons and librarians do not initiate
the question–answer situation but have it presented to them. They can follow
the scheme by making schematic preparation and review of their questioning
practice. Physicians and psychiatrists have lists of questions in their manuals
to ask of various cases; therapists have strategies of questioning for various
purposes; librarians respond to typical reference requests, and they are
trained in these cases. All of these practitioners can prepare and assess their
questions for typical cases or habits of action, much the same as a personnel
interviewer who devises a semi-structured interview schedule for any applicant. All of these practitioners can first specify their purposes for asking questions. All can afterwards ponder the questions that they have put in the moment.

All other practitioners can follow the scheme step by step as they use questions – teachers, lawyers, investigators and interrogators, journalists, survey
interviewers, examiners of various types. They can address the first two

generic questions (see Table 11.1) long before entering the question–answer situation; the next two in the actual exchange; and the last two thereafter. For instance, a teacher can prepare the questions at home in an evening, put them in class on the morrow, then reflect on the question–answer that night.

Without exception, all practitioners who use questions will *also* run through the scheme in a trice during the circumstance of practice – thinking for a moment before and a moment after posing the question. The duration of the action of questioning does not matter. All of the acts in Table 11.1 are involved in using questions, like it or not, whether the scheme is stretched out over three days or rushed through in three minutes. These acts are done willy-nilly, whenever they are done and however well.

The scheme schedules the action of using questions. The schedule may be followed at leisure. *In addition* it must be hurried through in the heat of the exchange. That is a necessity of practical action.

Better, then, to discipline ourselves to face the questions of practice *also* over a protracted time. Otherwise we abandon our practice solely to the devices of the moment. The first act is to prepare the questions for the asking.

Prepare the questions

Preparation is the most practical thing we can do to use questions rightly. Before stepping into the question–answer exchange, and again in the moment before putting a question, we wisely govern our step in face of two practical issues: *what are the questions for? which questions to ask?* We resolve these issues by preparing the questions to purpose.

Purposes – what are the questions for?

At issue are our general purpose for using questions and our particular purposes for using specific questions. So our first step is to recall and specify our

Table 11.1 Generic scheme of questioning

Prepare the questions

1	Purposes – what are the questions for?
2	Formulation – which questions to ask?

Put the questions

3	Question – how to put the question?
4	Answer – what to do with the answer?

Ponder the question–answer

5	Evaluation – how did the questions work?
6	Redesign – which next questions might work better?

purposes, making them plainly known to ourselves. Then we will know why we are asking and which questions to ask. Otherwise our questions are pointless.

A good way to recall general purpose is to formulate it as a question. We have some purpose in mind: how can we express that purpose to ourselves as a question? To help us formulate that question of purpose we might repeat to ourselves, 'What am I asking questions for?' Then answer, 'I'm asking questions in order to _____.' The blank that we fill in is then easily reworded into a question – our general purpose phrased as a question.

Bearing this purpose in mind as a general question, we next summon our particular purposes for using specific questions. We don't yet know what these specific questions are, only that we are going to be using some. We find out what they are by first specifying our purposes for using them. Otherwise we will never know why we are asking, which questions to ask, and whether our questions can serve to any known and good purpose.

The only way to know our particular purposes is to *specify purpose in circumstance*. We do not hold purposes all by themselves, as it were, but always attached to some particular things. We do not ask questions in general but always *these* questions; and not questions up in the air, so to speak, but always questions grounded in concrete circumstance – in a time and a place, put to a body about a topic, and so on. These particulars of circumstance sharpen the purposes we have. The point of specifying our purpose in circumstance is to make sure that we will know what we are doing. Otherwise we should be doing it somewhere else for some other purpose.

So the general question, 'What am I asking questions for?' becomes 'Why ask questions here?' and 'Why ask this question here?' We answer in terms of purpose in circumstance. Circumstance helps us to specify purpose; purpose in circumstance helps to specify the questions – those questions which promise to serve our purpose in this circumstance. Circumstance is constituted of time, place, space, activity, people, and topic or subject-matter. So we ask, 'Why ask this person about that matter?' and so forth.

Because we hold purposes in view of some end, we can start our planning at the end instead of the beginning. A smart way to proceed is to plan right away in terms of *answers* rather than questions. Using the notion of answers helps to discover and clarify our purposes for asking; and it helps again to devise particular questions that will serve these purposes.

Faced with a situation in which we are preparing to use questions, we skip in our mind right to the end, when all is finished, and we ask ourselves:

What would the situation look like if all were accomplished and purposes were achieved?

Next we describe that end-situation in terms of answers having been given.

Which answers together constitute the achieved situation?

That brings us pointedly back to the questions which we should prepare for the asking:

Which questions might permit these answers?

By this little manoeuvre we adroitly step forth and back between outcome and purpose, answer and question, finely turning each towards the other. It is an answer dance, a *pas de deux* whirling about answers while twirling out questions to achieve purpose in circumstance.

There is no end to the purposes that questions can serve. One generic purpose for asking questions is to obtain answers in return. (The use of questions for other generic purposes, including *not* to get an answer, may be apt in other circumstances but in no circumstance of question–answer practice at issue throughout this book.) Hence the question of purpose can be answered by discovering our intents with respect to answers. The question of purpose, 'What am I asking questions for?' assumes this form: 'What do I want the answers for?' Related general questions include:

– What is it that I want to know or to find out?
– What kind of answer do I need?
– How will that answer work to tell or to show me that which I intend the answer to do?
– What will I do with the answer?

Asking these questions raises to our mind in a clear and pointed way our purposes for using questions, then clearly points our way towards the specific questions to prepare.

Formulation – which questions to ask

Having figured out our purposes, we now configure the questions. At issue are the specific questions to ask, and how to ready them for the asking.

In general, it is a practical blunder to put questions that have not been specifically prepared, fitted to purpose, and suited to circumstance. Without preparation we may be asking a lot of questions – impulsive, idle, diffuse, everyday questions – with little discipline and little service to purpose. It is impractical not to prepare the questions beforehand.

All the detailed things that might need to be done will come to light as we write, arrange, and rehearse the questions. At each step we get good help from the guiding notion of answers.

Write the questions. That means literally to write the questions down on a piece of paper, laboriously forming each one word for word and continually reforming it until satisfied that it expresses the question we have in mind. Then we look over the formulation to see if it is the right question. The fastest way to tell is by looking ahead to the answers. The best way to do that is to make a *dummy answer*. We model the answer by sketching out all the possible answers we can imagine for this question and that are permitted by this form of the question. The dummy answer is not the particular answer that will eventually come to the question, yet any answer that does come will be just like the dummy – the same sort of shape, size, number, colour, texture, composition. Without making the dummy we might get a true and genuine answer that is still no good to our purposes, because there was something wrong with our question to begin with – the wrong question, the wrong formulation, and the like. The problem is that we would not know that until too late, if ever. So we construct a dummy and quietly ask of it such things as:

- Is this what I am looking for?
- Is this the kind of thing I want to know?
- Can I use something like this?
- What would I do with that one?
- And how about this model over here?

Guided by the dummy, we smartly reformulate our question until it permits the kind of answer which we judge desirable. That is to model the question after a model of the answer. So, first make a dummy of the answer before the answer makes a dummy out of you.

Arrange the questions. Next we arrange our questions in an order that we judge suitable. We use any principle of ordering and any mode of displaying the order on paper. It would be silly of us to arrange our questions in a logical order if logic is not suitable to disposing our questions – which is most often the case. Psycho-logic may do, or intuition, or interest, or chronology, or certainty (known to unknown), or yet size (general to specific) – any principle at all that we judge suitable to purpose in this circumstance. Several arrangements emerge from our tracing the interrelations among the answers we have sketched and the various other questions we have formulated. Another arrangement is a simple question-outline, displaying the main and subordinate questions as best we perceive them to be related. Like the alphabet and the number system and library shelving, the outline is an illogical but serviceable ordering system. The result is the same as any outline save that the items are questions.

I QUESTION
    (a) Question
        (i)   question
        (ii)   question
    (b) Question
        (i)   question
        (ii)   question
II QUESTION
    etc.

Whatever the arrangement, we will, thanks to it, know the interrelations among our questions and their answers. We might not go on to ask the questions in that order. No matter. The order in which we ask questions depends on other things and people, such as the answers that respondents give. But having arranged the questions we will know those questions that we must ask, and we will further know the appropriate next question to ask. Without carefully and thoughtfully arranging the questions that we have laboriously formulated beforehand, we will stumble at every step in the exchange. With our arrangements made beforehand we can keep in step and even ahead of the game, moreover moving quickly into the sudden good openings that develop – *and* get out of them again. In that way even our seemingly 'spontaneous' questions are well prepared, even rehearsed.

Rehearse the questions. We must find a way to practise the questions. One way is to review them in our head. A better way is to speak the questions aloud to ourselves in our practitioner voice and manner (reading or whispering will not do). Then we speak aloud two or three (not one) alternative answers to the questions *as spoken*. It will help to clear away the anticipated or desired answer by stating it mentally before putting the question aloud. Speaking the question as it will be spoken lets us hear the sound and sense which the question makes to the ear; and it will yield novel, unanticipated answers which we surprise ourselves to speak after the question. These tell us to revise the question or to complete the set of answers. The best way is to hold a dress rehearsal by putting the questions to a collaborator, seeing how someone else makes sense of the question and actually answers it. Or we could switch roles and have the collaborator put our questions to us. Marvellous things emerge from our mouth as we struggle to answer our own craftfully wrought questions, producing answer after strange answer that moves us to rework the question. As the fruit of our rehearsals we use the question–answer (not the question) to touch up our final preparations.

The hard part is over. Now our questions are ready for the asking and answering on the stage of practical action. The questions still might not work. That much we know about the uncertainties of practice, the varieties of circumstance, and the peculiarities of people to whom we shall put our redoubtable questions. But we shall have done every possible thing in advance to ready the questions to serve our purpose. Only one thing remains to be done, and that cannot be done in advance. First we must put the questions and they must give the answers. Thereafter we can see whether our questions worked.

Put the questions

Now arrived on the scene of action we put the questions that we have prepared for the asking. Again we discipline our behaviour so that the act of putting the questions serves to purpose in circumstance.

As we proceed through the intensity and complexity of the exchange, other questions too come to mind and appear good to ask at the present moment. The same principle applies. These spontaneous questions too must be prepared before they can be put to purpose in circumstance. Hence we do not ask questions on the spur of the moment or off the cuff, as they happen to pop into our mind and roll off our tongue. Rather, we give one moment's forethought to the question. We hesitate to ask, as it were, taking a second to examine and to formulate the question. Then, on second thought, we ask the question or not. Without this discipline we will most likely be asking everyday questions. Better not to ask questions on the spur of the moment but only on second thought.

Although essential, this part of the scheme is the smallest part of the practice of questioning. It is minimal in right perspective. To put the questions takes less time, effort, thought, skill, and discipline than to prepare them beforehand and to ponder them afterwards. And it is of far less moment. We could even bungle this part and still practise questioning rightly enough, if we situated this act between forethought and afterthought. We have no good reason to think that the act of questioning will go rightly – to the contrary, all evidence, experience, and even common sense informs us that in this enterprise, unlike in certain others, things readily go wrong half of the time. What counts is the continuous application of the scheme of practice – preparing, putting, pondering questions.

Question and answer are the two main events at this stage. The two issues for practice are *how to put the questions* and *what to do with the answers*. Again it is the answers that deserve our practical emphasis, even while putting the questions.

Question – how to put the question

We have already prepared the question. At issue now is the manner of putting it. What is the apt manner of asking?

The particulars of manner describe aspects of delivery, such as tone, voice, diction, inflection, attitude, pace. Every one of these is particular not only to each different field of practice but also to individual circumstances of practice in any one field. No one way of putting questions is appropriate for all, even for most, circumstances of practice. For instance, in many cases the questions are best put at an unhurried, even slow pace – far more slowly than most practitioners do it; they should slow down. Yet in other cases the questioning is best at a rapid pace.

The only generalization that is useful is to put questions *with interest in the answer*. Our manner of asking displays our interest, whatever it is. In everyday communication it is the norm for people to hide their interest in the answer. Yet in circumstances of question–answer practice that is not strategic but aimless. We do well to ask as if the answer were a matter of some interest to us. And so it is, for it is in the interest of answers that we are putting questions. Hence, whatever the details of our manner of asking, they should in particular favour the answering.

Answer – what to do with the answer

Although answering is an act of the respondent, it requires intense activity of the questioner. Signal qualities of the answer depend on what the questioner is doing. At issue here are the actions of the questioner during the moment of answering. How to act during the answer? How to react to the answer? How to act upon the answer once given?

Of all the things to do in this moment, the one essential act is to *listen to the answer*. Yet oddly enough, listening is the most faded activity in this moment. And we are surprised to find that we cannot perform this simple and obvious act without effort and discipline.

We are forced to discipline our behaviour just to listen to the answer. Otherwise we only half listen, if at all. We might be thinking of the next question to ask. We might be wondering about the respondent. We might start marshalling objections and criticisms of the answer, formulating all manner of 'ifs, ands, buts' before we have so much as heard the answer. We might complete in our minds the other half of the answer that we are not attending to, especially when we have some official, anticipated, preferred, or preconceived answer in mind. Then we substitute our thoughts for the still forthcoming thought of the respondent.

All of that is perfectly normal but entirely contrary behaviour. It is contrary to the purpose of our practice, and contrary to the purpose for putting the question in the first place. As practitioners we are enjoined to behave in peculiar, disciplined ways instead of normal, everyday ways. Question–answer practice is not conversation. We are not passing the time. Answer time is not time off for the practitioner. It is time to exhaust our powers in attending to the answer.

As a certain result of not listening we will miss the answer or some part of it, together with its character, and pass up the opportunity of discovering what the respondent knows and how he know it – for all of which we had just asked the question! Listening gives us two kinds of information. It gives us the information we need to judge the kind of answer that is given, and whether it is an answer at all or one of the multiple non-answer responses that people give to questions. Listening also helps us to obtain the desired topical information and to ascertain the desirable next question to ask.

For a practitioner, the counterpart to questioning is not answering but listening. Listening aright is at least as hard as questioning aright, and it takes more sure effort and discipline. Once the question is put we might wish to step back while our partner takes a turn. But if we relax our step we may miss the whole point and defeat the purpose of our question.

Ponder the question–answer

Reflection completes the act of questioning that begins in preparing the questions to ask. It is a practical matter of comparing question–answer against purpose. Reflection answers two questions: *how did the questions work*? *which next questions might work better*?

Evaluation – how did the questions work?

At issue are the questions actually put and the answers actually given, and how these served to purpose in circumstance. To find out how they worked we must first know what the question–answers were. To accomplish either task we will need system. Like all other aspects of using questions, this reflective act is a disciplined behaviour, again in favour of purpose in circumstance.

System is required for finding out the question–answers that transpired in the exchange, and for ascertaining their characteristics. Recollections and estimates seem good enough alternatives, yet only when we have nothing better available. They are in fact next to worthless. The reason is simple. As practitioners we cannot report with any accuracy the events that transpired in the heat of the exchange. We remember one, or two, or three; but we may have asked 100 questions. We have impressions, but we need observations. And we cannot observe while engaged in doing vital things in the moment of practice.

Therefore we need a systematic way of capturing the question–answer that did in fact occur. Then we can reflect on this record, examining how the questions worked.

We can choose among a small number of systematic devices. All are useful to some extent in some respects but not others. All are cumbersome and otherwise unsatisfying. None the less, these are the things we shall have to use:

- *tape-recording*, audio and/or video;
- *transcript*, stenographic or reproduced from recordings;
- *tallies* or other check-lists and schedules filled out by a collaborating observer during the session;
- *notes* or other memoranda made immediately after (not during) the session – perhaps annotations made directly on our prepared list of questions.
- *interviews and questionnaires*, or other debriefing devices for respondents to report their perceptions and reactions to the questioning, and to give an account of their answering.

One and another of these five kinds of devices can be used now and again to capture this and that aspect of the question–answer, to the point where we are satisfied of making systematically a reliable record for us to reflect on. For instance, we might choose to apply one of the devices to our next five episodes of questioning; one different device to each one of the next five episodes; all five devices to the next episode; one selected device to every fifth episode; or some device to some episode every five months; and so on.

Having obtained some record that is systematic and reliable, we compare the record against our purposes. To do this we need yet more system, first in the form of some written criteria, check-list, guidelines, advice, categories, and so forth for describing questions and their use. Several written forms are at hand to help:

- the scheme of questioning in this chapter;
- the elements of questioning in the previous chapter;
- the tables and descriptions of questioning throughout Part One;
- the list of questions we prepared to ask.

For instance, one of the first evaluative tasks might examine the record to see whether the questions on our prepared list were actually asked or otherwise answered, in which manner and order, and so on. We might count the questions, classify them by types of one sort or another, time their pacing or rate, check whether they were answered, classify the answers, time the answers, and so forth.

Having ascertained from the record the characteristics of the question–answer, we proceed to reflect on their functions and effects. A useful guide to reflection is to pose a series of evaluation questions. Basically we want to find out how the questions worked to purpose. We will have to become particular about that, examining each question before making a judgement about 'the questions':

1 What was the purpose (motive, intent, and so on) to this question? – and to that question?
2 Wherein was that question suited to the broad purpose in this case of practice?
3 To what observed extent, and how, did the question achieve or serve that purpose?
4 Which purposes, and which aspects of purpose, were served by the questions?
5 Which purposes were not served by the questions?

For all questions that we put we have purposes. And all questions serve to some purpose. But not all purposes are condign to our practice, or serve in this circumstance. And not all questions serve to good purpose. Some fail to serve to purpose; others serve to contrary, neutral, or irrelevant purposes. It is the simple but arduous task of evaluation to find out how our questions served to purpose – which questions, to which purposes.

Here again the best guide is the notion of answers. To stretch a point, we might evaluate our questioning without referring to the questions at all, examining only the answers. The principle is to look to the answers, always including the answer and the respondent in any assessment of question and questioner. Thus the assessment of purpose, function, and effect of questioning is accomplished through scrutiny of the answers given. The evaluation questions would run:

1 What purposes did the answers serve?
2 What did I and my respondent *do* with the answer?

Sometimes we have done nothing at all with the answer, or nothing to any known and good purpose of practice. We might then wonder about our use of the question. This wonderment is essential to the practice of questioning.

Redesign – which next questions might work better?

At issue is a new design on action, renewing the practice of questioning. Re-design is essential if our questions have not worked quite rightly. In the odd case where all has gone well, the question of redesign arises none the less – because circumstances, and with them our purposes, will now have changed.

Having revealed to us how our questions worked, reflection moves us to devise the questions to ask next. Again we make a design to serve purpose in circumstance. Again we prepare the questions to ask, again we put them, and again we ponder them. That is the right practice of questioning.

Chapter twelve

Alternatives to questioning

Alternatives to questioning are non-questioning techniques that enhance communication. Used together with well-chosen questions, a mix of alternatives gives the greatest promise of enriching the cognitive, affective, and expressive processes of participants in both group and dyadic settings such as discussion and certain kinds of interview.

'Alternatives' imply choices: to use questions or alternatives, whether overall or at a given juncture; and which alternative to use in place of a question. The choice is properly made on the practitioner's judgement as to which technique will most likely advance purpose in the given circumstance of communication.

To help inform choice, we will describe the practice of alternatives and research on alternatives. This chapter sets out all the alternative techniques available for choosing. The next chapter details how these alternatives prove to function in communication.

The practice of alternatives consists of substituting non- questioning techniques for questions. At any given juncture of talk the practitioner can choose either to ask a question or to use an alternative. The most common juncture for choice is where the partner has just finished making a contribution, as in response to a question:

Practitioner: Question
Partner: Response
Practitioner: Question or alternative.

What else can the practitioner do at that point other than ask a question?

The practitioner may use four different kinds of alternatives, encompassing a dozen specific ones – declarative statements, speaker questions, signals, and silences. There are also various other alternatives of mixed kinds. These latter alternatives will be reviewed briefly after systematically describing the dozen alternatives of four different kinds.

At the juncture where the partner has just finished a response the practitioner can, instead of asking a question, choose to:

1 make a *statement* of his selected thought in relation to what the speaker has just said; or
2 provide for a *speaker's question* related to the speaker's contribution; or
3 give some *signal* of receiving what the speaker is saying, without himself taking and holding the floor; or yet
4 say nothing at all but maintain a deliberate, appreciative *silence*.

As for specific alternatives, fourteen are set out in Table 12.1 (from Dillon 1988a), listed by type: statements, speaker questions, signals, and silences. For each alternative Table 12.1 gives the definition, the generic example, and a counter-example (namely, a question). Here in the text we will follow the scheme in the table, adding detail and commentary, the rationale for using the given alternative, suggestions for learning to use it, and examples of its use in actual discussions and interviews. The research on these alternatives will be reviewed (see Chapter 13) after considering all of these points of practice.

Statements

Instead of asking a question, *state your selected thought in relation to what the speaker has said*. Contrary to what might be obvious, people do respond to statements. And responses to statements promise to be longer and more complex than answers to questions.

Any number of thoughts can be stated, and various kinds of statements made of them. Six kinds of statements are identified in Table 12.1. When a speaker has just made a contribution, you can choose to make a declarative statement or a reflective restatement, state your mind or your interest, make a speaker referral or give a practitioner reddition. The first two of these will be treated at greater length so as to clarify the scheme in the table and to establish the rationale for using other alternatives of this type.

1 Declarative statement

State the (pre-question) thought that occurs to you as a result of what the speaker has just been saying.

For example (Table 12.1), the speaker has just said that something is the case: 'X is the case'. The thought occurs to the practitioner that Y is the case. So he says: 'Y is the case'. For a counter-example, instead of stating that Y is the case the practitioner *asks* the speaker, 'What other letter is the case?'

That is the *generic* example – the one example that describes all of the specific, individually different examples that can be thought of. Accordingly, the speaker doesn't actually say the very words, 'Something (or X) is the case', and the practitioner doesn't actually say back, 'Y is the case'. Nor is it an argument. The speaker is stating his thought and the practitioner is stating his related thought; the thoughts can be complementary as well as opposed. Here is a general example and counter-example.

The speaker has just said something, as in answer to a question. Whenever the speaker says something, he is averring that something is the case – X. 'Roses are red.' That's X. While the speaker is talking, you the practitioner are thinking something in relation to that (among many other thoughts occurring to you at the moment). You too are thinking that something is the case. 'Violets are blue.' That's Y. 'You look like a monkey that lives in the zoo.' That's Z. You do not state your thought Z because it offers less promise of serving to purpose in this circumstance. Instead you state your *selected* thought, Y, in relation to the speaker's contribution X. Your 'Violets are blue' complements his 'Roses are red', and there you have, the two of you, a nice communicative couplet.

Any counter-example to this alternative is, naturally, a question. The speaker has said that X is the case ('Roses are red'). You are thinking Y ('Violets are blue'). Instead of stating Y you *ask*, 'What other letter is the case?' (What colour are violets? What flowers are blue?) The speaker has just told you what letter he thinks is the case. You've just told him that you will not tell him what letter you think is the case but that he must tell you what letter you think the case is. Eventually he will come to say Y, whatever he thinks, and you will say 'yes' and then state that Y is the case. The alternative is to state at the outset that Y is the case. Then the speaker has the immediate benefit of your thought in relation to his thought, and now discussion of the two related thoughts can proceed forthwith.

Here are specific examples drawn from recordings of actual classroom discussion (transcripts in Appendix). In each case some student has just said something of the kind, 'X is the case'. Here is the teacher's statement of 'Y is the case', together with a possible counter-example for the statement actually made by the teacher.

1. 'Or even sometimes you see X along with Y. That sometimes happens too, I think.'

   – What letter sometimes goes along with Y? What else sometimes happens, do you think?

2. 'Well, I'm not sure that's their basic argument. I don't think – I think the basic argument is just the fact that they're X.'

   – What is their basic argument?

3. 'Well, X – first of all, X is not located in Y.'

   – Where is X located? What is located in Y?

4. 'OK, I think that there is a difference, that X does this whereas Y does that.'
   – Is there a difference between X and Y? How do X and Y compare in what they do?

5. 'That's a little bit unfair, I would say.'
   – Is that fair, would you say?

Table 12.1 Alternatives to questioning

Alternative	Generic example	A counter-example (viz., a question)
A STATEMENTS		
1 *Declarative statement* State the (pre-question) thought that occurs to you as a result of what the speaker has just been saying.	*S: X is the case. † P: [thinking Y] Y is the case.	Any post-thought question, e.g., What other letter is the case?
2 *Reflective restatement* State your understanding of what the speaker has just said. (a) Repeat it	S: X is the case. P: X is the case.	What do you mean?
(b) Summarize or characterize it	S: A, B, Q, H, O, V, G, C, J, M, A, T and Z is the case. P: the alphabet is the case, or maybe some jumble of letters.	Do you mean X? Do you mean Y? What are you trying to say?
3 *Statement of mind* Describe in truth your state of mind, and none other, in relation to what the speaker has just been saying.	S: X is the case. P: [mind is square] My mind is square about what you're saying.	What do the rest of you in here think about what S just said?
4 *Statement of interest* State whatever it is that you are interested in hearing further about what the speaker has just been saying.	S: X is the case. P: [interested in Y about X] I'm interested in hearing Y about X.	Why do you think X? What are some aspects of X? What about Y?
5 *Speaker referral* State the relation between what the speaker has just said and what a previous speaker has said.	S1: X is the case. S2: Anti-X is the case. P: So you're saying anti-X and S1 is saying X, the opposite.	How does that relate to what S1 said?

table continues...

179

Table 12.1 *Continued*

	Alternative	*Generic example*	*A counter-example*

6 *Practitioner reddition*
  Give an account of your own
  status (knowledge, experience,
  feeling) regarding the matter
  at hand.

  S: X is the case with me.
  P: With me, the case is .... And what's the case with you, S2?

(B) **SPEAKER'S QUESTIONS**

7 *Speaker's question*
  Provide that the speaker
  formulate a question about
  what he is struggling to think
  and say.

  S1: Something is the
  case, I don't know.
  Pa: Relax for a minute
  and think up the question
  that's still bothering you
  about that.

  What exactly do you think the
  case is?

8 *Group question*
  Provide that another participant pose a question
  about the speaker's
  contribution or the
  matter under .discussion.

  b: Let's take a minute to
  hear the question that
  somebody else might be
  thinking of about that.
  c: Maybe it's time now to
  hear a few suggestions as
  to the kind of question we
  should be asking now,
  given everything that's
  been said up to this point.

  Anybody else? What is the
  case here?

  Let's move on to the next
  question: what is the case
  over there?

9 *Discussion question*
  Provide that participants formulate the question that now
  appears at issue in the
  discussion.

  S1 or 2: Is X the case?
  P: You're wondering if X
  is the case.
  Good question.

  Any answer, e.g., yes/no.
  Any counter-question, e.g.,
  Well what do *you* think? – Is X
  the case?

(C) **SIGNALS**

10 *Phatics*
  Uttering a brief phrase, quietly
  exclaim feeling in reaction
  to what the speaker has just
  finished saying.

  S1: X is the case
  P: [phatic] Oh, X is nice.
  [filler] Mm-hmm.
  S1: And Y is the case, too.

  Any question.

11 *Fillers*
  Emitting some word or sound,
  indicate attentive interest in
  what the speaker has said or is
  in process of saying.

12 *Pass*
  By gesture or statement, pass
  the next turn at talk to the/
  another speaker.

  S1: X is the case.
  P: [pass] Yes, S2.
  S2: Y is the case.

  And what about you, S2?

table continues...

These examples show some of the more obvious ways of stating corrective and complementary kinds of thoughts. But the thoughts need not be corrective or anything else, only *informative* of the practitioner's thought in relation to the speaker's contribution. 'Roses are red. – Violets are blue.' Yet why on earth would someone then *respond* to a statement like 'Violets are blue'?

In the first place it should be noted that 'Violets are blue' does not come out of the blue but is related to the speaker's previously expressed thought.

A second general reason is that you are the practitioner and this is a communicative setting – for example, a teacher in a classroom. Students must respond to things that the teacher says to them. This social constraint also operates in other circumstances involving superiors and subordinates, and it fur-

Table 12.1 *Continued*

Alternative	Generic example	A counter-example
(D) SILENCES		
13 *Deliberate silence* Say nothing at all but maintain a deliberate, appreciative silence for 3-5 sec. until the original speaker resumes or another speaker enters in.	S1: X is the case.	*Any question is counter-example*
	P: [rehearses in mind: 'Baa, baa, black sheep, Have you any wool?']	...while rehearsing in mind: – nod, nod, does S1 have any more?
	S1: And Y, too, come to think about it.	
	P: ['Yes sir, Yes sir, Three bags full.']	Nod, nod, hold for 3 seconds!
	S1 or 2: But not Z.	
	P: ['One for my master, And one for my dame, And one for the little boy Who lives down the lane.']	look at speaker look at a girl look at a boy look down the back rc
	S2 or S1: Z isn't the case because....	
14 *Non-deliberate silence* You'd better figure out something to do. If in trouble, start asking questions.	S1: X is the case.	
	[confusion, trouble]	
	P: Question. S2: Answer. P: Question. S3 :Answer.	*Discussion is counter-example.*

Notes: *S=Speaker
         †P=Practitioner

Source: J.T. Dillon (1988a) *Questioning and Teaching: a Manual of Practice*, London: Croom Helm; New York: Methuen.

ther operates in some everyday encounters between apparent peers. Try not to respond to a statement addressed to you by a friend, or yet by a stranger, in some harmless circumstance, say, in a bar or queuing for a bus or for a cashier in a shop. 'Hey, I'm *talking* to *you*!' Polite response is the social norm.

But people will not merely respond. In most communicative settings, they respond at some length and complexity to relevant practitioner statements. And their responses to statements can be expected to be longer and more complex than answers to questions. By contrast to questions of any type, statements are more *open* in response initiative, content (including topic), process, and duration; they are in *direct* relation to what the speaker has just said; they are more *informative*, supplying information and intelligence, more likely unknown to the speaker and certainly unknown to him as being our thought in relation to his. Finally, the statement requires *accommodation*. The information that is supplied must be accommodated in relation to the speaker's expressed thought. In accepting or rejecting the information, the speaker makes some adjustment of the complex of his knowledge and thinking about the subject; and in making that adjustment and speaking that accept/reject, he will first have to examine and construe that statement, elaborate and explain his accept/reject, evaluate and justify, illustrate or give counter-examples, ponder and wonder, and so on. That is more complex thought as well as more lengthy talk.

To use this alternative requires first that we deliberately break the connection between a question and the thought that precedes it. ('State the pre-question thought.') Before the question comes to our lips a thought has occurred to our mind. With teachers and interviewers especially, this connection seems automatic and nearly instantaneous. We have a fleeting thought and immediately form a question to ask. This connection must be broken and the thought spoken.

It takes effort to break the connection, and practised effort actually to speak the thought instead of the question. The question comes so readily to the lips and rolls off the tongue. In part that is because we may think that questions are the proper thing for us to speak. Interviewers and teachers commonly speak in questions and commonly think that questions will keep an interview or discussion going. In other part that is because we may not know what else to speak at that moment, yet we have to speak and we have to get the partner to respond. The alternative of making a declarative statement instructs us as to what else to do, it satisfies the need to speak, it gets the partner to respond, and it keeps the process moving. A third part to the effortlessness of questions is the fact that we pay little attention to the thought that precedes a question in our mind, and we leave it without much formulation. So it is hard to state the thought; we go right to the question.

The connection between pre-question thought and question has to be broken, the question stayed, and the thought attended to, formulated, and then enunciated. You can learn to do that by being analytical and introspective, catching yourself in a question and then looking for the prior thought; and by deliberately practising and disciplining yourself to formulate and state that thought. But there is an easier way to learn this alternative, especially for a beginner.

All you have to do is to *answer* your own question aloud. Don't ask it, just give the answer. That way you will not have to be analytical and slow about it, all the while looking as if you don't know what you are doing. Take the question that so quickly comes to mind and go right ahead and answer it.

For example, Hernandez says: 'Roses are red'. You say: 'Violets, Hernandez – violets are blue'; or 'Blue, Hernandez – some flowers are blue, like violets'. Which version you speak depends on your question: which flowers are blue? what colour are violets? Similarly, when Gloria is talking about the price of tea in China, you say: 'No tea, Gloria – we don't import any tea from China' (how much tea do we import from China?); or, 'India, Gloria, not China – India is where we get our tea from nowadays' (where do we get our tea from?). And when LeRoy is trying to prove his point by citing unemployment rates in the 1930s, you merely say: 'But when the war broke out, LeRoy, unemployment dropped' (what happens to unemployment in time of war? what causes a drop in unemployment?).

The key to the alternative is to give the speaker the benefit of your thought. Using a declarative statement, state the selected thought that occurs to you as a result of what the speaker has just said.

2 Reflective restatement

State your understanding of what the speaker has just said, giving your sense of it in one economical and exact sentence. There are two basic ways to restate the contribution (Table 12.1).

(a) *Repeat it.* The speaker says, 'X is the case'. You say, 'X is the case'. As a counter-example, you *ask,* 'What do you mean?'

(b) *Summarize or characterize it.* The speaker says various letters from A to Z, in some jumbled order. You say, 'The alphabet is the case, or maybe some jumble of letters'. As a counter-example, you ask, 'Do you mean X? Do you mean Y? What are you trying to say?'

To this alternative the speaker will respond with something like 'Right' or 'Well, what I meant was – '. In either case he will almost invariably go on to discourse at greater length and with richer thought on the matter, enhancing his original response by extending and improving it. Even when you do no more than to repeat the speaker's 'Roses are red', the response will most likely be, 'Right, and violets are blue'. In this case it is the speaker who forms the nice couplet, completing and enriching his original contribution.

Here from actual classroom recordings are some examples of reflective re-statements, showing what they can look like and how students have responded to them.

In Mr T's lesson on European history (transcript no. 1B in Appendix), Diane is speaking about Louis XIV's reasons for persecuting the Huguenots, and the teacher characterizes her contribution.

T.: So you feel that he was justified in what he was doing, as far as he was concerned – he could justify it to himself.

S.: Yeah, he could justify it to himself. But then ... *(continues for 11 seconds).*

In a sensitive discussion about sexual topics in the students' home life (transcript no. 11) Marilyn is speaking about her family's way of talking about sex. Mr SN, the teacher, reflects her statement and she elaborates, connecting her contribution with that of a previous student.

T.: You do this all together.

S.: Yeah, my mother and father and all the rest of us. And just like he said ... *(continues for 21 seconds).*

George then speaks about his case. 'See, and in my case ... ' The teacher summarizes and George expresses a shorter but more emotive contribution (as appropriate to the subject and purpose of this discussion):

T.: She won't listen.

S.: Right. So I feel, I get angry with her, you know. *(5 seconds)*

Other reflective restatements used by this teacher begin with the phrase, 'So you're saying that ... '; for example, 'So you're saying that your parents never sat you down and talked about sex'.

A simple, apt example of restatement is the physician's mere reiteration of the patient's statement of not having had headaches for years (exchange 20 in transcript no. 6C), since this point forms part of his careful determination, at the very close of the interview, that nothing has been left out. The point is pursued, in response to the restatement, that the headaches occurred decades before in the course of raising a family. The doctor then checks the point yet again by a light but pertinent remark about the cause of the headaches, followed by 'I don't know' and a pause to see if any other 'headache' information would be forthcoming. Dozens of examples of restatements are found in the transcripts of client-centred (no. 4) and eclectic (no. 5) psychotherapy. The eclectic therapist favours starting with 'It sounds like ... ' (exchanges 4, 15, 18). The client-centred therapist favours 'You feel as though' (6, 10, 11, 12). This therapist is a past master at capturing in a very few words precisely the meaning *and* the feeling of something that the client confusedly and profusely expresses without seeming to understand or even to recognize it. Every one of his 'reflective restatements' seems perfect and nearly every one is followed by further, greater client talk and self-understanding.

In using this alternative you might find it helpful to begin with some introductory phrase making it plain to yourself as well as to the speaker that you are trying to make a restatement rather than your own statement or interpretation. For example:

- So, you feel/think that ...
- So, you're saying that ...
- I get from what you say that ...
- Oh, in your mind, the ...
- So what you're talking about is ...
- You think/mean, in other words, that ...

But these are mere preliminaries, and they are not even necessary. The essence of this alternative is what you say *after* such an introduction.

What you say is your understanding of what the speaker has said. It is no easy matter to catch someone's sense and then render it in just the right few words. It is even hard merely to repeat what someone has said, and, in repeating it, to convey just the sense that the speaker had in saying it to begin with – the correct twist, the right tone, the same measure of certainty, and so forth. You cannot even begin to do any of this if you have not disciplined yourself to listen to the speaker in the first place.

First you must attend to the speaker, listening to what he is saying and listening for what he is meaning and for the way in which he is meaning it. Then you make the reflective restatement, giving your understanding of what the speaker's understanding is. By contrast, most people will give their understanding of the point at issue, substituting theirs for the other speaker's understanding. Most listeners do not intend to grasp the speaker's meaning as the speaker would have it but as they would construe it. Many people do not even listen to what is being said but spend the waiting time getting ready for their next turn at talk – formulating questions, objections, corrections, positions, tangents. Then in their turn they base their move on their imaginary construction of the previous speaker's words and meanings. 'Yeah, I know what you mean' – followed by a demonstration that they have no idea of your meaning.

In such a case it seems polite enough to ask the other person, 'What do you mean?' But it is pointless to ask, as he has just told you what he means. Furthermore, he has no idea of what to say in answer, other than to repeat or to reword that which he has already said and which you have ignored or dismissed in the first place. Hence to be polite but not boring he will customarily answer by saying something *different* from what he had said; and you, rather than impolitely asking once again what he means, may choose to accept the second, novel contribution as merely a version of the first. The alternative is to inform him at the outset of what you understand him to have meant. Then he can know which part of his meaning to clarify or reaffirm, and so on.

Above all the speaker is motivated to make that try because you seem *interested* in understanding what he means before you go on to give your own meaning. In that way real rather than imagined meanings, and shared rather than private ones, come to form the basis of your communication.

We commonly misconstrue the meaning and often enough mis-hear the words. The proof is when you try this alternative for the first 100 times or so, only to discover that you don't know what the speaker is talking about. Time and again he responds with some such phrase as, 'Well, what I meant to say was … ', if not, 'No, that's not what I meant at all'. But that negative response is a fruitful one, as fruitful as a 'Yes, that's just exactly what I meant!' For, the restatement gives the speaker an opportunity, invariably taken, to clarify, elaborate, and establish his meaning, sometimes discovering it for himself only on the second time around.

A reflective restatement permits the speaker (and other partners) to infer, rightly, that what he thinks and says *matter*. It confirms the speaker in his effort to contribute. It helps him to express thoughts gradually more clearly and fully. It assures him of understanding. And it makes a public possession of a private meaning. The result is to encourage participation, both speaking and listening, and to facilitate relevant discussion of actual rather than imaginary meanings.

The key to this alternative is actually to make the try at it. Beginners can do it effectively, even when they don't quite get the speaker's meaning right or don't state it in just the right words. To do *that* takes a master. But you don't have to be a master to use this alternative. All you have to do is to state your understanding of what the speaker has said. Your understanding may be wrong but your use of the alternative right.

3 Statement of mind

Describe in truth your state of mind, and none other, in relation to what the speaker has just been saying.

A speaker has said that X is the case. Your mind is in some state – let us say it is square. You so inform the speaker: 'My mind is square about what you're saying'. Then the speaker knows your state of mind and responds directly to it. A counter-example is to ask, 'What do the rest of you in here think about what he's just said?' That way no one in the group will know your state of mind. You will not reveal it, although they are to reveal theirs.

During a discussion or interview the practitioner can experience any number of states of mind and use various ways to state them. All the variety is of no concern. The key is to describe the state of your mind, and none other.

One of the most common states of mind is to be *unclear* or *confused* about what the speaker is saying. You so inform him: 'My mind is unclear about what you're saying'; 'I'm confused about what you're saying'. In this state you want to respond but you don't have anything clear to say, so you describe your state of mind.

- I'm not sure I understand, exactly.
- I don't quite follow you there.
- I'm afraid I'm just not getting your point.
- I must be missing something about what you say.

Of course, there is no use tiptoeing around with such delicacies of phrase if they do not in truth describe your state of mind.

For goodness' sake, don't say, 'I'm afraid I'm not quite getting your point' when in truth you have it nailed down and object to it. Say rather, 'I object to what you are saying', and then state your preferred point. 'I don't agree with you there, because an X is a Y'.

But if in truth you don't understand, state that which you do not understand. 'Ah, Willie, what I don't understand is you saying, "I'm not knocking it, but it's stupid".' If you are confused, state your confusion; if opposed, state your opposition. If you understand and disagree, say so: 'OK, I can see where you're coming from, but I don't know if I can totally agree with that'. On the other hand, if you are agreeable, state your agreement: 'OK, I'll go along with that'. If surprised, state your surprise: 'I'm surprised that you feel X. Somehow in my mind you'd think it'd be kinda Y, in some way'. All of that is to describe in truth the state of your mind, and none other.

During a discussion it commonly happens to me that I am in a *lost state*. I find myself at a loss witnessing exchanges between people with no trace of understanding any more the connection between them. This is not a fruitful state to be in either as practitioner or participant. Then someone starts talking at length to me! Although I understand the words, I can't construe the speech for lack of understanding its purpose and relevance. So I say something like, 'I know that you're saying something important to me but I'm not getting the connection between what you're saying and what she just said'. In response the person commonly informs me that he is saying X because she has said Y – whereupon *she* commonly remarks, 'But I meant Z', and he says, 'Oh'. Now I understand, and so does he and she. We three are back on track, together, and I discover from scattered murmurings that other people in the room have also only now found themselves following along.

A statement of mind enhances the discussion itself and also teaches appropriate communication behaviour. First, it informs the person who is speaking to you of your state of mind, and it evokes the speaker's response to your exact state. Second, it get you back into the swing of things, and other people too. Third, it establishes norms of responsible participation, such as the norm of speaking the truth of your mind and not bespeaking something else. It is a demonstration *against* the norms of sitting there and pretending that you get the gist of things; of listening to people while ignoring their meaning; of speaking back and forth without having any idea of what is being exchanged. These are the norms that make of 'discussion' a series of alternating monologues.

Two other states that I am frequently in during conversations and discussions are distraction and muddling. When in a *distracted state* I say: 'I'm sorry, I'm distracted right now' or 'I was thinking about something else just then'. In response, the speaker can make another try at his point or he can seek to discover that supposedly more absorbing point which was preoccupying me. When in a *muddled state*, I say things like: 'Something about X bothers me, I don't know'; 'I'm trying to decide if X or Y is the case here'; 'I was just wondering whether X would make any difference'. Those sound very much like questions, but in this muddled state I am in no condition to ask a question, nor do I want to. I'm engaged in muddling through for the moment, and a question to the speaker would neither communicate to him my state of mind nor get from him the kind of response I want. So I describe my state of mind and he responds to that.

When, on the other hand, I am in a *perplexed state* – when I don't know and I need and desire to know, and when I want help with knowing and I believe the participant(s) can give that help – then I ask a question. That becomes the alternative of choice at that juncture.

4 Statement of interest

State whatever it is that you are interested in hearing further about what the speaker has just been saying.

The speaker says that X is the case. You are interested in Y about X. You say: 'I'm interested in hearing Y about X'. A counter-example is to ask, 'What are some of the aspects of X?' or worse, 'What about Y?'

This alternative is simplicity itself but strangely difficult to do. If you would like to hear more of the speaker's views on X, say, 'I'd like to hear more of your views on X'. That is an invitation to elaborate, somewhat more inviting than 'Elaborate on that' or 'What else do you think about X?' 'Roses are red' – 'That's interesting, I'd like to hear more of your views on that' – 'Well, Violets are blue'.

Here are some things that teachers and interviewers are interested in but do not state their interest, rather putting a question or directive about them. To state the interest requires both straightforwardness of thinking and some delicacy of phrasing.

Definition. 'I notice you keep stressing X, and I'd be interested in your definition of "X".'

Example. 'It would help me to understand better if I had an example of X.'

Reasons/applications. 'I'm interested in knowing the reasons behind/uses of X.'

Objection. 'I'd like to learn the objection you have to X.'

Background. 'I think it'd really be interesting to hear about your background thinking/experience with X.'

Of course, if you are not interested in these things there is no use in stating your interest in them. This alternative is useful only when you choose to reveal your interest, and to reveal it in a direct and enticing way. You can choose other things to do when you are not interested or prefer to veil your interest.

5 Speaker referral

State the relation between what the speaker has just said and what a previous speaker has said, referring one to the other.

Speaker One has said that X is the case. Later Speaker Two (or in dyads, Speaker One again) says that anti-X is the case. You say to Speaker Two: 'So you're saying anti-X and Speaker One is saying X, the opposite'. As a counter-example you ask Speaker Two, 'How does that relate to what Speaker One said?' – asking her to state the relation that you perceive but will not tell her until she tells you first what relation you perceive. You prove that by saying no to the relation that she perceives. She answers your question: 'Well, I dunno, he was saying, you know, kinda the same thing, I think'. You retort: 'He was saying the exact *opposite* of what you said!'

The alternative is to state the relation you see. Then the two partners can look at each other, examine their contributions for any relation, and discuss the relations they might begin to have. 'Roses are red', says he; 'Violets are blue', says she; 'You form a couple, he and you', says the romantically poetic practitioner.

In Mr T's history discussion (transcript no.1B) the teacher first refers students to what Marty said, then refers Marty to what Sean says:

T.: All right, Marty raised an interesting point just a few seconds ago. He said that X is the case.

Sean: I think Marty was wrong, because even though X, Y is still the case today.

T.: All right, so he's totally disagreeing with what you had to say, Marty.

Marty: Yeah, well – No, he brought up a good point. ... But what I'm saying is ... .

The relations can describe complementarity as well as contradiction, similarity or inconsistency, and so on; and they can be stated in any number of ways. The variety is no matter. The point is to make a speaker referral. There seem to be three kinds of referral to make.

(a) *Refer speaker to speaker/s.* 'I don't think Victor would go so far as to agree with you.' – 'OK. And yet, as Regina was saying, ... '
(b) *Refer speaker to self.* 'Like you were saying, Pam, X is the case.' – 'All right, X is the case – going back to what you were saying earlier.'
(c) *Refer speaker/s to speaker.* Mr T's Marty- students-Sean referrals are examples. Here is a more extensive referral: 'OK. I think, ah, we can go backwards to Marilyn's point and take off from that a bit. She said – and I think that some of you are agreeing with her – that X is the case. But Stacey said, and I think that Bonnie's saying the same thing, X is a case of Y.'

6   Practitioner reddition

Give an account of your own status (knowledge, experience, feeling) regarding the matter at hand.

The speaker has just finished saying, 'X is the case with me'. You say, 'With me, the case is ... '. In response he or another speaker says, 'That's the case with me, too' or 'See, and in my case ... ' A counter-example is to ask, 'And what's the case with *you*, Speaker Two?' Speaker Two will respond but might not say what the case is with him – especially if the case is a touchy one and he has noticeably not been saying anything about it before.

In this discussion (transcript no. 11) about a sensitive subject, sexual attitudes in home life, the teacher is trying to induce students to speak about three topics, one of which is physical affection witnessed between their parents. At one point in an on-going exchange with Larry, during which Larry is not speaking to that topic, the teacher directly asks him about it; Larry evades the question with a comment that produces nervous laughter from the class.

T.:   What about affection?
Larry: Yeah. I mean, it's not like I'd see my folks naked on the couch, no.
   (Laughter)

So the teacher moves to give an account of the case with him. Larry then responds in kind, and so does Marilyn:

T.:   Right. So quickly, one problem I know I have when I think about this question, I can't ever imagine my parents having sex, or whatever. But the thing is, you know, at least the kids – my parents had 10 kids, so I know they went to bed together at least 10 times, you know. *(Laughter)* You know, but I still have this trouble connecting that – the reality.

Larry: Yeah, I have that trouble too. I just couldn't – ...
   (continues for 11 secs)
Marilyn: In our family, you know, we have something like ...
   (continues for 12 secs).

Here there are two responses, by students of different sexes, both responses on the topic, in the right manner, and at considerable length.

A point-for-point contrast to this fruitful development can be seen in two other classes discussing similarly sensitive topics. In both classes a student has just stated the case with him/her, and the teacher asks a named student of the other sex (and other than the teacher's) what the case is with her/him. In both classes the student evades the question, the exchange stalls, and the teacher gives up – only to start doing it again with yet another student. Here first is Mr B and Nydia:

T.: Nydia, do *you* agree with that?
S.: What? I didn't hear –
T.: What Leandro said, in terms of personal satisfaction being your goal, in sex?
S.: I didn't hear what he said.
T.: I just restated it.
S.: Restate it again.
T.: Would you like me to restate it again? He said, personal satisfaction in terms of being the goal in sex. Would you agree that that would be your goal in entering into sexual relationships? Primarily for personal satisfaction?
S.: I don't know.
T.: You don't know what your goal would be, huh?
S.: *(No response, 5 secs)*
T.: Gina?

The very same happens with Mrs K and Wally:

T.: Wally, what do *you* think? Do you agree with her? That you can pretend?
S1: Pretend what?
T.: Explain it again, please, Maryanne.
S2.: You can pretend that you like being with this guy, but you really don't. You do it, you're just there.
S1.: Just to pass one night, you're gonna tell him, just so you can – *(Laughter)*
T.: Would *you*, Sue?

In both of these classes the teacher had asked of Student Two, 'And what's the case with *you*?' That didn't work with Student Two. So the teacher turned to do the same thing with Student Three. 'And what's the case with *you*?' An alternative move at either juncture would be teacher reddition: 'With me the case is ... ' In response, as shown in the fruitful first example, Student Two *and* Student Three, boy and girl, tell at length what the case is with them.

Practitioner reddition is *an* alternative at this juncture. You don't have to use it. Furthermore, the topic does not have to be a sensitive one, and the reddition need not exhibit personal feelings or intimate experiences. The topic can be a touchy or a stuffy one, the issue moral or intellectual, and the reddition an account of your knowledge, background, studies, feelings, and so on.

Whatever the issue, an excellent way to start the reddition is to imitate the teacher in the first example: 'One problem I know I have when I think about this question ... ' Another teacher started this way: 'You know, the way I understand the problem is ... '. Or, 'Well, I look at it like this ... ' Finally, in a senior class students are amazing the teacher with their preferences for getting married in a civil rather than traditional religious ceremony, sparse rather than elaborate; and he gives this telling account of his status:

> Well, that's good, I'm glad to hear some of these things. 'Cause, see, I've lived in my own little world here for so many years, and I don't run into a lot of people that would have a differing opinion from what I have. So that's why I always tell you people that you got 30 good ideas in here against one of mine, and that's why I like to discuss things with you.

What a wonderful reddition for any teacher to give and any student to hear! – or for any participants in any discussion.

Speaker questions

Instead of asking a question, *provide that the speaker* (or other partner) *ask a question related to what the speaker has just said*. When well provided for, speaker questions of themselves enhance group as well as individual processes. And participants' responses to speaker questions are longer and more complex than their answers to practitioner questions.

There are multiple ways of providing that speakers ask questions. But the alternative is only *that* they be provided for. There are three cases, and one and the same general way of enacting the alternative in each case. Whether the case is of the speaker's question, the group question, or the discussion question, the alternative involves providing for a speaker's question and then sustaining it.

Four generic steps or moves are involved (see Table 12.1), two by the speaker and two by the practitioner. The case begins, as all alternatives do, at the juncture where a speaker has just said something, as in answer to a question.

1 Speaker contribution.
2 Provide for a speaker question.
3 Speaker question.
4 Sustain speaker question.

There next begins a new sequence involving discussion of the speaker question. By contrast, the counter-example proceeds as follows:

1 Speaker contribution.
2 Practitioner question.
3 Speaker answer.
4 Practitioner
   (a)   evaluation of answer plus,
   (b)   further question.

At this point a new sequence not involving discussion has already begun.

The alternative is to provide for a speaker's question. Here the point is not the manner but the *act* of providing for speaker questions as an alternative to practitioner questions. There are endless ways of accomplishing this act. The details of how it might be done are far less important than the act that is being done. That is, the example or particular instance must not be taken to stand for the act itself. One summary example is the employment interview (transcript no. 7 in the Appendix). At the start, the recruiter *provides* for applicant questions (exchange 4). Towards the end he *invites* them directly (exchange 42). The applicant demurs: 'Well just maybe comments'. But the recruiter does not resume asking questions. Rather he responds declaratively to the various comments: 'Sure, yeah. I agree with you. Completely'. Then the applicant actually begins, quite hesitantly, to ask questions (49, 52, 53, 55). The recruiter sustains the asking not only by not asking questions but also by actively using other non-questioning techniques such as statements, phatics, and fillers (for example, exchange 55) in the midst of the applicant's hesitant efforts to express questions. Another summary example is the classroom discussion (transcript no. 13) where the teacher frequently – not always – uses student questions. For instance (exchanges 15–17), he has the student repeat the question; he praises it ('That's a good question'); he repeats it; he supplies background to it; and again he restates it, offering the student question for class discussion, while himself exclaiming, 'I don't know'. But these are merely *instances* of some of the ways in which speaker questions may be provided for.

As a general caution, it should be noted that this act of providing for speaker questions consists of more than mere words: actions and attitudes are required, along with appropriate conditions, purposes, and subject-matters. Therefore the *words* that are cited as examples in this section are merely instances of how in part to provide for speaker questions.

7   *Speaker's question*

Provide that the speaker formulate a question about what he has just said or is struggling to think and say.

A speaker has just said, 'Something is the case, I don't know' (Table 12.1). You act so as to provide that he ask a question about that. For example, you say: 'Relax for a minute and think up the question that's still bothering you about that'. In response the speaker poses a question, 'Is X the case?' You act to sustain the question. For example, you say: 'You're wondering if X is the case. Good question.'

As a counter-example to the first act, when the speaker has said that 'something' is the case, you ask: 'What exactly do you think the case *is*?' He has just told you that he does not know what the case is, and you have just told him to tell you what the case is. 'Is it X? Is it Y? What do you think?' He thinks that some letter is the case but he doesn't know if it is X, if it is Y, if it is Z. 'Which letter is the case?' you ask. 'Roses have some colour, I dunno' – 'Which colour do roses have, exactly?'

As a counter-example to the second act, when the speaker does pose a question you either answer it or counter it.

(a) *Answer*. He says, 'Is X the case?' and you say 'Yes' or 'No'. He has just told you that he is wondering whether X is the case and you have just told him that you do not wonder whether X is the case, you *know* that it is the case (or not). In that way you settle the issue, putting a stop to enquiry by substituting your certainty for his wondering. 'I wonder if roses are red' – 'I know that roses are red, I don't wonder about it'. It is as much sense to say, 'No, violets are blue'.

(b) *Counter*. The other way not to do the alternative is to ask the speaker a question. When he asks, 'Is X the case?' you wittily counter with 'Is X the case?' He has just told you that he is wondering whether X is the case, and you have just told him to wonder whether X is the case. Or you say, 'Well, what do *you* think?' after he has told you what he is thinking. First he tells you that he can't tell, then you tell him to tell. In that way you supply him with the question that he came up with in the first place, and give back to him the question that he has just contributed. 'Are roses red?' – 'What do *you* think? Are roses red?' It is as much sense to riposte, 'Are violets blue?'

The alternative is to provide that the speaker ask a question and then to sustain it. In that way the speaker who is struggling to think and say something gets just the kind of help he needs to work his way out: help with identifying and formulating the question confusedly at issue in his mind. Once he gets his question, and only if he gets it, he can pursue the answer. Often enough you will hear the speaker begin working out the answer in the same breath as bespeaking the question. Now the earlier struggle, confusion, and difficulty with thinking and speaking begin to dissipate as energies mobilize and concentrate upon the newly discovered issue that gives sense and direction to effort, by contrast to the earlier muddling and flailing about over scattered fragments of unseen but not unfelt issues.

The speaker's effort may still be difficult but now it is disciplined and promising, yielding one of two fruits. The speaker will work out the thought he was earlier, fruitlessly, struggling to express. Or, if unable to answer his question, he will provide a new and perplexing question to consider. The alternative helps the student to deliver himself of a stalled thought or to yield up a tough question as the fruit of his struggle to think. Either one is a good contribution.

8 Group question

Provide that another partner pose a question about the speaker's contribution or the matter under discussion.

A speaker has said that something is the case. You say, for example, 'Let's take a minute to hear the question that somebody else might be thinking of about that'. The rest follows as before. In response some partner says, 'Is X the case?' and you sustain the question by saying, for example, 'You're wondering if X is the case. Good question.'

The counter-example is to ask the group for another statement of the case. One speaker has already made a statement, a confused and hesitant one. 'Something is the case, I don't know.' The practitioner treats this contribution by ignoring it, turning to someone else for a clear and confident statement. 'Anybody else? What is the case here?' Whether the next speaker's statement is clear or not, the key issue is the treatment of the first contribution. What is to be done with it (as also with the next one)?

The choice is either to ask a question or to use an alternative. Any of the alternatives might be chosen at this juncture, but the kind being described here is provision for a speaker's question. The previous case provided for the speaker's question; this case provides for the group's question. Instead of asking a question, then, you treat the contribution ('Something is the case, I don't know') by providing that another participant pose a question related to it.

The choice seems odd: instead of a question from the teacher, for example, a question from some student. But it is a well-grounded choice. First, of itself it enhances enquiry because *participants* are formulating and posing questions. And it stimulates participants' thought and response, for the response consists of a question and questions stimulate the thought of those who ask them. But furthermore it encourages participation and enriches the exchange. That is because (1) students more readily address questions to students than to the teacher – a variant of the general case with social peers vs. subordinates; (2) students respond to student questions at greater length and complexity than they do in answering teacher questions. Hence the teacher's act of providing for students' questions has the overall effect of enhancing discussion on all counts.

9 Discussion question

Provide that participants formulate the question that now appears at issue in the discussion.

Some speaker has conclusively said that X is the case, and/or several have said that something is the case, X, Y, Z. At this juncture the practitioner – such as the chairman, teacher, or group leader – provides that the question for discussion be formulated by a participant(s). You say, for example: 'Maybe it's time now to hear a few suggestions as to the kind of questions we should be asking now, given everything that has been said up to this point'. As before, some speaker says, 'Is X the case?' and you sustain it by saying, for example: 'One question we might discuss now is whether X is the case. Interesting question.'

The counter-example is to state the next question for discussion. 'OK, so X is the case here. OK. Let's move on to the next question: what is the case over there?' In that way you save the participants from wondering about what question comes next in the process. You also move discussion right along without making a big issue of what makes sense to be talked about at this point. You tell them what to talk about, and generally what to say: answers to your question – otherwise, there are a lot of people in the room with different ideas that would take a lot of time to sort through and come together on; they're not very clever to begin with and they probably wouldn't agree anyway, even if somebody did come up with a good idea. Sensibly enough, you give them the next question to answer.

The alternative is to provide that participants formulate the question that is now at issue. In that way you take steps to help them learn how to identify and formulate questions, how to connect question with question in a sequence of enquiry, how to join together in deliberating and deciding among competing and compelling issues, and how to act together under uncertainty. The result is a public question for discussion, one that arises from the group. This is the question that *must* be discussed, so the discussants feel and experience. By contrast, the practitioner's question need only be answered. And to do that, as everyone knows from long experience, requires no discussion.

Signals

Signal your reception of what the speaker is saying, without yourself taking or holding the floor. Signals are modest devices with substantial functions. There is nothing much to doing them, yet they encourage the speaker and they open the floor for further participation. All the while they give the practitioner something to say without actually holding the floor.

10 Phatics

Uttering a brief phrase, quietly exclaim feeling in reaction to what the speaker has just finished saying. He will then say more, and more than he will say in answer to a question.

When the speaker has said that X is the case (Table 12.1), you exclaim, for example, 'Oh, X is so nice', and he will go to say that Y is the case, too. 'Roses are red' – 'Oh, red roses are lovely!' – And violets are blue.' He has made a poem because of you.

The phrasing of phatics will depend on the peculiarities of language around you. Perhaps people around you don't say things like 'lovely/nice'. You might say 'wonderful', 'amazing', 'interesting', 'awful'. Around me I used to hear 'Good gravy!' and 'Good night!' Other available phrases include: 'goodness', 'gracious', 'gosh', 'wow', 'no', 'well', 'my', 'you don't say!' For example, the recruiter in the employment interview (transcript no. 7, Appendix) favours 'really' as a phatic (exchanges 11, 15, 19), along with 'No kidding? That *is* large' (9). The physician (transcript no. 6C) also uses 'really' (exchange 2) and 'sure' (10) and 'good, I'm glad' (5).

Phatics are not reactions to the fact that the speaker has said something, nor evaluations of the way he has said it – as in, 'Good answer/lad'. You are not saying that the speaker, the move, or the wording of 'X is the case' is nice, you are saying that X is nice. Of course, if you don't feel that X is nice, don't exclaim so. And if you have no feeling at all about X, don't exclaim any feeling – that is, don't use a phatic but choose a more suitable alternative.

There is nothing to using phatics, but although modest in themselves, they serve important functions and have substantial effects on discussion. Indeed, phatics are among the most powerful alternatives available. Responses to phatics are longer and richer than answers to questions of any type. X is indeed nice.

11 Fillers

Emitting some word or sound, indicate attentive interest in what the speaker has said or is in process of saying. He will go on to say more.

When the speaker says that X is the case, you emit, for example, 'Mm-humm'. He goes on to say that Y is the case. 'Roses are red' – 'Mm-humm' – 'and violets are blue'.

Fillers are more than modest, they are minimal. They are 'mm – humn, uh-huh, mm, huhn, yes, yeah; I see/understand; good, fine, right, OK'. These are normal conversational devices for signalling reception, and are also called back-channel feedback or verbal encouragers. They encourage the speaker by showing him that what he is saying is falling on not altogether deaf ears, and that the mind between these ears shall not for the moment venture forth to displace his own.

People respond positively to fillers, as in interviews. Examples are found throughout the interviews in the Appendix. The employment interview (transcript no. 7) shows the use of 'I see, I see' (exchange 7) and many uses of 'um hm, uh huh' (17, 18, 24, 55). The medical interview (transcript no. 6C) has several 'hm hm' (exchanges 4 5, 9). The client-centred therapy session (transcript no. 4) has a strong 'M-hm. M-hm' (exchange 9), and the eclectic session (transcript no. 5) an especially strong 'uh huh' (11). Fillers remain a useful alternative if only for letting the practitioner say at least something, *and* to say it without taking the turn at talk away from the speaker.

12 Pass

By gesture or statement, pass the next turn at talk to another speaker. The obvious response is more speaker talk, and talk by more speakers.

Speaker One says that X is the case. You pass by saying, for example, 'Yes, Speaker Two'. Two says that Y is the case. 'Roses are red' – Pass – 'Violets are blue'. Here two participants join in to form a nice couplet by the practitioner's gracious leave.

If you the practitioner choose to pass, it is necessary that you do something to signal that choice. For instance, students will not barge in, as peers will do with or without your leave. You might pass to a volunteer or supplicant by saying 'Yes' and/or by naming him; or by nodding, gesturing, smiling at him. You can pass to a non-volunteer or someone who is reticent by gazing contentedly and expectantly about the room; and/or by saying something like 'Some people haven't had a chance to speak yet'. But by all means do not make a pass at some reluctant participant by saying something like a question: 'What do *you* think about it, John?' John and other wallflowers and fading violets will not be responsive; they will indeed answer, but certainly not with 'Violets are blue'.

By now you should know that the response will go as it did in this child-care class. At the end of a rich discussion over how children feel when their parents divorce, and after several students have related their personal experiences and feelings at considerable length, the nice lady of the teacher gently but awkwardly passes to Karen and others who had not spoken.

T.: How did *you* feel, Karen?
S.: Oh, my parents got divorced when I was 4 or 5.
T.: How did they tell you?
S.: I don't remember.

Next over to Kathy:

T.:   How about you, Kathy?
S.:   I don't remember.

Then over to Debbie:

T.:   Debbie, what about you?
S.:   No, not then.

Having come as far as to arrive at this twelfth alternative to questioning, you should by now know in general that questions are not the way to get Karen, Kathy, and Debbie to discuss; and you should know in particular 11 other ways to encourage them to join in. Specifically you should know how to make a pass at them. The alternative of 'Pass' by definition excludes asking a question and does not include much speech at all. But you must do something.

Pass is a minimal act but a substantial move on the practitioner's part, ceding the turn and yielding the floor to participation. It may seem to be a nothing, but the practitioner is actually doing something to good purpose. In moments that you adjudge promising, your pass is a fundamental alternative with immediate beneficial effect on discussion.

Silences

Instead of asking a question, *say nothing at all*. Silences are either deliberate or non-deliberate. Only the deliberate kind are positive practitioner behaviours, serving to purpose; the other kind reflect lack of practice, serving to no good purpose.

13   Deliberate silence

Say nothing at all but maintain a deliberate, appreciative silence for 3–5 seconds or so. The original speaker will resume or another will enter in.

Against all appearances, silence is a positive practitioner behaviour; and seemingly against all expectations, people respond positively to it. They respond to silence with both further talk and more complex thought.

For example (Table 12.1), a speaker has just made some contribution, saying 'X is the case'. The practitioner chooses not to ask a question and not to make a statement, nor to utter anything at all but to maintain an appreciative, attentive silence. After a few seconds the speaker says, 'And Y too is the case'. 'Roses are red' – a noticeable pause – 'and violets are blue'. The speech is the speaker's, the intervening silence is the practitioner's.

The practitioner is doing something, not nothing. In a positive, active behaviour he is deliberately maintaining silence, an appreciative, attentive one; and the silence itself is noticeable. To be noticeable the silence must achieve at least 3 seconds or so, because exchanges are commonly rapid, following one upon the other with nary a pause. Also, teachers are rarely observed to use silence and genuine examples of this alternative are hard to find in class-rooms.

Here a civics or government class is discussing capital punishment. A boy excitedly jumps in with a conclusion, phrased as a rhetorical question. The teacher remains silent and the boy resumes, now giving the antecedent reasoning.

S.:   So that's not consistent with the law, then, is it?
T.:   [3 seconds]
S.:   – If rehabilitation is an object of sentencing and then they know that a [executed] killer is never going to be able to function again in society.

Or a different student may enter in after the silence to offer a divergent opinion, as in this discussion about life after death.

S1.:   I think it depends on what your definition of life after death is. And then I think, that each person has a different outlook on what it is like, what it'd be for them, for themselves.
T.:   [3 seconds]
S2:   It's already determined, the way that you live your life on earth.
        (Continues for 12 seconds)

Numerous examples of silence are easily found in certain kinds of psychotherapy and counselling, where therapist silence is routinely prescribed as an active intervention in place of questions. The transcript of client-centred therapy (no. 4) marks no fewer than 11 silent pauses in only 15 exchanges. For instance (exchange 14):

Client: Yeah. And there's somehow no dodging it now. You see, I'm much more aware of it.

Therapist: [silence]

Client: I don't know. Right now, I don't know just what the next step is. I really don't know.

Therapist: [silence]

Client: Fortunately, this is a kind of development, so that it – doesn't carry over too acutely into – I mean, I – what I'm trying to say, I think, is that I'm still functioning.

This use of silence not only helps the client to express self but to come to an understanding of self. Moreover, the second episode of silence sustains the 'speaker's question' in the midst of a struggle to understand and express something of importance to the speaker and to the very process itself.

Deliberate silence is the simplest alternative available and one of the most effective. Yet it is also the hardest alternative to learn and to use. First of all, silence seems to be an awkward affair at best, if not a void, a waste of time, or worse, counter-productive. Practitioners such as interviewers and teachers feel responsible for the flow of talk and the response of the client. They are concerned to keep entering in and saying something so that the student or interviewee will keep saying something back. Moreover, teachers feel responsible for moving through the curriculum and over the subject-matter, keeping pace and covering ground. Lastly, teachers are responsible for managing the classroom, in some sense of discipline and crowd control. Silence threatens on each count. Actually to choose to use it seems not an alternative communication behaviour but an alternative to communication.

The facts are otherwise. Deliberate silence can well serve to purpose in classroom discussions and various interviews. The practitioner remains in control and the partner responds. Indeed, they respond with considerable length and complexity of thought. There are very good reasons that things turn out that way.

It is obvious that time is needed for thinking and for expression of thought. But more time is needed for more complex thought, and that is not so obvious. The sustained expression of thought is marked by hesitations, false starts, and *pauses* in speech. It is at these precise points that practitioners habitually enter in to ask a question. But the partner has only ostensibly finished speaking. Were the practitioner to maintain silence at this juncture, he would probably hear not only further talk but also richer thought.

Silence is an appropriate communication behaviour and furthermore it models appropriate behaviour for participants to imitate. For instance, it models due attentiveness and appreciative listening until such time as a participant will have succeeded in delivering self of an entire thought – not just a phrase or sentence or two. To speak up at the first second's pause or on the first flawed phrase is to grab the floor and to dismiss the speaker. It is no less an interruption than when someone is speaking. Indeed, someone *is* speaking – and thinking, too. The alternative asks only that speakers be given 3 seconds' grace when they falter in giving expression to a complex thought that they are in process of forming about the issue before them.

Silence is a very odd practitioner behaviour which you, the practitioner, will just have to learn in the first place – before trying to use it. The first thing you have to learn is just how long 3 seconds last, the empirical duration. You can learn this at home, as I did, with the second hand of a clock or stop-watch, or a metronome. The second thing to learn is timing. You can practise timing as you recite something – separate sentences – before a mirror or other friendly face which might provide helpful cues. The third thing to learn is how to do it in your classroom or interview in the heat of the exchange.

There, where everyone is accustomed to rapid exchanges and when the partner expects you to speak up within less than a second's lapse, 3 seconds of silence will seem an eternity, especially when manifold concerns press upon you while nothing seems to be happening. So, *despite* good intentions and earnest practice, you rush things and start talking to get something going. That is the hard way to do things, as I did them. Now here is an easier way. It is foolproof. All you have to do is sing 'Baa, baa, black sheep'.

The speaker says, 'X is the case' (Table 12.1). You sing in your mind:

> Baa, baa, black sheep,
> Have you any wool?

On the 'Baa, baa' you nod, nod to the speaker, hoping he has more wool. That takes up a good four seconds which you will run in two or three. At that point, unbelievably enough, the speaker says, 'And Y too, come to think about it'.

Then you decide what to do next with this response – which other alternative to use, or which question to pose. You might even choose again to use deliberate silence, pursuing what you judge to be a particularly rich development in the process at hand. If that is the case, sing the rest of 'Baa, baa, black sheep'.

The full pursuit, should you judge it promising at the moment, starts as before with a speaker who says that X is the case (see Table 12.1). You do your 'Baa, baa' and he adds that Y is the case, too. Again you maintain a deliberate silence for 3 seconds or so, singing along in your mind:

> Yes sir, yes sir,
> Three bags full:

And with a nod, nod, hold for 3 seconds!

If you hold out for the three bags full, that speaker or another will say, 'But not Z – Z isn't the case'. So you sing on:

> One for my master
> And one for my dame,
> And one for the little boy
> Who lives down the lane.

– looking gently at the speaker and – if in a group setting – looking next at some girl, then at some boy, finally glancing down the back row. You are going the full course of silence at this rich juncture, fully 8 or 9 seconds which you do in 5, whereupon a participant starts explaining that 'Z is not the case here, because ... '.

All this may sound silly enough, but it is serious business to enhance the participants' cognitive, affective, and expressive process. And it is hard to do. 'Baa, baa, black sheep' is merely an artifice for enacting the choice of an alternative behaviour, deliberate silence, in service of purpose in this circumstance. That is good practice.

14 Non-deliberate silence

When silence occurs that is not deliberate, *you had better figure out something to do*. Non-deliberate silence is not of your choosing and acting, and describes a situation where no known and good purpose is being served. Confusion and trouble surfaces or events and people are suspended while you are silent for want of speech and action.

Figure out something to do. For example, in the case where things are troubled and you sense you are losing control, start asking questions. Chances are that you will regain control of participants' social and verbal behaviour.

For the moment you have chosen and enacted the best alternative available to your judgement in service of your purposes in present circumstances. Later you will reflect on your enacted choice, assessing and replanning. Then you will try again on the morrow. That is good practice.

Various alternatives

This baker's dozen of alternatives of four different kinds – statements, speaker questions, signals, silences – systematically covers the possibilities of practice in dyadic and group settings. But still other alternatives can be identified – various ones proposed for this or that particular setting or purpose but undoubtedly useful in other settings as well. Most of these further alternatives are individual variants of the types already described, or otherwise resemble them. There is no end to the specifics and variations. A review of these various alternatives will help the practitioner to grasp the general notion and function of alternatives, to perceive the possibilities of practice and, most importantly, to devise individual alternatives especially suited to his/her particular purpose and circumstance.

This variety of technique includes comments, self-questioning, reactions, a pot-pourri of statements, and still other practices in place of asking questions.

Comments

In social field work and research, 'interviewing by comment' is proposed as an adjunct or alternative technique supplementing or complementing the use of questions (Snow *et al.* 1982). 'Interviewing by comment constitutes an attempt to elicit information from a respondent by making a statement rather than by asking a question' (p. 287). Eight types of comment are identified, the first four more general and commonplace, the last four more narrowly focused.

1 *Puzzlement*. These comments imply that the interviewer or researcher is confused and in need of assistance; they can be used to probe and to encourage the respondent to elaborate. 'I do not recall all the particulars'; 'I don't quite follow you'.

2 *Humour*. These are spontaneous and situation-specific comments that allow the interviewer to explore the respondents' inclination to discuss a sensitive issue, and to assess indirectly the stress or embarrassment involved, or yet to ease the tension. Humorous comments can open a delicate area for discussion when questions or other forms of comment would fail. For example, to respondents laughing and drinking beside their building levelled by a tornado, one interviewer commented: 'Some people will do *anything* to have a party'.

3 *Replay* is a restatement of what the respondent has said, calling for clarification or elaboration. A replay comment can be used immediately after a response, or sometime later in the interview to compare present with earlier responses. The comment can also be either a verbatim restatement or a muddled one; the deliberately muddled replay is used to check the interviewer's understanding and interpretation. For example: 'That is the part you like best, if I understood what you said' – 'No, I said X. Let me explain more'.

4 *Description*. These are observations made about some social event or interaction episode. They function to elicit further information and to check the validity of the interviewer's perception of the event, thus stimulating corrective and elaborative responses. Descriptions can be stated matter-of-factly or by using analogy. For example: 'Those people sure seem to be having a good ole time' – 'Those people are just pretending to be happy. To be really happy, you have to X'.

5 *Outrageous comment*. These comments challenge the respondent's view of the situation, in order to discover the boundaries and norms in that view, and the tolerance for people who deviate from them. For example: to anti-pornography crusaders discussing possible speakers for their decency rally, one researcher commented, 'Linda Lovelace would be a good speaker' (a celebrated sex-film actress). The crusaders, at first shocked, later surprisingly agreed.

6 *Altercasting comments*. These cast the respondent into a role, identity, or personality type congruent with the purposes of the interview. The respondent is then obliged either to conform or to explain non-compliance. The casting can be direct or indirect. The indirect casting says, for example, that a friend or colleague suggested that the respondent would be a reliable informant, candid and informed about this topic.

7 *Motivational comments*. These comments indirectly gather information about the motives and attributions that respondents use to account for behaviour. Rather than asking 'why?' the interviewer offers a 'because' or 'in-order-to' statement. 'You couldn't attend the peace rally because you had to

study.' The respondent reveals the motivational system while indicating whether the account in the comment is appropriate and legitimate.

8 *Evaluative comments*. These comments elicit information about the respondent's feelings, values, and opinions. 'Gee, since you have several young children, you must have thought a lot about busing' (that is, transporting children out of their neighbourhood to another school in order to achieve racial integration).

In general, these comments serve better than questions for purposes of discovery and data gathering, on two grounds: 'interviewing by comment allows the interviewee to define the response field in accordance with his or her frame of reference'; and 'comments tend to be less demanding and threatening than direct questions' (Snow *et al.* 1982: 289). Comments are more effective for obtaining responses and data about sensitive and threatening matters, about the hidden side of social life, and about the perceptions and behaviours of respondents with different cultural orientations or world views (p. 305).

Self-Q

Self-Q is a self-questioning interview technique proposed to uncover the 'cognitive maps' – knowledge, beliefs, attitudes – of members of organizations (Bougon 1983). Instead of asking questions, the interviewer or researcher has the respondent ask questions.

In the initial interview, the purpose is to obtain concepts from the respondent without their being mentioned by the interviewer. The interviewer says:

> I would like to interview you about your view of the X organization. It is evident that you are the expert on your own view of X. Therefore, what I would like to do is have you ask yourself questions about X. Please do not answer these questions. While you are asking yourself these questions, I will be writing them down verbatim. Please, let's begin by you asking yourself an easy question.
>
> (Bougon 1983: 183)

After 50 minutes, the respondent's questions have identified anywhere from two dozen to 200 useful concepts for the remaining interviews (pp. 184–5), where the concepts will be mapped and verified in order to describe the respondent's knowledge of the given social territory.

By contrast, the interviewer's questions will 'plant' a concept rather than uncover one in the mind of the respondent, and they will restrict rather than open the range of social territory covered (p. 182). Furthermore, persistent and elaborate questioning after other notions related to the concepts that the respondent is actually attending to 'remains fruitless' (pp. 185–6).

Reactions

In classroom discussions 'reacting moves' are proposed to encourage student participation (MacDonald 1989). A reacting move is a comment that follows a response – as in a response to a question. Instead of asking a further question, the teacher (or other discussant) uses one of five types of reacting moves.

1 *Restatement* – to state again in a new form.
2 *Repetition* – to state again in the same form.
3 *Highlighting* – to call attention to, single out, make particular note of. 'That's a very important fact about slavery.'
4 *Amplifying* – to add to or extend prior discourse. 'Extending Harriet's ideas, slaves were considered property.'
5 *Recapitulation* – to summarize; to relate to and/or connect with prior information or discourse. 'So, according to Steve's comment, we know that Washington had slaves, and Cynthia explained why he waited to free his own slaves. He was not what one, today, would call a liberal.'

By contrast to a question at this juncture of discourse, a reacting move has 'an invitational effect on student participation' (MacDonald 1989: Ms p. 10). It is likely to be followed by further responses from more students, whereas a question would initiate a cycle involving one response from one student.

Other alternatives

Various other alternatives are recommended for use in personnel, psychotherapeutic, and medical interviewing.
   1 *Declarative statement*. In personnel interviewing, 'the use of direct questions is to be avoided wherever possible' (Lopez 1965: 252); 'the interviewer substitutes, wherever possible, declarative statements', for statements 'subtly invite the interviewee to speak more freely' (p. 119).
   Three other commonly recommended techniques have been found in research on employment interviews (McComb and Jablin 1984):
   2 *Restating* – restating what the applicant has just said, in the interviewer's own words. 'Now let me get this straight. ... '; 'This is what I think you mean ... '
   3 *Verbal encouragers* – short acknowledgements of understanding interjected during the applicant's speaking turn that encourage conversation: 'Hm-hm, yes, right'.
   4 *Silence* – lack of interruption in addition to the use of silence as encouragement for prolonging responses.
   These alternatives take their inspiration from well-known techniques in psychotherapy, where other techniques in addition are recommended accord-

ing to the particular orientation of therapy, such as interpretation in psycho-analysis and clarification of feeling in client-centred therapy.

Interpretation – a 'causal-correlative' statement in the form of 'X because Y', used to inform the patient of a proposition that the analyst believes remains unrecognized. By direct contrast to a question, this kind of statement elicits longer and more fruitful responses (Colby 1961).

Clarification of feeling – a short, economical summary of the feeling expressed by the client in typically long and confused speech. In contrast to a question, this kind of statement results in the client's increased understanding and insight (Frank and Sweetland 1962).

A good summary example of many of these alternatives can be found in sessions of client-centred and eclectic counselling and psychotherapy (transcripts nos. 4 and 5 in the Appendix). These therapists use restatements of client response, clarification of feelings expressed, interpretation, fillers or encouragers, and silent pauses.

Related in spirit to these therapeutic techniques are the 'alternative practices' identified by contrast to routine practice of questioning in medical interviews (Mishler 1984). Alternative practices include several broad strategies such as using less scientific and more everyday language. They also include asking fewer questions, listening to the patient's account without interruption, referring to the patient's responses and feelings in the patient's own terms, and specific linguistic techniques in place of questions. The summary example (transcript no. 6C in the Appendix) shows the physician making comments and self-declarations, restating the patient's response, using phatics and fillers. By contrast to the continual questioning in routine practice, these alternative practices help the patient to construct a coherent and meaningful narrative of the medical problem, and to join with the physician in identifying and addressing it.

Chapter thirteen

Research on questions vs alternatives

The apt use of alternatives depends on the practitioner's informed choice of that technique which promises to serve purpose in circumstance. To help inform choice, the practitioner can attend not only to considerations of practice but also to understanding from research. By contrast to questions, how have alternatives proved to function in various processes of communication? The answer will give a clue as to how alternatives might function in particular practice, and whether their function will be to advance purpose in that circumstance.

Statements

This alternative is to state, declaratively, the thought that occurs to you in relation to what the speaker has just said. The rationale is that people do respond to statements, and with greater length and higher quality than to questions. Observational, correlational, and experimental studies in various communicative contexts – different interviews, conversations, discussions in dyads, trios, and groups small and large – have revealed the contrasting responses that adults, special children, and students at all levels have given to questions and statements.

Adults

In psychoanalytic sessions, the task is to enhance the patient's awareness and understanding of unrecognized beliefs governing behaviour. The tool for this task is 'free association'. In order to amplify free association, the analyst in one experiment (Colby 1961) systematically intervened either with a question or a statement following five sentences of talk about a given personage or topic.

The interrogative input consisted of a simple question, put with the intent to elicit information about that topic; for example, 'What did your father have against you?' The statement input was a 'causal-correlative', a compound statement with 'because', put with the intent to inform the patient of an inferredly unrecognized proposition; for instance, 'You think of this couple because you would like to have that sort of power over Julie'. Following either type of intervention, the analyst remained silent for the free-associational flow.

The statement input proved to have a significantly greater amplifying power than the question. The patients spoke at greater length after the statement, and their talk contained a higher incidence of references to the topic for free association.

| Analyst | Patient response | |
	Number of sentences	References to topic (%)
Question	19.1	49.8
Statement	26.1	58.4

Note: data from Colby 1961

'Because of this greater amplifying power, an increased use of causal-correlative inputs might represent a more effective heuristic in clinical discourse' (Colby 1961: 238). The reason might be that questions direct the respondent to 'find answer, then *stop*', whereas a statement supplies information for 'accept–reject'. A statement is thus more informative and more ambiguous regarding the response to give beyond accept–reject; 'what direction to develop and when to terminate are less clearly defined than in the case of an interrogative' (p. 238).

Similarly, in a study of client-centred therapy sessions (Frank and Sweetland 1962), questions and statements were shown to have opposite effects on the client's 'understanding and insight'. The questions were Direct Questioning and Forcing the Topic (for example, 'Would you like to tell me more about your mother?'). The statements were 'Clarification of Feeling', summarizing a complete area of confused emotionality in one or two careful sentences; and 'Interpretation', stating cause–effect relations much like the causal-correlative statements in the psychoanalytic study. Ratings of the subsequent client talk showed that the therapist's questions significantly decreased the client's understanding and insight, whereas the statements significantly increased them.

Therapist	Client Understanding and Insight
QUESTIONS	
Direct Questioning	−153
Forcing the Topic	−120
STATEMENTS	
Clarification of Feeling	+340
Interpretation	+225

Special children

The same effects are also seen in various kinds of research, from different fields, with children who are hearing-impaired, language-delayed, and non-standard or second-language English speakers. In all of these cases, the task of practitioners is to enhance the child's expression of language. The children respond to statements with greater length and quality than to questions.

In a series of observational, correlational, and experimental studies with deaf children aged 6–11 years, the children's 'initiative' and length of talk was found to vary systematically with the question or statement put to them (Wood *et al.* 1982; Wood and Wood 1984). Initiative represents the proportion of child responses marked by unsolicited or voluntary material: elaborated answers, spontaneous contributions, ideas, and questions asked by the child. Length of talk represents average number of words per response.

The sessions initially studied (Wood *et al.* 1982) were naturally occurring 'news' sessions of 30 minutes during which the children, in groups of 4 to 8 with their teacher, were to talk about their experiences. The children exhibited greater initiative and talked at greater length in response to teacher statements than to questions, whether closed or open (p. 303):

	Response
2-choice questions	2.1 wds
wh- questions	2.7
Statements	3.2

In a second study (Wood and Wood 1984), questions and statements were experimentally manipulated in a series of 10-minute sessions where the teacher, with two children, was to use a specified type of intervention for each session. Again both the children's initiative and length of response were found greater for statements than for questions. For instance, of one teacher (p. 51):

Session and intervention	Response	
	Length (wds)	Initiative (%)
1 Habitual style (base-line)	2.0	34
2 Ask 2-choice questions	1.9	25
3 Ask wh-questions	2.5	46
4 Make comments	3.7	83
5 Habitual style (return to base-line)	2.6	41

The same children with the same teacher spoke longer and showed more initiative (elaboration, contributions, ideas, questions) when the teacher refrained from questioning them and substituted instead declarative statements (such as 'I like going to the park, too'; 'That must have been awful').

With language-delayed children the task of parent and practitioner is to facilitate spontaneous talking, or expressive language not specifically elicited by controlled stimuli. Various studies with these children at home and in clinic and school (reviewed by Hubbell 1977) reveal that questions and commands are 'inhibiting stimuli' rather than facilitative. Parents, teachers, and clinicians often rely primarily on questions and commands in attempting to elicit talking from these children, whereas the fact is that the children talk little in response (pp. 228–9). The recommended strategy involves 'minimal emphasis on direct elicitation of talking' and the use of 'non-constraining' techniques (p. 225). The research uniformly shows that this works (studies as reviewed by Hubbell 1977).

First, children of nursery-school age were found to respond to teacher questions and directions, compared to non-constraining techniques, with a smaller vocabulary and little discussion. In the non-questioning condition the children responded with greater diversity of vocabulary and greater length of semantic unit; whereas 'conditions of constraint, which included questions and directions from the teacher, elicited talking from the children of lesser quality and breadth' (p. 219).

Second, when one mother was trained to model utterances rather than ask questions and give commands, the child's rate of verbal responses increased from 10 per cent to 56 per cent.

Third, when mothers were trained to decrease questions and commands, while increasing their comments and reflecting and expanding the child's utterances, the children increased the number of their utterances and the mean length of responses.

A similar contrast between questions and statements was discovered in an 'inadvertent experiment' from sociolinguistic field research with first- and second-grade Hawaiian children (Boggs 1972). The researcher's only purpose was to prolong a conversation in order to obtain as much speech as possible, so he asked many questions and made few comments. The answers were so sparse that he abandoned the attempt to elicit answers in this way, instead expressing interest, surprise, and disagreement by making comments and remarks.

The two months of recorded speech under the question-condition contained only six volunteer narratives of speech from the children, compared to five hours of narratives over the three months of the comment-condition. In 37 conversations with 14 children, the children's response to comments was nearly three times longer than to questions (p. 318):

	Response
Questions	1.0 lines of transcript
Comments	2.7

Moreover, in 78 per cent of the comparisons, response to comments was longer than response to any type of question, whether yes–no or wh-type: 'Thus one can conclude generally that answers to questions are briefer than other responses' (p. 319).

The children also *asked* more questions themselves when not being questioned. Thus the comments elicited longer responses, more narratives, and greater initiative and enquiry.

Students

The same contrasting responses to questions and statements as found with adults and special children in various settings is also found with ordinary students at various levels of schooling.

Preschool children, aged 3–4 years, paired in conversational sessions with a teacher, responded to statements with greater length and initiative than to questions, whether closed or open (Wood and Wood 1983). For instance of one pair:

	Response	
	Length (wds)	Initiative (%)
2-choice questions	2.7	28
wh-questions	3.4	32
Comments	5.5	69

The same results were seen with other pairs of children, notably those for whom English was a foreign language. The correlation of teacher questions and all measures of child response was strong and negative. 'The more questions a teacher asks, the less likely children are: (a) to take up any opportunity to show initiative; (b) to follow her 2-choice questions with additional, unrequested information; (c) to elaborate on their answers to all questions – including wh- type questions; and (d) to give long utterances overall' (Wood and Wood 1983: 157).

In *middle-school* social-studies classes (MacDonald 1989), the teachers' use of 'reacting moves' in place of questions generated greater student engagement in discussion. A reacting move is a comment that follows upon a response. There were five types: restatement, repetition, highlighting, amplifying, and recapitulation. Over half of the discourse ran in a five-move cycle, compared to the usual three-move cycle involving questioning:

Questioning		Reacting	
1	Teacher question	1	Teacher question
2	Student response	2	Student response
3	Teacher evaluation	3	Teacher reaction
	+ next question	4	Student reaction
		5	Student reaction

As a result of the reacting move instead of another question at step three, more students talked and students talked more – far more than the teacher. Students made three moves to the teacher's two, compared to the questioning cycle with one move for the student and three for the teacher. 'The teacher reactions seemed to have an invitational effect on student participation, and suggests that teachers might generate greater student engagement by asking fewer questions and listening more carefully to students' comments' (MacDonald 1989: MS p.10).

In *senior high school* social studies discussions (Dillon 1981), students responded for the same amount of time to statements as to questions – 17.9 vs. 18.1 seconds, based on a statistical grand average of classroom averages. That shows statements to be at least as effective as questions. However, averaging all of the individual responses across all classrooms reveals a small superiority of statements over questions, whether factual or opinion:

	Response (secs)		
	All	Fact	Opinion
Questions	14	10	15
Statements	16	13	18

Moreover, apart from length, the *cognitive level* of responses to statements was on the whole higher than for questions (Dillon 1982). A response can be either at the same cognitive level as the question or statement, or at a higher or lower level. Statements elicited responses at higher levels than the information in the statement itself, and at comparatively higher levels than questions did.

Response level	Questions (%)	Statements (%)
Lower	13	13
Same	49	33
Higher	38	54

That is, half of responses to questions were at the same level as the question, whereas half of responses to statements were at higher levels. Even the *lower*-level statements elicited higher-level responses:

	Lower-level	
Response level	Questions (%)	Statements (%)
Higher	29	65
Not-higher	71	35

That is, two-thirds of responses to statements were at levels higher than the statement, whereas for lower-level questions less than one-third of responses were at higher levels. Hence the statements enhanced cognition of respondents twice as much as did questions. The rule for practice would run: 'Ask a high-level question, get a lower-level answer – but make even a low-level statement and get a higher-level response' (p. 550). For instance, a factual-level statement might get responses at levels of explaining or justifying.

Furthermore, students in these classes showed much greater *initiative* in response to statements than to questions. These very same secondary classrooms were also analysed by other researchers (Wood and Wood 1988), who found that student initiative following the statements was twice as great as after questions (91 per cent vs. 45 per cent). These are the same researchers who had studied preschool and primary school children, and who in addition studied mothers and toddlers conversing at home while watching TV. A summary of all of their studies (Wood and Wood 1988: 290) provides a good picture of research on statements compared to questions.

Group		Child initiative in response	
N	Level	Questions (%)	Statements (%)
16	Secondary (ages 16–18)	45	91
16	Primary (ages 6–11)	18	66
16	Preschool (ages 3–4)	25	76
30	Home (ages 2–3)	16	67

In every case, at every level, the contrast favours the use of statements as an alternative to questions. All of the respondents – toddlers at home, children in pre-school, pupils in primary and students in secondary schools – responded to statements with greater length and greater initiative than to questions – two, three, four times as great. They not only talked more but better – going beyond to elaborate, to volunteer contributions and ideas, and to ask questions themselves.

Furthermore, the use of statements instead of questions also enhances the cognitive and expressive processes of special children: deaf, language-delayed, and second-language children. Their responses to statements are marked by greater frequency and length, and by higher quality. And statements enhance the cognition and participation of adults in psychoanalysis and counselling sessions. Their responses to statements are longer and they are more fruitful to the essential processes of free association and understanding and insight.

Where such effects are desirable to purpose in circumstance, the practitioner may elect to use declarative statements as an alternative to questioning.

Speaker's questions

This alternative is the opposite of the practitioner's questions. It consists of providing for the speaker or another partner to ask a question, and then using that question. The rationale is that the speaker's question enhances his/her cognitive, affective, and expressive processes, while the very questioning itself enhances the communication process at hand.

In various (but not all) communication settings it is fruitful for practitioners to use the speaker's or other partner's question – the child at home, student in school, patient in clinic, applicant in job interviews, colleague in conversations and discussions. Their questions too are part of the communicative process, and tend to enhance it. Yet in all settings the practitioner's questions prevent the partner from asking questions. Thus to use this alternative entails a reversal – first, *not* asking questions so that the partner can ask some, then using the questions to suit purpose in circumstance.

Not all research on question-asking is relevant to this alternative. Nor is the research that demonstrates various techniques of providing for speaker's questions (reviewed by Dillon 1988c) apt here, for it concentrates upon these questions only – not in their comparative character as an *alternative* to practitioner questions. Rather, here are some considerations from theoretical and empirical research touching upon the contrast between practitioner questions and partner questions.

In all settings the practitioner asks far more questions than the partner in communication (such as doctor with patient, adult with child). The more the questions the practitioner asks, the fewer are the questions from participants. For instance, teacher questions are strongly and negatively correlated with student questions – and with student voluntary declarations (Susskind 1969). Over the class hour, researchers in both elementary (Susskind 1969) and secondary (Dillon 1988c) classrooms have counted the same average of 84 questions per hour from the teacher, compared to two questions from all the students combined.

What is more, the questioning cycle commonly observed by sociolinguistic research in all settings provides no social or linguistic opportunity for the partner to ask a question. For example, in classrooms the cycle runs:

1 Teacher question,
2 Student answer,
3 Teacher evaluation + question.

When the practitioner is asking questions, all that the partner can do is to give answers.

Compared to the passive, dependent, reactive dynamics of answering questions, the partner's very act of questioning engages his/her active, independent, and energetic participation in the process. That follows as if by definition of the questioning-answering acts. For instance, analysis of the presuppositions and presumptions entailed in the student's act of asking a question revealed these summary features:

A student's act of asking a question exhibits for pedagogical appreciation and action a set of cognitive, affective, and behavioral dispositions describing the student's individual character and dynamic relation to the world. Moreover, of itself it instantiates those very propensities that educators otherwise labour to instil into the learner. ... For, the very act of questioning signals that attention has already been engaged and thought already stimulated; expression has been given, motivation is in force, readiness in evidence; action is undertaken, and participation joined. The question represents a perfect opening for teaching to enter, for enquiry is already under way and learning already sought.

(Dillon 1986: 337)

So much for the individual who asks; when more than one partner is involved in a communication setting, using the partner's questions evidently multiplies and spreads these effects towards the enhancement of the whole process at hand.

In group settings, moreover, children's response to questions from other children are longer and more complex than to adult questions (Boggs 1972; Mishler 1978); for instance of first-grade children (Mishler 1978):

216

	Child response	
	Adult questions (%)	Child questions (%)
Length		
1 wd	37	20
2–5 wds	32	38
6 + wds	31	42
Complexity		
fragment	37	20
phrase	41	47
sentence +	22	33

Hence, questions from the partners in a group setting serve to enhance participation and discussion.

On a broader scale, studies from various fields (reviewed by Dillon 1989) support the general proposition that question-asking on the part of the speaker or self (versus being questioned by a practitioner) enhances human development over a range of cognitive, affective, and behavioural features such as learning and information-processing, autonomy and mastery, linguistic and social interaction.

In certain contexts such as cross-examination, a partner's questions are not suitable to ask at all, let alone to be used by the practitioner. But where appropriate to purpose in circumstance, the practitioner may elect to provide that the partner ask questions, and then use these questions as an alternative to his own questioning.

Signals

These techniques signal to the partner the practitioner's attentive receptivity, without at the same time taking the turn at talk away from the partner. They are minimal devices with surprisingly large effects on the partner's response.

Two types of signal are fillers and phatics. There is little research on these but widespread agreement about their facilitative effect on participation.

Fillers

Fillers are nothing more than 'mm-hmm', 'uh- huh', 'I see', and like interjections. Studies of various interview settings commonly show that fillers actually encourage the partner to continue talking, such that he will speak longer than where there are no fillers (Matarazzo *et al.* 1964; McComb and Jablin 1984).

For instance, in employment interviews (McComb and Jablin 1984), where the filler or 'verbal encourager' was found to be used every two minutes, the effect was to enhance the response in talk and in estimation of the communicative process. The average response to the fillers was an additional 6 seconds of talk and a higher rating of the interviewer's empathy. 'Verbal encouragers do reinforce an applicant to continue his/her response behavior, and, in turn, this is associated with perceptions of the interviewer as an empathic listener' (p. 368).

Phatics

Phatics are brief exclamations of sentiment related to the speaker's ongoing utterance; for example, 'oh really', 'how lovely!', and the like. These have a remarkable effect. In studies with both deaf and hearing children (Wood *et al.* 1982; Wood and Wood 1983), the teacher's phatics enhanced the length and initiative of children's responses more than did questions, whether open or closed; for instance, of the hearing pre-school children:

| | Response | |
	Length (wds)	Initiative (%)
2-choice questions	2.7	28
wh-questions	3.4	32
Phatics	4.6	57

This effect of phatics has also been experimentally demonstrated (Wood and Wood 1984) by having teachers use the various techniques in specified sessions; for instance, of one teacher:

| Session | | Response | |
		Length (wds)	Initiative (%)
1	Habitual style (base-line)	2.0	34
2	2-choice questions	1.9	25
3	wh- questions	2.5	46
4	Phatics	3.5	67
5	Habitual style (return to base-line)	2.6	41

In every case, observational and experimental, the use of phatics proved to enhance response more so than did questions, whether open or closed. The children talked longer and showed greater initiative – more elaborated responses, spontaneous contributions, and child questions. Moreover, the same results have also been observed in secondary school discussions and in mother–toddler conversations (Wood and Wood 1988). These are the same studies that examined the use of comments or statements by contrast to questions. The general conclusion runs:

> In all of these studies, we had found that a simple measure – how many questions were asked by teachers in various sessions – was significantly

related to how much initiative was displayed by the children in those sessions – in a negative direction. A great many questions produced a great many answers, but little else, whereas fewer questions and more comments and phatics were met by children giving more spontaneous contributions, elaborated answers, and asking questions themselves.

(Wood and Wood 1984: 45–6)

Thus, phatics as well as comments prove to enhance cognition and expression more than do questions of any type. For instance, the experimental line-up with pre-school and primary school children runs as follows (Wood and Wood 1983, 1984):

	Pre-school response		Primary school response (deaf children)	
	Length (wds)	Initiative (%)	Length (wds)	Initiative (%)
QUESTIONS				
2-choice	2.7	28	1.9	25
wh-	3.4	32	2.5	46
ALTERNATIVES				
Phatics	4.6	57	3.5	67
Comments	5.5	69	3.7	83

In every case, phatics as well as comments prove to be useful alternatives to questions. They are useful for enhancing cognition and expression, whereas 'the more the teachers question students, the less initiative they show and the less they say' (Wood and Wood 1988: 294).

Signals such as fillers and phatics are minimal devices with mighty effects on the communicative process. They encourage the partner to speak at greater length and with higher quality than when responding to questions. Where purpose in circumstance is advanced by enhancing the partner's participation and cognition, the practitioner may elect to signal attentive receptivity by a filler ('hm-mm') or phatic ('oh, lovely!') instead of asking a question.

Or the practitioner may use a technique even more minimal than a filler or phatic: he may choose to say nothing at all. For, silence too is a golden alternative to questioning.

Silences

As a communication technique the practice of silence is to maintain a deliberate, appreciative silence for 3–5 seconds after the partner has finished speaking (for example, after a student has responded to the teacher's question) until the partner resumes speaking or another speaker enters in (for instance, another student). The rationale for this technique lies in the unexpectedly salient role that silent pauses play in speech; the justification for it lies in the demonstrated relation of silence to participants' cognitive and expressive processes.

Silence in speech

Normal speech is filled with silent pauses. (It is also marked by filled pauses – 'ah' – and other hesitations.) The silent pauses may conveniently be viewed as occurring *within* a speaker's utterance and *before* it; those before may be a 'switching' pause between speakers or a latency or hesitation at the start of a lone speaker's utterance. Both of these junctures are appropriate for the practitioner's use of silence: maintaining silence when the partner pauses (1) in the midst of utterance, as it were, and (2) at the end of utterance. The result is that the partner (1) continues to speak, and (2) resumes speaking. The contrary, of course, will result from not using silence; a question, for example, terminates the on-going utterance and forestalls the forthcoming one.

The reason that the silence must be maintained for a minimum of 3 seconds is that the majority of pauses in speech are far shorter than that. At its most fluent, the greater part of speech – two-thirds of it – flows in segments of less than six words, punctuated at either end by pauses. Half of speech is emitted in groups of less than three words. A mere 10 per cent consists of phrases of ten words and more (Goldman-Eisler 1968: 17).

The duration of these pauses varies by communicative setting: they are longer in dyads than in groups. For instance, half of the pauses in psychiatric interviews have been found to last 2 seconds or more, while half in discussions are a half second or less – 99 per cent are less than 2 seconds long (Goldman-Eisler 1968: 14–15).

The same is observed for between-speaker pauses: overall they are short; longer in dyads than in groups; and longer in dyadic interviews than in conversations. For instance, various studies have clocked the between-speaker pauses in interviews to be 1.4 seconds, compared to 0.9 in dialogues (Jaffe and Feldstein 1970; 137–9); 2.4 seconds in interviews with nurses, compared to 0.5 in nurses' group discussions (Matarazzo and Wiens 1972: 38–9). And it is uniformly less in classroom discussions. For instance, in hundreds of science lessons, the average time that elapsed between a student's answer and the teacher's next question was 0.9 seconds (Rowe 1974b).

At all of these points the practitioner can intervene, swiftly or no, vocally or no. He can intervene after a few words from the partner, or after more words; before a second's lapse in some contexts or before 2 seconds' in others. He can intervene either with speech or with silence. The speech, such as a question, will interrupt and terminate the partner's flow of speech and thought; the silence permits and encourages the flow to continue and to expand. If silence is judged to be the technique appropriate to purpose in circumstance, its communicative effect will be to enhance the partner's participation and cognition. The partner will respond with more talk and more and better thought.

Expressive processes

People do respond to silence. A variety of observational and experimental studies of interviews of various types and of classrooms at all levels demonstrate that silence enhances participation in the process at hand.

Numerous recent studies in classrooms (reviewed by Tobin 1987) have examined the effect of 'wait-time'. When the teacher maintains a silence to the criterion level of 3 seconds after a student response to a question, student participation increases. The observed elements of participation are:

1 increase in overall student talk-time;
2 increase in number of student words spoken;
3 increase in number of student utterances;
4 increase in length of student utterances;
5 increase in student-initiated discourse;
6 increase in student–student interactions;
7 decrease in student failure to respond.

For instance, the pioneering studies on wait-time (Rowe 1974a, 1974b) showed these effects as the teacher increased wait-time from 1 to 3 seconds after student response:

	1 sec	3 sec
Response length	7 words	28 words
No. of unsolicited responses	3	37

These effects are desirable to pedagogical purpose in the classroom circumstance of discussion. In general, they are also desirable to purpose in certain kinds of interviews, such as psychotherapy.

Interviewees also respond to silence. Experimental research (Matarazzo *et al.* 1968: 375–6) on employment and therapy interviews has demonstrated that the frequency of response increases systematically with the length of interviewer silence:

Silence (sec)	Responses (%)
1	0
5	25
15	65

That is, how often an interviewee will take the initiative and speak again following his own last utterance varies with the length of time that the interviewer waits for that response (p. 356). Yet *how very long* to wait probably varies with the particular circumstance, as well as the purpose, of various kinds of interviews.

In one field-interview study (Gorden 1954), the interviewer spoke with people about a tornado that had just hit their town. These people responded less frequently, and gave shorter responses, as the interviewer's 'silence-probe' increased in duration. The average response to silences of 3 seconds was 3.8 lines of transcript, compared to 2.5 lines for silences of 10 seconds and more. For 8,000 silences in 500 interviews, the longer the silence the fewer the responses (p. 177):

Silence (sec)	Responses (%)
2	78
3	65
4	57
5	44
...	...
15	16

Past some time of silence, the citizen respondent might pick up his hammer and go back to boarding up his house (p. 178). This was an open-air, on-site, free-interview situation unlike those involving job applicants, patients, and students. Still, even on their own terms, these townspeople responded to most of the silences (for example, 2–4 seconds).

In psychotherapy, the therapist's use of silence enhances various participative processes, just as claimed in the theoretical and clinical literature (for instance, Lief 1962; Weisman 1955). One study (Hunter 1957) found that the therapist's silence – a full ten minutes – results in more information from the client, and more expression of attitudes. This experimental finding accords with Carl Rogers' (1942) clinical caution that, in place of a question, a pause would elicit further attitudes from the client (p. 289). Other studies have found more positive process-ratings and overall success for sessions with therapist silence. Clients rated the therapist's 'empathic understanding' as low when silences of 3 seconds were used, and as high for silences of 6 and 9 seconds (Adana 1979). A lack of therapist silence characterized unsuccessful cases of therapy, compared to the use of silence in successful cases (Cook 1964). Highest ratings went to sessions showing between 4 and 20 per cent of silence (p. 44):

Silence		
Range (%)	Average (%)	Process rating
0–3	0.1	2.6
4–10	6.0	3.4
11–20	17.0	3.4
21–38	28.0	3.0

Hence, although the length of silence may appropriately vary in different circumstances, people clearly do respond to the practitioner's deliberate use of silence. The recommended length of 3–5 seconds is demonstrably long enough for group circumstances (such as classrooms), and just long enough for dyadic circumstances (for example, interviews). Partners will respond to the use of silence. Moreover, the silence will enhance their participation – the frequency and length of their responses, their initiative and affect, their sense of the communicative quality of the practitioner and process at hand.

Cognitive processes

The practitioner's silence does far more than enhance participation. It enhances cognition, and for very good reasons.

In classroom studies of wait-time (Tobin 1987), the teacher's use of silence – during and after student response – has repeatedly been demonstrated to enhance the student's cognitive as well as expressive processes. In addition to the seven elements of participation cited in the last section, the use of silence results in:

1 more complex student responses;
2 higher cognitive level responses;
3 more alternative explanations;
4 more student questions.

For instance, the pioneering research (Rowe 1974a, 1974b) demonstrated these effects as the teachers increased their wait-time from 1 to 3 seconds:

	1 sec	3 sec
No. of evidence-inference responses	6	14
No. of speculative responses	2	11
No. of student questions	4	18

These results are desirable to pedagogical purpose in classroom circumstances of discussion, certainly for the science and social-studies lessons most often studied.

In classrooms, where student talk has long been conditioned to bursts of speech punctuated by teacher questions asked less than a second after the student's first breath, the teacher's question 'intervenes between bursts to prevent completion of thought'; the teacher 'hears only a fragment of an idea' (Rowe 1974b: 81, 87). But were the teacher only to maintain a silence of 3 seconds, he would hear not only more talk but also more and better thought. The reason is simple: *pausing in speech* correlates with *processing in cognition*.

First, it takes more time to say more complex things. In senior high school discussion classes (Dillon 1983), students took twice as long to state a fact as to recite a definition, twice again longer to give an explanation, and again twice longer to proffer a justification:

Response	Duration (sec)
Defining	3.2
Fact-stating	6.0
Explaining	12.2
Justifying	20.2

In middle-school discussion classes (Rowe 1974a), students paused successively longer as they worked through a description of some phenomenon, and as they worked through an explanation of it; and at each successive step they paused longer while explaining than while describing (for example, 17 vs. 10 seconds). In primary schoolrooms (Arnold *et al.* 1974), pupils took longer to start a response involving analysis than one involving synthesis, and longer for synthesis than for knowledge and comprehension responses:

Response	Start-time (sec)
Knowledge	2.0
Comprehension	2.1
Synthesis	3.6
Analysis	6.3

It takes more time to produce the more complex utterances – longer to start them and longer to complete them. The teacher's deliberate silence at junctures of speech gives students the time to start and finish a thought.

Second, and more pointedly, it takes more *pausing* to produce more complex speech and more complex thought. Pausing is the reason that it takes more time – not necessarily to say more words but necessarily to form and express more thought.

Psycholinguistic research has revealed the details. Consider first the simple case where adults view a very short film and then are asked merely to describe what they saw: 'Tell what happened in the movie' (Chafe 1985). At the onset of their speech there is 'a considerable period of floundering', illustrated by this initial sentence:

OK.
Um –
let's see.
Uh –
the first part of the
m ...
movie,
uh well,
the ...
the – ...
the basic action,
i – s that there's –
a man
uh ...
on a ladder,
uh picking pears from a pear tree.

Quite apart from fillers, lengthened syllables, false starts, and repetitions, this adult speaker paused *5 seconds* in the midst of producing a single-sentence description of a man on a ladder picking pears from a pear tree – not even an original account but a mere *recounting* of what the speaker had just seen. 'When one begins a narrative, some time-consuming mental processing usually needs to be devoted to the finding and clarification of an initial focus' (Chafe 1985: 81). But there is far more yet to come – pauses when moving from focus to focus within a sentence, and still longer pauses when moving from sentence to sentence:

focus to focus	0.8 sec
sentence to sentence	1.2

'The degree of hesitating is correlated with the degree of difficulty' (p. 87).

The difficulty in this task of *description* increases when a speaker moves from description to *explanation*, and from the concrete to the abstract. And with that, so do the silent pauses increase.

College students were found (Taylor 1969) to take more time to produce sentences with an abstract topic word (for instance, 'expect', 'proper') than a concrete one ('shout', 'soft'), and longer for infrequent than frequent words ('affluence', 'car'). This 'content-difficulty' led to longer latencies or start-times and more and longer pauses, reflecting the different 'amount of concep-tualizing' needed. The difficulty variable 'affects sentence production not only prior to the first word, as reflected in latency, but throughout the entire sentence, as indicated by more frequent within-sentence hesitations on the difficult topics' (p. 174).

Primary school children were found (Levin *et al.* 1967) to pause far more frequently and for twice as much time while explaining a curious event than while describing it (for example, the event of one balloon rising and another falling).

	Description	Explanation
No. of pauses	2.2	12.8
Duration of pause	0.4 sec	0.9 sec

'In short, *to think* is not automatic and results in slow, pause-filled, hesitant speech' (p. 564).

In a series of pioneering experiments (Goldman-Eisler 1968), adults were shown to pause more and longer according to the information load, complexity, and quality of the thinking involved.

Asked to fill in a gap in a sentence, people paused an average of 20 seconds before producing words of low-information content, compared to 37 seconds for high-information content (p. 45). Asked first to describe and then to interpret a concrete event (an uncaptioned magazine cartoon), people paused longer while interpreting than while describing.

	Description	Interpretation
Average pause	12 secs	20 secs
Silence/speech ratio	1.2	2.3

The ratio of silence to speech means that interpretation required twice the pausing *per word produced*. It is not that the people had to say more words while interpreting; they had to take more pauses. They took more pauses to produce the same amount of words but a superior level of thought.

The quality of their interpretation also varied with the pausing. Quality was the degree of generalization, or the level of generalizing from the particular to the universal by abstracting meaning from the concrete event of the cartoon. When idiosyncratic pause patterns were removed from analysis, the higher-quality interpretations were found to result from still further pausing. 'The additional time of pausing determines the intellectual quality of verbal statements' (p. 68).

The conclusion is that pausing accompanies cognitive operations:

At every step in the psycholinguistic continuum, preliminary to, as well as concomitant with, the vocal utterance, the interpretation of meaning, i.e.

abstracting and generalizing from perceived events requires more time in pausing than does their description.

(Goldman-Eisler 1968: 58)

The implication for practice is to use deliberate silence in order to enhance participants' cognition.

For the practitioner, these are the experimental grounds that both explain and justify the deliberate use of silence as a communicative technique. All speech is filled with silent pauses. The frequency and duration of pausing increases with the difficulty, complexity, and quality of the thought being expressed – from low to high information content; from restricted to universal generalizations; from concrete to abstract and from frequent to infrequent notions; from description to interpretation and explanation, inference and speculation; from knowledge and comprehension to synthesis and analysis; from reciting definitions and stating facts to explaining and justifying them; from answering to questioning. It is with these cognitive processes that people respond to the use of silence, all the while engaging self more expressively in the process at hand. People respond to silence with greater participation and higher cognition, with more talk and with more and better thought.

The ultimate justification for the use of silence resides not in research but in practice. Where appropriate to purpose in circumstance, the practitioner may elect to use silence at suitable junctures where the partner has paused or ostensibly finished speaking. The practitioner maintains a deliberate, appreciative silence for 3 to 5 seconds until the partner resumes speaking or another partner enters in. The silence will probably enhance the partner's cognitive and expressive processes. Where these effects advance purpose in circumstance, the use of silence is the alternative of choice. Where not to purpose, silence is not golden. It is better not used at all; rather, questioning may better serve to purpose.

Multiple alternatives

A mix of alternatives may be used in a given setting – various declarative statements, speaker questions, signals, and silences. Their effects on communication are shown through case study, or analysis of samples of talk taken from a naturally occurring case of practice. Here are selected cases from dyadic and group settings – interviews in psychotherapy and discussions in classrooms.

Interviews

The use of questions varies by school of therapy. But the *effect* of questions does not vary. To illustrate, we can take the cases of rational-emotive therapy (transcript no. 3 in the Appendix), client-centred (no. 4), and eclectic (no. 5) therapy.

The rational-emotive therapist speaks nothing but questions. The client-centred therapist speaks no questions at all. The eclectic therapist uses questions half or more of the time. As a result, the clients' expressive processes vary among the three sessions. Measured by lines of transcript (in the Appendix as typewritten), the amount of expression varies systematically.

1 The clients in the two 'alternative' sessions speak at greater length than the client in the questioning session (namely, the rational-emotive session).

2 The client in the *non*-questioning session speaks more than the client in the *semi*-questioning session, who in turn speaks more than the client in the questioning session.

3 The clients in the two 'alternative' sessions spoke more than their therapists did, whereas the questioning therapist spoke more than his client did.

4 The therapists in the all-questioning and all-non-questioning sessions spoke for the same amount of time, yet the non-questioned client spoke twice as much as the questioned one.

5 Client response to questions was shorter than to alternatives, as compared both between sessions (client-centred vs. rationale-emotive) and within session (eclectic).

In place of questions, the client-centred therapist (transcript no. 4) used these alternatives: *fillers* (at exchange 9), many *silent pauses* (for example, exchanges 5, 11, 12, 14), and *reflective restatements* (such as exchanges 11, 13, 15), especially clarification of feeling. The eclectic therapist (transcript no. 5) also used *fillers* and *silence* (6, 11), *declarative statements* (17, 21), and *reflective restatements* (4, 8, 15). His technique of restating began, 'It sounds like ... ' and the client's response began, 'Yes, that's exactly how I feel' or 'You bet!' By contrast, the rational-emotive client (transcript no. 4) began his responses to the first questions with 'Oh, ... ' or 'Well, ... ' (exchanges 1, 2, 3, 5), while his responses to the final five questions ran 'No, OK, OK, Right, No' (8–12).

Apart from expressive processes, the questions and alternatives also affect cognitive and affective processes and the quality of the therapeutic process itself. The appropriateness of these effects may vary – although the effects themselves will not – according to therapeutic school and purpose. On this point each therapist will make the judgement. Indeed, each of the therapists examined here has used these very cases to illustrate a 'good' therapeutic session (Ellis 1977; Long *et al.* 1981; Rogers 1961).

Other research has shown the effects of questions vs. alternatives on the particular therapeutic process. For instance, a study of client-centred therapy (Frank and Sweetland 1962) showed that questions decrease clients' understanding and insight, whereas interpretation and clarification of feeling enhance it. A study of psychoanalytic sessions (Colby 1961) showed that 'causalcorrelative' statements, or interpretation, enhanced response and free association more than do questions. In both cases the effects of the non-question alternative are more desirable to purpose in circumstance.

But for certain other purposes and circumstances these effects will not be desirable. Worse, they might be counter-productive. The mistake in practice is to use techniques, whether questioning or alternatives, that do not serve to purpose in circumstance. An even worse mistake is to use techniques with the intent of serving purpose X, when their effect is demonstrably anti-X. This is the case with the practice of group discussion. Teachers, for example, regularly use questions with the intent of promoting discussion whereas the effect is to prevent it.

Discussions

The two major processes of group talk in classrooms are called recitation and discussion. Recitation is characterized by a teacher–student question–answer pattern, illustrated by the typical case of HK's class (transcript no. 1A in the Appendix). Discussion is properly characterized by a mix of questions and statements from a mix of students and teacher, as shown in TG's classroom (transcript no. 1B). Case study comparing these processes in these two classrooms (Dillon 1988d) shows the distinctive features of group communication characterized by a predominant question–answer pattern in the one case and not in the other.

Another research approach examines questions and alternatives used within one and the same class discussion. Case study then reveals the contrasting functions of questions and alternatives in determining characteristic features of communication within one group during one process; showing, that is, how the same participants respond differently to questions and alternatives. Case studies of individual discussions are then compared to see the general function of alternatives, by contrast to questions, in the process of discussion. Their function in discussion may then be compared to recitation.

Below are case studies (Dillon 1985) of three classroom discussions. Each is an instance of a different kind of discussion. Thus the study examines not merely three different discussions but discussions of three different kinds. They are: teacher SN's 'informational' discussion (transcript no. 11 in the Appendix); WB's 'dialectical' discussion (transcript 12); and PR's 'problematical' discussion (no. 13). All are from senior high school classrooms, with adolescent students aged 16–18. (These same cases have been studied by two dozen researchers from various disciplinary perspectives, in a collection by Dillon 1988b. The classification of these three discussions is from one of these researchers, Roby 1988.)

First, each case will be reviewed, then the general case summarized and compared to the other general case, recitation. These case studies are used to illustrate the general proposition that 'teacher questions foil discussion, whereas nonquestion alternatives foster discussion' (Dillon 1985: 109).

1 Informational discussion

In his senior Marriage class, teacher SN (transcript no. 11 in the Appendix) is conducting in a most sensitive way a discussion on a rich but touchy subject: sexuality in the students' early home life. SN wishes to hear and to understand what students say, for that is essential to the kind of discussion he proposes. Here is how he begins the hour:

> Today we want to spend the time sharing the kinds of things that we can remember going on in our family during our childhood. Now the goal here is to help us understand, that as we begin to recall what went on during our childhood, we might have a better insight into why we are the way we are today. ... And again, let's proceed or keep in the back of our mind that we're also working on how to disclose ourselves to someone else. We're also continuing to learn how to divulge information, and share.

Beyond clarifying one's own present feelings as learned from childhood experiences, SN continues, one of the purposes of the discussion is to discover which attitudes and behaviours one might wish to change, and which to pass on to one's children.

In favour of this kind of discussion SN regularly speaks to students in declarative sentences. The statements summarize in an economical way what the student has just said, or otherwise express SN's understanding of the student's meaning or experience. The effect is to encourage discussion. But his occasional questions have the contrary effect. The transcribed episode illustrates these contrasting effects in exchanges with six students.

Larry. Larry opens with some clarifying questions (student questions) and successively longer contributions. SN makes the 'reflective statement', 'It wasn't that strict' (9a). Before that statement, Larry had spoken for 9 seconds, and now he elaborates for 13 more seconds. Next the teacher asks a question and Larry responds for only 3 seconds. A further question brings a response which evokes class laughter (12b). Then the teacher discloses something of himself ('reddition') and Larry responds at some length that he too has that trouble (13b).

Marilyn. Next Marilyn volunteers a 12-second contribution and SN utters, 'You do this all together' (14a). Marilyn continues at twice the length as before, moreover connecting her remarks with those of Larry some eight to nine exchanges back. Then the teacher asks a question and we hear her meagre 'um-hm'. Next he offers an interpretive statement: 'I don't know, you seem to feel good about that'. This is the interesting result: Marilyn expounds on her feeling 'good about that', whereupon Larry enters in to say that he too thinks that is good, and he too expounds (16c).

However, after these fruitful exchanges with Larry and Marilyn, SN has two exchanges of another kind, produced by his questions about what a student has just said.

Shawn. She is exploring something she doesn't understand (21b) and, after an external interruption and the teacher's apology, she expansively continues, revealing that her mother has told her about sex when Shawn was 8 years old (22b). Now SN asks her a question, then another. Shawn's responses drop abruptly and the last produces class laughter (24b).

Girl. Another girl then volunteers to say that she too can talk with her mother about sex, even about this class. SN's interest is alerted and he asks the girl a question, then another. Again the responses diminish and provoke class laughter (26b).

Sharee. Sharee follows with an expansive contribution which diminishes in response to the teacher's question, then recovers when he states, 'OK, so you're saying they're not so willing to listen or hear your story' (28a).

Shan. Lastly Shan enters in and no questions are asked. She refers to Shawn's contribution from 9 to 10 exchanges back and speaks at length but somewhat confusedly. The teacher offers a summary interpretation and Shan is able to clarify her meaning (29b).

One way of summarizing the contrast between questions and alternatives in SN's class is to note that student response to statements was significantly more expansive, in four ways.

First overall, students responded for an average of 8 seconds to SN's questions, but 13 seconds to his statements.

Second, an individual student's successive contributions were enhanced by the teacher's statements, then abruptly diminished by the questions. Larry's contributions fall from 10 seconds to 3 in response to a question, and Marilyn's from 21 to 1 second; while contributions by Shawn, a girl, and Sharee wane from 16 to 3 seconds, 5 to 2, and 26 to 11 as each answers questions.

Third, other students joined the original respondent in discussion after teacher statements. By contrast, questions involved only a single respondent.

Lastly, the statement-exchanges produced student references to one another's contributions, thereby continuing and deepening discussion. By contrast, the question-exchanges in several cases produced class laughter, thereby disrupting and relieving the discussion.

2   Dialectical discussion

WB's class (transcript no. 12) offers a second illustration, in contrasting circumstances. Compared to SN, he has a large class (41 vs. 24 students), all but a few students white compared to all but a few black in SN's class. The two teachers take the same proportion of turns at talk (42 per cent, 45 per cent), but the pace is more leisurely in WB's class – he intervenes only once a minute, compared to thrice a minute for SN. Everyone in WB's class speaks at length, far longer than in the other classes. None the less, students in both classes respond still more expansively to the teacher's statements than to his questions.

The lesson bears on changes in society from past to present times. Students have a worksheet listing various aspects of society, on which they were to have written examples of changes. WB asks them to take out their worksheets: 'We'll use them as the basis for our discussion today.' He goes on to say:

I'd just like you to volunteer those examples of change that you've been able to come up with, try to explain why, how you see it changed from the past to the present, and we'll try to analyse that in the same way that we have the rest of our society, some of the examples that I gave, like the influence of electronic media.

In the transcribed episode the aspect at issue is changes in parent–child authority relations.

As the lesson progresses, the teacher praises the students' contributions (3a, 5a), makes connections among them by name (la, 8a, 10a), and asks discussion-like questions: Why do you think? (2a), How do you mean? (6a), and the interesting How to do X and maintain an apparent anti-X, Y? (8a). Students as well as teacher speak at considerable length. Yet overall the students respond at nearly three times the length to teacher statements as to his questions (40 vs. 15 secs).

Regina's initial contribution of 83 seconds diminishes to 39 and 1 second in response to questions, then rises to 23 seconds after a statement. Student talk continues to increase, with Steve and Anna at 30 to 50 seconds, then it decreases to 7 seconds after a question. Next after a statement, student talk again rises to 24 seconds, again falls to 14 and 12 in response to questions, and once again recovers to 66 seconds after a statement.

But students do not merely talk more, they talk *differently* when not responding to questions. Their talk has a pronounced flavour of exploration, personal revelation, interpretation of experience, questioning, and interconnectedness. More students join in. Students refer to one another's contributions. Students combine, elaborate, and build upon previous contributions.

At the start, after the teacher has suggested that Paul's and Steve's viewpoints might be two different ways of looking at the same thing, Regina (1b) goes on to connect Paul's and Steve's views with each other, and then the two with her own. 'I don't see what Paul and Steve said as two separate ideas', she begins. The teacher praises Regina's illustration and Steve comes in with, 'I agree with her almost all the way up until the end, where she said ...' (5b). Anna too contributes to the point (5c).

Towards the end, Chris and Tommy offer contributions and Regina follows at length (10e). She begins by citing Tommy and Chris to make her own interpretation. 'I think he has a point of view or whatever, but I think, taking from what Chris said, that ... ' She then incorporates another boy's remarks from 4 to 5 exchanges back, to build to her conclusion. 'And just like he said, some parents are ... So, ... '

That is not the kind of talk that follows teacher questions – neither in length nor in quality.

3 Problematical discussion

A third illustration in yet different circumstances is PR's Psychology class (transcript no. 13). His 27 seniors, almost all of whom are black, have read *The Three Faces of Eve*, and their experienced teacher leads them through an interesting discussion on the problem of multiple personality. He starts by mentioning that they have previously studied the construction of consciousness and today are going to work on the dissociation of consciousness. 'You've read the material. So let's see, ah, summarize that, and then open it up for your observations – or whatever.'

In this episode we hear about one question per minute – but from *students*. Other odd events follow. Whereas SN would ask the occasional question and WB would alternate questions and statements, PR uses *series* of questions and series of non-question techniques. But the overall effect on discussion is the same: conversational ups and downs, with series of questions that depress student participation alternating with series of non-questions that enhance it. That happens despite the 'good discussion questions' that Mr PR asks, including Suppose X, what then? (15, 18, 22), and What would/why not/how come? (13, 23).

Student questions appear in the midst of both series, leading to two different results. Three times student questions (12b, 22b, 23b) appear in the midst of teacher questions, and participation declines and stays meagre. But when Mr PR takes the alternative of *using* student questions, participation surges and discussion gets markedly richer.

When Duane raises a questions (15c), the teacher asks that it be repeated, then he praises it, reiterates and extends it, offering it for discussion. Mitchell (16c) follows by formulating a corollary question, and the teacher exclaims, 'I don't know' (17a). Yvonne then gives it an extensive try. Mr PR stops her with a question and Yvonne explains, 'I don't know! That's what we're looking for!' (19b). So the teacher says, 'OK, come on, let's find it!' Whereupon Mike and Darryl (21bc) offer two possibilities.

There follows a series of teacher questions and declining participation, including two student questions that come to nothing. But the next four exchanges (25–8) are quite different. The teacher asks no questions.

Mr PR praises a girl for suggesting something that was not in the book, 'trauma', and Duane (25b) suggests another possibility. The teacher connects it with 'the trauma model'. Yvonne enters in and the teacher identifies her suggestion as 'the idol model'. Then Mike contributes something which the teacher also praises as not derived from the reading, and which he identifies as 'the conflict model'. Whereupon Anthony suggests yet a fourth possible explanation.

In these last four exchanges the teacher has not used questions but alternatives. In response, four students have proffered, two in a questioning way, different explanations to consider. And each student has spoken at length: Duane for 26 seconds, Yvonne for 37, Mike for 22, and Anthony for 31. Earlier, three possibilities had been offered at length, again in response to non-question interventions: Yvonne (17b), Mike (20/21b), and Darryl (21c).

To characterize the contrast, students in PR's discussion respond twice as long to his non-question alternatives as to his questions (15 vs. 8 seconds). In addition, students raise questions, explore possibilities, speculate beyond the reading, and speak to one another's points. They do not do these things when responding to questions

4 Discussion in general

In all of these classes, it is as if we see discussion diminishing in the face of teacher questions, resurging when alternatives are used, and again receding when the questions resume. These twists in discussion are the natural consequences of what questions and alternatives do.

Table 13.1 summarizes data from this study (Dillon 1985) and another (Wood and Wood 1988) which examined these same discussion classes. It also compares the discussions with a case of classroom recitation conducted by teacher HK (transcript no. 1A). Three conclusions are evident in Table 13.1.

First, in every case student response was longer to teacher alternatives than to questions. Even in the case of recitation, where 5 to 6 questions are asked and answered every single minute, constraining student response to a few seconds' burst, the response to alternatives is longer. To be sure, it is only 1 second longer. But in this breathless class the 1 second represents a 25 per cent increase over response to questions. In the discussion classes, the response to alternatives was two and three times longer than to questions.

Second, in every case student initiative was greater after alternatives than after questions. To the teacher's comments and phatics students did not just respond at greater length but with more active and energetic dynamics – elaborations, spontaneous contributions, unsolicited material, ideas, and questions of their own. Their overall initiative is apportioned in a way as to significantly discriminate questions and alternatives, the one diminishing initiative, the other enhancing it.

Table 13.1 Questioning vs alternatives in classroom group talk

Features of talk	Recitation HK (transcript 1)	Discussion Problematical PR (transcript 11)	Informational SN (transcript 12)	Dialectical WB (transcript 13)
Teacher questions				
*overall (%)	76	54	20	26
†rate per min.	5.2	1.8	1.2	0.4
†*Student response* (sec)				
to questions	4	8	8	15
to alternatives	5	13	13	40
**Student initiative* (%)				
overall	39	65	80	93
after questions	30	44	45	100
after alternatives (comments & phatics)	100	100	88	100
†*Student talk* (%)				
overall	41	64	78	67
student–student turns	12	39	42	43

Sources: * Wood and Wood (1988)
              † Dillon 1985

Third, discussion distinguishes itself from the question–answer process of recitation both by longer student response and greater student initiative. And, even within that differential, questions and alternatives in both cases are further finely distinguished by longer response and greater initiative after alternatives.

In summary, students responded at greater length to the alternatives than to the questions, and they showed greater initiative. The students did not merely talk more, nor was it mere talk. In response to the alternatives, but not to the questions, their participation exhibited these additional features:

1 more student questions;
2 more exploration and speculation;
3 more reference to personal experience and outside factors;
4 more contributed topics and unsolicited material;
5 more participants overall and in each exchange;
6 more references by students to other students' contributions;
7 more student initiative (e.g., spontaneous contributions, ideas).

The alternatives were followed by more student talk and also by more complex thought, deeper personal involvement, wider participation, greater cohesion, stronger dynamics and richer enquiry – in short, by more and better discussion.

These are plainly desirable features of communication in a discussion class. They serve to educative purpose in that classroom circumstance, enhancing the students' cognitive, affective, and expressive processes. Accordingly, the practitioner with like purpose and circumstance may elect, as these teachers did, to use a very few questions together with multiple alternatives to questioning.

Appendix: Transcripts of questioning

1   Classroom questioning

A   *Recitation class*

1   *T.* *(Teacher):* OK, so we've kind of covered leadership and some of the
    things that Washington brought with it. Why else did they win?
    Leadership is important, that's one.
   S. *(Student):* France gave 'em help.
2   *T.:* OK, so France giving aid is an example of what? France is an example
    of it, obviously.
   S.: Aid from allies.
3   *T.:* Aid from allies, very good. were there any other allies who gave aid to
    us?
   S.: Spain.
4   *T.:* Spain. Now, when you say aid, can you define that?
   S.: Help.
5   *T.:* Define 'help'. Spell it out for me.
   S.: Assistance.
6   *T.:* Spell it out for me.
   S.: They taught the men how to fight the right way.
7   *T.:* Who taught?
   S.: The allies.
8   *T.:* Where? When?
   S.: In the battlefield.
9   *T.:* In the battlefield?
    (and so on)

B   *Discussion class*

1   *T.:* The treatment that Louis XIV gave to the Huguenots is anything but
    acceptable, and yet some people say that he was justified in his treat-
    ment of the Huguenots, in respect to the point that he was trying to
    take care of his country. Do you feel that Louis was justified in his
    treatment of the Huguenots? – Rosa.
   S1: I think, you know, they had their religion and stuff like that. I don't
    think he should have gone as far as totally kicking them out of the
    country and giving them, like, social disgrace, you know, like taking
    their jobs away from them. If they wouldn't interfere with his way of
    ruling, and their religion, why should he interfere with them? (*T.:*
    Ken.)
   S2: He's partially right in what he did, but I don't feel he should've kicked
    them out, like she said. 'Cause who is he to say how they can (–), you

know? Even though it's all Catholics, he gave 'em, like, religious freedom. (*T.:* Barb.)

S3: I feel, I feel that he had hardly any justification at all. He wound up at the end, as Lydia said, having to almost be persuaded by all the people around him that were saying, 'Well, look at the Huguenots'. You know, 'Why don't you do something about the Huguenots? We don't like the Huguenots'. *(continues)* It was one of the last places that he had to conquer, so he figured he'd just go out and then kill 'em. I think it was totally unfair.

2   *T.:* OK, I can see where you're coming from, but I don't know if I can totally agree with that. Is there anyone who disagrees with what these people are saying? – Marty.

S1: I don't really disagree, but you know the story, how everything worked out. *(continues)* They wanted to get rid of the Huguenots. And just like that, you know, us here, we don't like somebody, like, you know, Italians and Nazis – sorta the same thing, something like that, in their eyes. I don't think he was justified himself. (*T.:* Diane.)

S2: OK, in those days the church and state were like the same thing and everything, and so I think, well, like Louis – well, it isn't like today, when you can be a member of a country, just a member of a country. In those days, the church and the country meant the same thing, and when he saw people breaking away from the church, then he thought that they were breaking away from him. And he wanted to stop it. That was about the only thing he could do.

3   *T.:* So you feel that he was justified in what he was doing, as far as he was concerned – he could justify it to himself.

S.: Yeah, he could justify it to himself. But then, before then they really didn't have a separation. So all he could see was an allegory. And he wanted to pull back on that.

4   *T.:* All right, Marty raised an interesting point just a few seconds ago. He said that *(continues)*.

2   Courtroom cross-examination

(from Brennan and Brennan 1988)

83   And when your Uncle David came in to your room, did he turn the light on?
     – No.

84   You do not know?
     – No.

85   Did he close the door after him?
     – I think so.

86   And that is when he came in?

- Yes.

87   And he closed the door?
- Yes, I think so.

88   And you say you think so?
- Yes.

89   Are you not sure?
-Yes, I'm not sure.

90   You are not sure. You usually sleep with your bedroom door closed or open?
- Closed.

91   Did you hear him come into your room?
- No, because I was asleep.

92   You were asleep? And did you hear Sonia leave the room?
- I don't really know.

93   You do not really know?
- Yes.

94   So you do not remember if you heard Sonia leave the room do you?
- Yes.

95   When your Uncle David came into the room, did you look to see where Sonia was?
- No.

96   She was not sleeping in your bed that night, or was she?
- She wasn't.

97   Was there any reason for that?
- She doesn't sleep in my bed every night.

98   I see. Just when you want to talk or not?
- Yes.

99   What did, what did he do, sorry, did you wake up as soon as Uncle, your Uncle David came into the room?
- Yes.

100   And did he say anything to you?
- No.

101   And you saw him close the door behind him did you?
- No, because it was dark.

102   I see, so you did not know whether it was Uncle David did you at that stage?
- No.

103   So somebody came into your room?
- Yes.

104   And somebody, that person, then pulled the blankets down from your bed is that right?
- Yes.

105 And that person who you do not know, who you did not know at that stage?
– Mmm.
106 Took your nightie off?
– He didn't take my nightie off, he took my knickers off.
107 Took your knickers off? And you did not say a thing?
– No.
108 You were frightened?
– Yes.
109 Did you scream?
– No.
110 Why did you not scream?
– Because I was frightened.
111 Did you try and get away?
– No. I tried to get my blankets.
112 You tried to get your blankets to cover up?
– Yes.
113 And, but you did not know who this person was?
– It must have been Uncle David because there's no one else would come into my room and do that.
114 I see. But you had no idea who it was but you thought it was your Uncle David?
– Yes.
115 Is that right?
– Yes.
...
157 Just before the school holidays? And what happened on this occasion?
– He rooted me.
158 Well can you tell me how that came to pass?
– No.
159 Sorry?
– No.
160 You cannot tell me what led up to?
– No.
161 You cannot remember?
– *(No verbal answer)*.
162 You cannot remember anything about it at all?
– No.
163 You have forgotten everything about it?
– Yes.
164 You have forgotten where it took place?
– No.

165   Where did it take place?
       – Horsley.

166   Horsley. Apart from the fact that it took place in Horsley, there is nothing else you can remember about it?
       – Yes.

167   Is that, is what I have said correct?
       – Yes there's nothing else.

168   There is nothing else you can remember?
       – No.

169   Sorry, keep your voice up?
       – No.

170   Do you remember the day of the week?
       – No.

171   Do you remember whether it was night or day?
       – It was night.

172   It was night. Do you remember if it was early at night? Or late at night?
       – No.

173   You do not? Do you remember if you were in bed, or you were up?
       – I can't remember.

174   You cannot remember. Do you remember who was home?
       – My sisters and brothers.

175   Your sisters and your brothers? And do you remember where you say Uncle David rooted you?
       – No.

       ...

244   Thank you, and do you say there were two incidents, or more than two incidents at the Commission house?
       – Two incidents.

245   Two incidents. Now you are certain about that?
       – Yes.

246   And when did those incidents take place, at the Commission house at Horsley?
       – I don't remember.

247   You do not remember. Do you remember if they took place this year?
       – No they didn't take place this year.

248   Sorry?
       – No they didn't take place this year.

249   They did not take place this year?
       – No.

250   Are you certain about that?
       – Yes.

251 Where do you say, when do you say these incidents took place? Do you say last year or the year before that?
– I don't remember.

252 You do not remember?
– No.

253 And do you think it might be 1984?
– I think.

254 You think it was 1984?
– Yes.

255 And do you remember whether it was in the summer-time or the winter-time?
– I think it was summer.

256 You think it was the summer, and can you remember if these incidents took place during the school holidays or during school times?
– No.

257 You do not remember?
– No.

...

269 Now you said before you did not like your Uncle David, is that not right?
– Yes.

270 Do you remember he saved your life? Remember that?
– Yes.

271 You are an epileptic are you not Beverley?
– Yes.

272 And sometimes you stop breathing and you have a fit, is that not right, and your father saved your life on one occasion that you know about, or your step-father I mean, sorry.
– Yes.

273 And do you support a Rugby League team?
– Yes.

274 And is that the same team that your Uncle David supports?
– Yes.

275 And he has bought you T-shirts and jumpers in Manly colours has he not?
– Yes.

276 And you got on very well with your Uncle David, did you not?
– Yes.

277 You are very close to him, were you not?
– Yes.

278 True to say that you loved him at one stage?
– Yes.

279 And he is hard on the girls is he not, when you were all living together, strict, he is hard on you, is he not?

- Yes.

280 He is very strict? Sorry, do not shake your head or nod because...
- Yes he is.

281 He is. And if you do something wrong he punishes you does he not?
- Yes.

282 And you admit that you have done things wrong in the past, have you not?
- Yes.

283 And he has punished you, is that right?
- Yes.

284 Now did he not punish you for smoking?
- Yes.

285 And do you remember when that was?
- Oh a while ago.

286 Do you not think it could have been the August holidays this year?
- ...(inaudible)

287 You do not think it was the August holidays?
- No.

288 Just before you ran away?
- No.

289 Do you remember him saying to you 'We'll give you the cigarettes, we'll buy your cigarettes for you if you give up all your school outings and your sport', do you remember him saying that?
- Yes.

290 And you told him that you did not want to do that you would stop smoking, do you remember that?
- Yes.

291 Did that happen in August this year?
- I don't know.

292 You do not know. Do you remember how you came to be punished for smoking, do you remember that?
- Yes we were made to smoke a cigar.

293 And do you remember another occasion your father, or your step-father asked you if you were smoking, did you not say no?
- Yes.

294 So you told him a lie, did you not?
- Yes.

295 And he found you smoking on another occasion, did he not?
- Yes.

296 And this was about August this year, or September this year, just before you ran away?
- I don't know.

297 Did he not yell at you?

	– Yes.
298	He was angry, was he not?
	– Yes.
299	Did he tell you he was very angry with you because you told him a lie?
	– Yes.
300	And he shouted at you and told you to go to your room?
	– Yes.
301	Do you remember that he kicked you in the bottom as you went into your room?
	– Yes.
302	Now in September of this year just before you ran away do you remember that Uncle David and your mother went to Crowley for the day, do you remember that, and the girls stayed home?
	– No.
303	You usually vacuum your room do you not?
	– Yes.
304	And that is the room you share with Sonia. Do you remember that you hit Sonia on the arm with the steel part of the vacuum cleaner?
	– Yes.
305	And that hurt Sonia, did it not?
	– Yes.
306	Were you and Sonia having a fight?
	– Not a real fight we were just, you see Sonia was calling me names and I just hit her with the vacuum cleaner.
307	What names was she calling you?
	– She was stirring me.
308	What names was she calling you?
	– I can't remember the names.
309	Remember if she was calling you 'Iceberg'?
	– What, yes, they used to call me that at Pankhurst High.
310	See you did not like that, did you?
	– No.
311	Did Sonia call you that?
	– Yes, and they used to call me another name.
312	And what was the other name?
	– A two C tunnel cunt.
313	Two C tunnel cunt.
314	Did your Uncle David see Sonia after you had hit her with the vacuum cleaner?
	– Yes.
315	Sonia was in great pain, was she not?
	– Yes.
316	She was crying, was she not?

    – Yes.

317 And your Uncle David told you that he thought you had broken Sonia's arm?

    – Yes.

318 He was very angry with you, was he not?

    – Yes.

319 Sent you to your room did he not, again, he yelled at you?

    – Yes.

320 Shouted at you?

    – Yes.

321 Do you remember what he said to you?

    – No.

322 Do you remember him saying to you 'Your mother ought to put you in a home where you belong'?

    – Yes.

323 You remember him saying that to you?

    – Yes.

324 And that was after the incident with the vacuum cleaner, was it not?

    – Yes.

325 And you did not want to go to a home, did you?

    – No.

    ...

375 No. Did you have friends at this school?

    – Yes.

376 Boyfriends and girlfriends?

    – Yes.

377 Did you know a boy called Steve Donne?

    – Yes.

378 And that was this year, you knew Steve Donne this year, he was in your class was he not?

    – Yes.

379 Do you know what it means to have sex, do you know what that means?

    – No, I don't know what it means.

380 Do you know what it means to have sexual intercourse?

    – I ...

381 Do you know what that means?

    – I think so.

382 What do you think that means?

    – When someone forces you to do something.

383 And did you have sexual intercourse with Steve Donne?
OBJECTION:

3   **'Rational–emotive' psychotherapy**
      (from Ellis 1977)

1 *T.* *(Therapist):* Why should that be true? Why must a person be more
      than human? Ask yourself: 'Why must I, George, be more than
      human?'
   C. *(Client):* Oh, because I'd like to be more than human.
2 *T.:* You've read the books now, so you know the slogans. But stop and
      think. OK. 'I would like to be so effective that it would dazzle you.'
      Right? 'Because I would like to and because you would like to.' But
      why *must* you and how *can* you be more than human?
   C.: Well, the only reason I must is because I tell myself that I must.
3 *T.:* I know you do. But let's think it through! *Why* must you? Think about
      that notion that you have.
   C.: Well, it is not so much that I must, it's that I would really like to. Well,
      because it would really be neat to be very competent.
4 *T.:* OK. I am with you. But the reason you go through so much grief is be-
      cause you go over that border from 'My, that would be nice', to
      'therefore I must'. Once you step over that border, it starts getting
      uncomfortable. Now why *must* you – you, one human being in the
      universe – why *must* you always, or put to it a little differently in our
      terms, why *must* you in the next instant have to absolutely be on top
      of the situation? Not 'why it would be nicer', I know that, and we can
      both agree that it would be nicer, but why *must* you?
   C.: Logically thinking, there is no reason.
5 *T.:* What is the logic?
   C.: Well, logically thinking it through, there are a number of things. The
      first thing: my being is intrinsically separate from what I do so that
      just because I do well or do shitty in the next instance that doesn't
      make me well or shitty intrinsically.
6 *T.:* That's true, it doesn't. But why doesn't it though?
   C.: Why doesn't it?
7 *T.:* Yeah. Why does your performance in this next conference, say, not
      mean you are a good or evil person?
   C.: Logically, it doesn't. Because that would be assuming that you can
      have perfection. So that being good in the next instance, for that to
      make *you* good would mean that in *all* those next instances you
      would be good. You'd have to be perfect to say 'If I'm good in this
      next instance that makes me perfect'. You'd have to be perfect in the
      next instance and in the next one...and in the next one...and in the
      next one.
8 *T.:* And is that possible?
   C.: No. It is not possible.

9 *T.:* That's true. What does that mean?

C.: OK. That means that you can't perform as well as you would want to perform. Nor would I want to perform perfectly in every instance. You can break it down; even in a field, even in a part of your field, you can break it down as small as you want to, but the chances are of your performing perfectly every time are...it is not possible to do so. There is too much going against it.

10 *T.:* There is too much going against it, including your humanness.

C.: OK.

11 *T.:* If you were more than human you'd be godlike; you would either be dead or godlike. Right?

C.: Right.

12 *T.:* Everybody is human except those who are dead or those who are gods. I know no gods. I have never sat down and talked to a god. I never have! Have you ever met another human being, have you ever sat with another human being in this world whom you could in all honesty say has not made a mistake? I am talking about a living human being.

C.: No. *(laughs)*

4   **Client-centred psychotherapy**

         (from Rogers 1961)

0 *C.* *(Client):* I have the feeling it isn't guilt. *(Pause.)* Of course I mean, I can't verbalize it yet. It's just being *terribly hurt*!

1 *T.* *(Therapist):* It isn't guilt except in the sense of being very much wounded somehow.

C.: It's – you know, often I've been guilty of it myself but in later years when I've heard parents say to their children, 'stop crying', I've had a feeling, a hurt as though, well, why should they tell them to stop crying? They feel sorry for themselves, and who can feel more adequately sorry for himself than the child. Well, that is sort of what – I mean, as though I mean, I thought that they should let him cry. And – feel sorry for him too, maybe. In a rather objective kind of way. Well, that's – that's something of the kind of thing I've been experiencing. I mean – how – just right now. And in – in

2 *T.:* That catches a little more the flavour of the feeling that it's almost as if you're really weeping for yourself.

C.: Yeah. And again you see there's conflict. Our culture is such that – I mean, one doesn't indulge in self-pity. But this isn't – I mean, I feel it doesn't quite have that connotation. It may have.

3 *T.:* Sort of think that there is a cultural objection to feeling sorry about yourself. And yet you feel the feelings you're experiencing isn't quite what the culture objected to either.

   C.: And then of course, I've come to – to see and to feel that over this – see, I've covered it up. But I've covered it up with so much *bitterness,* which in turn I had to cover up. *That's* what I want to get rid of! I almost don't *care* if I hurt.

4 *T.:* You feel that here at the basis of it as you experience it is a feeling of real tears for yourself. But *that* you can't show, mustn't show, so that's been covered by bitterness that you don't like, that you'd like to be rid of. You almost feel you'd rather absorb the hurt you'd like to be rid of. You almost feel you'd rather absorb the hurt than to – than to feel the bitterness. *(Pause)* And what you seem to be saying quite strongly is, I do *hurt,* and I've tried to cover it up.

   C.: I didn't *know* it.

5 *T.:* M-hm. Like a new discovery really.

   C.: I never really did know. But it's – you know, it's almost a physical thing. It's – it's sort of as though I were looking within myself at all kinds of – nerve endings and bits of things that have been sort of mashed.

6 *T.:* As though some of the most delicate aspects of you physically almost have been crushed or hurt.

   C.: Yes. And you know, I do get the feeling, 'Oh, you poor thing'. *(Pause)*

7 *T.:* Just can't help but feel very deeply sorry for the person that is you.

   C.: I don't think I feel sorry for the whole person; it's a certain aspect of the thing.

8 *T.:* Sorry to see that hurt.

   C.: Yeah.

9 *T.:* M-hm. M-hm.

   C.: And then of course there's this damn bitterness that I want to get rid of. It's – it gets me into trouble. It's because it's a tricky thing. It tricks me. *(Pause)*

10 *T.:* Feel as though that bitterness is something you'd like to be rid of because it doesn't do right by you.

   C.: *(Long pause)* I don't know. It seems to me that I'm right in feeling, what in the world good would it do to term this thing guilt. To chase down things that would give me an interesting case history, shall we say. What *good* would it do? It seems to me that the – that the key, the real thing is in this feeling that I have.

11 *T.:* You could track down some tag or other and could make quite a pursuit of that, but you feel as though the core of the whole thing is the kind of experience that you're just having right here.

C.: That's right. I mean – I don't know what'll happen to the feeling. Maybe nothing. I don't know, but it seems to me that whatever understanding I'm to have is a part of this feeling of hurt, of – it doesn't matter much what it's called. *(Pause)* Then I – one can't go – around with a hurt so openly exposed. I mean this seems to me that somehow the next process has to be a kind of healing.

12 *T.:* Seems as though you couldn't possibly expose yourself if part of yourself is so hurt, so you wonder if somehow the hurt mustn't be healed first. *(Pause)*

C.: And yet, you know, it's – it's a funny thing. *(Pause)* It sounds like a statement of complete confusion or the old saw that the neurotic doesn't want to give up his symptoms. But that isn't true. I mean, that isn't true here, but it's – I can just hope that this will impart what I feel. I somehow don't mind being hurt. I mean, it's just occurred to me that I don't mind terribly. It's all – I mind more the – the feeling of bitterness which is, I know, the cause of this frustration. I mean the – I somehow mind that more.

13 *T.:* Would this get it? That, though you don't like the hurt, yet you feel you can accept that. That's bearable. Somehow it's the things that have covered up that hurt, like the bitterness, that you just – at this moment, can't stand.

C.: Yeah. That's just about it. It's sort of as though, well, the first, I mean, as though, it's – well, it's something I can cope with. Now, the feeling of, well, I can still have a hell of a lot of fun, see. But that this other, I mean, this frustration – I mean, it comes out in so many ways, I'm beginning to realize, you see. I mean, just this sort of, this kind of thing.

14 *T.:* And a hurt you can accept. It's a part of life within a lot of other parts of life, too. You can have lots of fun. But to have all of your life diffused by frustration and bitterness, that you don't like, you don't want, and are now more aware of.

C.: Yeah. And there's somehow no dodging it now. You see, I'm much more aware of it. *(Pause)* I don't know. Right now, I don't know just what the next step is. I really don't know. *(Pause)* Fortunately, this is a kind of development, so that it – doesn't carry over too acutely into – I mean, I – what I'm trying to say, I think, is that I'm still functioning. I'm still enjoying myself and –

15 *T.:* Just sort of want me to know that in lots of ways you carry on just as you always have.

C.: That's it. *(Pause)* Oh, I think I've got to stop and go.

Session with Mr Bryan

(from Rogers 1942)

0 *C.:* Well, to draw another analogy, I feel that I have so much energy, so much reservoir of energy – now, what I want to do is to get the negatives to desert to the positive side. Which will be a double-barreled gain, you see, and will probably occur very rapidly once the ball gets rolling. But when the negatives are in power, why, of course how can the ball begin to roll?

1 *T.:* Can you, uh – not today, but one question that you want to be thinking over is, what are these negative votes?

   C.: Well, as I have it analyzed now, it seems to be just a blanket feeling operative in all these realms. You mean, can I refer the feeling – you mean would there be any ideological aspects to it?

2 *T.:* I think we might get further if we talked about it in specific terms. You say you like to dance, for example. And still this thing creeps up there, too, and blocks you from enjoying dancing. Well, can you tell me more about that – I mean what your feelings are while you're dancing, or what it is that seems to –

5   **Eclectic counselling and psychotherapy**

    (from Long et al. 1981)

1 *C.* *(Counsellor):* Come in, Sally. How are you?

   Cl. *(Client):* Fine.

2 *C.:* Make yourself comfortable. What is it we can do for you?

   Cl.: Well, I'm having a real problem with my roommate and I really don't know what to do about it.

3 *C.:* Could you tell me a little about the situation?

   Cl.: Well, Jean, my roommate, and I have not been able to get along since school started. She seems so inconsiderate. Almost everything she does gets on my nerves. All we do is fight and argue about everything. I wish we didn't have to live together.

4 *C.:* It sounds like this situation is pretty upsetting.

   Cl.: You bet! I can't get any school work done. She always has her boy friends over, until all hours of the night. I really get angry and then I wind up leaving the room.

5 *C.:* Could you tell me a little bit about how you feel when you do leave your room?

   Cl.: Well, it really bothers me that I have to leave or give in. I mean, why can't she go somewhere with her boyfriend? It's just as much my room as it is hers.

6 *C.:* Uh huh.

Cl.: It really makes me mad the more I think about it.

7 *C.:* How do you mean?

Cl.: Well, I feel mad at myself for not being able to do something about it.

8 *C.:* So, on one hand you feel upset because of what your roommate is doing and on the other, you feel upset because of how you are reacting or are forced to react to the situation. Is that about right?

Cl.: Yes, that's exactly how I feel. I really need to do something about it.

9 *C.:* Could we back up for a second? Maybe you could tell me something more about the things that happen between you and Jean.

Cl.: OK, well, it started almost from the time we first met. She just has no feelings for other people – well, at least not for me anyway. She does whatever she pleases. I try to be nice and think of her. I even try to talk to her about it. But it doesn't seem to work. She just disregards my rights.

10 *C.:* Could you tell me about that?

Cl.: Well, at first I just didn't say anything. I kept it in. It really made me feel like a jerk. I was afraid to say anything because I didn't want her to dislike me.

11 *C.:* Uh huh. *(Pause)*

Cl.: Well, nothing ever changed. Then one day I was studying and she came in with her boyfriend and they just sat on the bed listening to the radio. I got so mad, I just lost my temper.

12 *C.:* It must be difficult wanting someone to like you and trying so hard and then getting so upset by it.

Cl.: Well, I've tried talking to her several times, but we just end up arguing. Now I really feel bad whenever I have to go back to my room after class.

13 *C.:* You've tried to talk to her about the problems but it hasn't seemed to work, and now you really don't know what to do next. Is that what you see as the overall problem?

Cl.: Yes, that's about right.

14 *C.:* Well, Sally, how would you like to see this situation resolved?

Cl.: Well, I guess I'd like to get a new roommate. But I don't suppose that's possible this early in the term. Sometimes I think that maybe I'm to blame, too. Maybe it would be the same with a new roommate or even worse!

15 *C.:* It sounds like you're feeling some responsibility for the situation too.

Cl.: I really don't know. I guess there are things I could have done, too, but I was just too angry with her. Maybe I'd feel better if we could both get along and work this thing out. I really don't want to move out anyway.

16 *C.:* Uh huh. How do you think you can resolve this problem?

Cl.: Maybe you could help me figure out some way to work out our differences so we could live together – some kind of compromise. Maybe I'm using the wrong approach when I try to talk to Jean. Maybe you could help me to do something about that.

17 *C.:* I think that might be a good goal to work toward.

Cl.: Well, it's worth a try. I've tried everything else.

18 *C.:* Okay. Well, let me summarize where we are then. It sounds like you want to work out some type of compromise with Jean. This would entail developing some effective ways to communicate with each other. So this is our goal for counseling. Does that sound correct?

Cl.: Yes. I don't think it's going to be easy, but I've got to work something out soon.

19 *C.:* Have you thought about what has happened in the past whenever you two talked about your differences?

Cl.: Well, no, I haven't. I've always just gotten so mad that I usually get up and leave or else she will. I usually try to forget what happens.

20 *C.:* How are things between you two after one of these incidents is forgotten?

Cl.: Very cool. We both are cordial to each other. But, boy, you can tell there's something icy in the air. You know what I mean?

21 *C.:* Well, I suspect that if you feel this way toward Jean, it's a good bet that she feels about the same way toward you.

Cl.: I never thought of it that way.

22 *C.:* This may be a good approach to your problem. Maybe you could think about some of the things you do that irritate Jean and some of the things she does that irritate you. Write them down on paper if you wish. These can be the issues we discuss at our next visit. Does this sound like something you would like to start working on?

6 Medical interviews

(from Mishler 1984)

Interview A

1 *D.* *(Doctor):* What's the problem?

P. *(Patient): (unintelligble)* had since last Monday evening so it's a week of sore throat (hum hm) which turned into a cold...uhm...and then a cough.

2 *D.:* A cold you mean what? Stuffy nose?

P.: Uh, stuffy nose yeah not a chest (hm hm) cold. Uhm.

3 *D.:* And a cough?

P.: And a cough which is the most irritating aspect.

4 *D.:* Okay. (hh) uh. Any fever?

  P.: Not that I know of. I took it a couple of times in the beginning but I haven't felt like –

5 *D.:* How about your ears?

  P.: (hh) uhm. Before anything happened I thought that my ears might have felt a bit funny but *(unintelligible)* I haven't got any problems.

6 *D.:* Okay...(hh) Now this uh cough what are you producing anything or is it a dry cough?

  P.: Mostly dry although a few days ago it was more mucusy 'cause there was more (cold). Now (there's) mostly cough.

7 *D.:* What about the nasal discharge? Any?

  P.: A little.

8 *D.:* What color is it?

  P.: uhm I don't really know uhm I suppose a whitish –

9 *D.:* hm hm what?

  P.: There's been nothing on the handkerchief.

10 *D.:* hm hm Okay. (hh) Do you have any pressure around your eyes?

   P.: No.

11 *D.:* Okay. How do you feel?

   P.: uhm Tired. heh I couldn't – I couldn't sleep last night uhm.

12 *D.:* Because of the cough?

   P.: Otherwise – Yup. Otherwise I feel fine.

13 *D.:* Alright. Now have you had good health before (generally)?

   P.: Yeah. Fine.

Interview B

1 *D.:* Hm hm. Now what do you mean by a sour stomach?

  P.: What's a sour stomach? A heartburn like a heartburn or something.

2 *D.:* Does it burn over here?

  P.: Yeah. It li – I think – I think it like – If you take a needle and stick it right there's a pain right here (hm hm) and and then it goes from here on this side to this side.

3 *D.:* Hm hm. Does it go into the back?

  P.: It's all up here. No. It's all right up here in the front.

4 *D.:* Yeah. And when do you get that?

  P.: Well when I eat something wrong.

5 *D.:* How – How soon after you eat it?

  P.: Well probably an hour maybe less.

6 *D.:* About an hour?

  P.: Maybe less...I've cheated and I've been drinking which I shouldn't have done.

7 *D.:* Does drinking make it worse?

P.: Ho ho uh ooh Yes. Especially the carbonation and the alcohol.

8 *D.:* Hm hm. How much do you drink?

P.: I don't know. Enough to make me go to sleep at night...and that's quite a bit.

9 *D.:* One or two drinks a day?

P.: Oh no no no humph it's (more like) ten...at night.

10 *D.:* Whaddya ta – what type of drinks?

P.: Oh vodka yeah vodka and ginger ale.

11 *D.:* How long have you been drinking that heavily?

P.: Since I've been married.

12 *D.:* How long is that?

P.: *(giggle)* Four years. *(giggle)* huh Well I started out with before then I was drinkin beer but um I had a job and I was ya know had more things on my mind and ya know I like – but since I got married I been in and out of jobs and everything so...I have ta have something to go to sleep.

13 *D.:* Hmm.

P.: I mean I'm not gonna – It's either gonna be pills or it's gonna be alcohol...and uh alcohol seems to satisfy me more'n than pills do. They don't seem to get strong enough...pills that I have got I had – I do have Valium but they're two milligrams...and that's supposed to quiet me down during the day but it doesn't.

14 *D.:* How often do you take them?

Interview C

1 *D.:* Now what brings you...to the clinic today? I notice that you haven't been here...according to –

P.: Well I was in last week.

2 *D.:* – your record. Oh really.

P.: I was in here two weeks ago.

3 *D.:* Two weeks ago. Okay. Yeah. This ull – Right. And what –

P.: But I came to screening.

4 *D.:* What happened that made you come to the screening clinic?

P.: Well uh...first of all I'd had a lotta trouble with my stomach which I thought probably was uh from my gall bladder condition and I *know* I (hm hm) was supposed to stay on a diet and I wasn't too careful in the last few months. For about two years I uh lived *(laughter)* right on it. And then I went myself back on it...and uhm that improved some but the vein in my right legs are beginning to bother me terribly...And uhm...Well I'll – First of all I had been to a doctor about a month or so ago and he said that my pressure was...high...and I took some pa-pills I brought them in with me because Mr Holloway asked me what I was takin and I said I didn't know. And –

5 *D.:* Oh good I'm glad you brought them in.

P.: And after a *week* I called the doctor cause I felt worse and he said ta cut down a half of a pill instead of the whole one. (hm hm) And then the following week I went back –

6 *D.:* How – How did you feel worse? What – What was going on?

P.: Well I was having weak spells. I think that was probably what started me to come in here in the first place *(laughter)* because I got to the point where I thought I wasn't getting any help...locally you know...and where you had my records and all my troubles *(laughter)*.

7 *D.:* Right. Where – Where – Where are you from?

P.: Revere *(laughter)*.

8 *D.:* From Revere?

P.: Yeah.

9 *D.:* It's kinda hard for you to get in? It's –

P.: No not too bad no. And so I thought ya know well this was the thing to do because you um had my records in here. But I had been (hm hm) having weak spells...not – I didn't faint and I wasn't *dizzy*.

10 *D.:* Sure...How would you describe this spell?

...

11 *D.:* Let me tell you one thing that they did draw some blood here. (Yes) And I notice that you are anemic. Your chromatica is 31 which is about 9 or 10 points lower than it should be and –

P.: Hm hm. Would that cause (...)?

12 *D.:* And I dare say that alone would make me feel a little dizzy.

P.: Yeah.

...

13 *D.:* Your stool that I sampled was negative so there's no blood in it uh but you are anemic. So let me just talk with you ask you a few questions to begin with about that. You – you cook for yourself?

...

14 *D.:* And uh your urine is fine. So you don't have any problems (hm hm) there. Let me ask you a few more questions though (hm hm). I – I think...the reason for your weakness and dizziness most likely is gonna turn out that – that your anemia can account for this and what...I think we should do is to find out now why you're anemic (hm hm) and what's happening to make you have low blood all of a sudden. (hm hm) So that uh we can fix ya up (hm hm) 'cause I think ya still – you look pretty healthy.

P.: 'Cause my – yeah *(laughing)* 'cause my age is going against me a little bit.

15 *D.:* Oh you don't – you don't look 76.

P.: But I'm never –

16 *D.:* You don't look 76 at all. You're still pretty.

P.: Yeah I've been very active and –

17 *D.:* Good. Have you had any *nausea* or vomiting at all?

...

18 *D.:* Is there anything that...we haven't talked about that's bothering you at all? Or anything like that?

P.: No.

19 *D.:* Okay. Fine. Good. So we haven't left too much of anything out, not a lotta headache or sore throats (hm hm) or colds or –

P.: No. I used to have terrible headaches [but] haven't had them for years.

20 *D.:* Haven't had them for years.

P.: Yeah. I guess it was trying to raise a family caused them *(laughter)*.

21 *D.:* Well I guess seven kids are enough *(laughter)* to give me a headache anyway I don't know. ...Okay. Well fine, I'll get some of this written up and we'll get some of your lab tests on under way and get you on the road to gettin better.

7 Employment interview

(from Jablin, personal communication)

4 *R.* *(Recruiter):* I think from your résumé I got the...highlights any-how...ah...what I'd really like to do is get to know you a little better, and this is probably just the tip of the iceberg...And in the 26 or 30 minutes, or whatever it is, I'd like to spend the first 10 or 15 minutes or something talking about you, then the next 10 or 15 minutes or so that we have I'd like to tell you about Applied Marketing Research and the position that we have open and the type of person we're looking for...ahm and answer any questions you have about the company after that. If you would ahm, to help me to get to know you better, tell me a little bit about your background of where you were born and where you've lived and ah and secondly your educational experience, how you decided where to go to school and what you majored in and some of those important kind of decisions, ah then finally any miscellaneous anything else that's important in your background – work experience, travel, or hobbies or whatever.

A. *(Applicant):* Story of my life?

5 *R.:* Right.

A.: I grew up in Omaha and I went all through high school there and I was active in high school.

6 *R.:* Uh huh. How large is Omaha?

A.: It's almost like Austin, except it's about 100,000.

7 *R.:* I see, I see.

   A.: But not really like Austin.

8 *R.:* No. There's not many places that are. Ha. Ha. Ha....

   A.: And my high school had a large graduating class of almost 800 people.

9 *R.:* No kidding? That is large.

   A.: Yeah, was pretty big. Um...editor of the yearbook.

10 *R.:* How did you get interested in that?

   A.: I've always been interested in journalism and writing.

11 *R.:* Really...

   A.: And I've always written, so it seems pretty natural and a lot of my friends do too...umm...then my search for colleges began and Texas was chosen because mainly I could afford it financially (uh huh, uh huh) but it has a good business school for a ...

   ...

14 *R.:* What does your interest in business come from?

   A.: I think I always knew that my independence is important and (uh huh) my father and mother believed independence was very helpful (uh huh) and I think that is important for anyone, any person, and that's why I'm in it. (uh huh). Um...marketing was the big decision and I did, and I'm glad I did it. My emphasis is in market research...

15 *R.:* Really.

   A.: ...in statistics, in statistics also real estate interests me.

16 *R.:* How did you get to marketing out of the whole business...spectrum?

   A.: I think because...ahm I saw you could use a lot of creativity and it wasn't straight like accounting, even though my emphasis is in research with numbers. I don't, you can still be creative with it and use your own input...that's the main reason that I'm interested in people-oriented things too.

17 *R.:* Uh hm.

   A.: In the market place.

18 *R.:* Um hm. Uh huh.

   A.: Um...I'm not that sure if I had to do it over again I'd stay with marketing.

19 *R.:* Really.

   A.: I think that, that's an honest evaluation.

20 *R.:* What would you consider as an option?

   A.: Definitely financing with a real-estate emphasis.

   ...

21 *R.:* Really? Why do you say that? That's interesting.

   A.: Well I have been working at a mortgage bank and *(continues)*.

23 *R.:* Uh huh. Um hm . . . how did you come across your job for mortgage banking?

   A.: I had a, to be honest, I had a friend working there *(continues)*.

24 *R.:* Um hm.

    A.: Ya know, it is a learning experience.

25 *R.:* You bet. You bet. How long have you been at this job?

    A.: Last year part-time, this summer full-time, and this year part-time.

26 *R.:* I see...a pretty extended period.

    A.: Yeah...definitely. I learned to look more sharply at management in a company that it is important what I like is I can spot people easier by working there.

    ...

30 *R.:* Um hm, uh huh, ah where did your interest in real estate come from?

    A.: I think it is booming right now in Texas *(continues)*.

31 *R.:* Ah ha. Okay. You said that ah Austin and Omaha are roughly the same. What would you say, or how would you compare and contrast the two cities?

    A.: I'd say Austin has *(continues)*.

32 *R.:* Uh huh. Uh huh. What do you see as the main advantages and disadvantages of growing up there either in Omaha or wherever with your background?

    A.: I think the main advantage *(continues)*.

    ...

37 *R.:* Okay. All right. Well let me take 5 minutes or so and tell you about Allied Marketing Research and I'll have some time for questions, if you have questions. Allied is a research consulting firm *(continues)*.

    ...

42 *R.:* And have you come up with any questions?

    A.: Yeah, well just maybe comments. Umm I like the idea that it's research oriented, and I like to dig up information too.

    ...

49 *R.:* Sure. Yeah. I agree with you. Completely.

    A.: Do you like...you know, say I went out and got accounts...is that... would I have time to do that...or do you advertise or...?

50 *R.:* We really don't have any kind of direct sales effort *(continues)*.

    ...

52 *A.:* Uh huh I have one question that ah this is the position of an assistant researcher. Is there just, like one, main researcher? or –

53 *R.:* Well I'd say two of our people *(continues)* so that you would have the exposure to move the various individuals.

    A.: So that's not just reporting to one person. I would...

54 *R.:* Right, you, yeah, as far as your specific job you'd be reporting to probably two or three people. Ahmm but for years and that sort of thing you'd be reporting to me.

    A.: Well just out of, like say three years a person was a good hard worker.

55 *R.:* Um hm.

A.: And did good, do you see that person in one of those main positions definitely or –?

56 *R.:* In three years, again ahh, there's no way to really know for sure but *(continues)*.

A.: Okay.

...

58 *R.:* Right, right, we have one slot open and we've talked to probably...oh somewhere between 30 and 40 individuals and what we're going to try to do is narrow that field to between 3, 4, 5...some manageable number and see what they look like, not only can they do it but also their career goals and interests and match what we have to offer. I would say within the next week to 10 days, we'll be back in touch with you and everybody we've talked to as soon as we make that determination.

A.: Okay.

8 Criminal interrogations

A *Structure and types of questioning*
(from Yeschke 1987)

1 I'm asking everyone the same things and I'd like you to work with me on this to resolve this thing of the missing money last Friday. Let me ask – How do you stand on this, did you take that money?

2 Well, let me ask you then: Do you know for sure who did take that money?

3 Okay then, even though you don't know for sure who did, let me ask – Do you have any suspicions of who may have taken the money even though you don't know for sure who did it?

4 Okay then, who comes to mind that you trust, that you think would not have done it? Of all the people that did have access to the money, who do you think would not have taken it?

5 After considering the situation, do you really think the money is actually stolen or do you think there is some other reason for it to be missing?

6 Life presents many temptations for all of us. Let me ask you this: Has anyone ever asked you to help them to take money from the company?

7 People have thoughts of doing many things in their life. Now, as far as you're concerned: Do you recall ever thinking of taking money from the company even though you never actually did?

8 Many people borrow money from the place where they work and they pay it back. What comes to mind on money you have borrowed from

the company and paid back later? How many times do you recall doing that?

9   If the investigation shows that you actually did steal the money from the company, would you be willing to pay it back and get this thing straightened out?

10 Let's assume that we find out who actually did it – what do you think should happen to the one that actually did that?

11 How about jail for that person?

12 What kind of person do you think did this thing?

13 Why do you think someone would steal money from this company?

14 Is there any reason for anyone to say they think you took the money?

15 Let's assume that the person that actually did steal that money was caught. If that person was standing before you, what would you say to that person?

16 Is there any reason for your fingerprints to be on the safe?

17 Do you mind having the investigation extend beyond the company into your family and social friends?

B   *Questioning from general to specific*
    (from Buckwalter 1983)

1   How far away was the red convertible when you first saw it? (A: 'A long way down the freeway.')

2   In front of you or behind you?

3   About how far in front of you?

4   Are you a pretty good judge of distance?

5   Can you judge a half-mile distance?

6   How far would you say it is from here to that skyscraper?

7   Was the red convertible that far away?

8   Would it be half that far?

9   Would you say it was more, or less, than a half mile away when you first saw it?

10 Was it closer to a half mile or a quarter of a mile away?

11 Which would it be closer to – the quarter mile or half mile?

12 Would it be reasonably accurate to say that the red convertible was a little less than a half mile away when you first saw it? (A: 'That's as close as I could come.')

C   *Questioning from known to unknown*
    (from Buckwalter 1983)

1   You were found in the city of Vancouver, in British Columbia, Canada. How did you get there from your home in Phoenix, Arizona?

2   Where did you go by car and where did you go by train?
3   You travelled by car all the way from Phoenix to Portland?
4   How long did it take you?
5   Whose car did you travel in?
6   Who drove?
7   Who is 'both' of us?
8   How many were in the car?
9   Who were they?
10   What were the names of the other two?
11   Where do Allen and Brandt live?
12   When did you arrive in Portland?
13   What date was that?
14   Here's a calendar. Can you figure out the date?
15   Where did you stay in Portland?
16   When did you take the train to Vancouver?
17   Who went with you from Portland to Vancouver?
       (and so on)

9   Broadcast Interviews

(from Harris 1989)

Interview A

1 *I.*   *(Interviewer):* Do you accept responsibility Mr Wade for the mass picketing – organized outside Mr Shah's works last night and on other occasions?

   P.   *(Politician):* What uh I accept or what my National Council accepts responsibility for is the call to members of my union and indeed members of many other unions to demonstrate their solidarity uh with the NGA and in particular with our six members who are being victimized.

2 *I.:*   Do you accept responsibility for the mass picketing – and I put that to you in those words because as you know the Home Secretary has explained and everybody knows that mass picketing can amount to a criminal matter.

   P.:   Well as I said Sir Robin – I tried to explain that uh we're not calling for mass picketing – what we've said all the way through is that we want uh trade union members – trade union colleagues – to demonstrate their support for our six members in Manchester and that's precisely what we've been doing and that's precisely what they've been doing.

3 *I.:* But do they have to do it outside Mr Shah's works?

   P.: Well that's the most effective – way – it's the only effective way it can be done.

4 *I.:* So you are accepting responsibility and endorsing the mass picketing are you not?

   P.: No I'm not ac – uh endorsing mass picketing – I'm endorsing the request of trade union members to demonstrate their support for six members in Stockport.

(from Radio 4, 'The World at One', 1983)

Interview B

1 *I.:* Whereas Arthur Scargill is blamed for helping you to lose the Brecon by-election – the Notts miners are staunch traditional Labour supporters – why don't you hold out a supporting hand to them?

   P.: The situation so far as the Labour party is concerned is very obvious – we have affiliations from trade unions – not from area groups of trade unions – or industrial groupings within trade unions – from personalities within trade unions – from leaders of trade unions – but with trade unions – and trade unions (uh) with whom we have affiliations are those either recognized by the Trade Union Congress under our own constitution or recognized as being bona-fide trade unions by the Trade Union Congress – so the question of the situation facing the National Union of Mine-Workers at this time – is primarily one of course for the NUM itself – and all the membership of the NUM – secondarily it may become a matter for the TUC and then on that basis it is conceivable that it will become a matter for the Labour party – until that time is reached any declaration by me can't assist in the objective that I want to see secured and that is – the unification of all coal miners in Britain regardless of coal-field – for the proper defence and advancement of the interest of the industry and therefore – the interest of the country.

2 *I.:* But what about the wider audience outside the TUC? – outside the Labour movement all together – which you say you want to impress – as they look on what they see is Mr Scargill on one side with his talk of class-warfare and on the other side Mr Link and his colleagues who seem probably to them much more the kind of sensible Labour people that you want to install in power – why on earth they say – why can't the Labour leaders speak out in support of them?

   P.: The looking on – as you put it – is assisted by a substantial section of the media that wants to treat the whole situation as if it were some second-rate Hollywood movie – it is a matter of the constitution of the Labour party and whilst there are parties in our country who act according to the leader's whim and are very deferential – and other parties whose whole policy consists of the leader's whim (uh) I never wanted that kind of leadership when I wasn't the leader of the Labour party – and it isn't either practicable or desirable in a democracy that we make the future of a party dependable (uh) on or dependent on the (uh) personal relationships that a leader may or may not have with an assortment of (uh) trade union leaders – so consequently if the public (uh) since quite rightly – you are concerned about their perceptions – understood that we have and have had for a very long time in our constitution a provision relating to the nature of trade unions that can be affiliated to the Labour party – then I'm sure they'll get the matter in perspective and understand that it's not a Boys' Own Paper escapade.

3 *I.:* But perhaps the public even unassisted by the media might like to know if the Labour party leader thought that people like Mr Link had a welcome place in the Labour movement.

    P.: My view is absolutely clear and I repeated it time and time and time again – I did it very directly at the Durham miners' gala last week – that it is in the interests of *all* miners and the mining communities – wherever they are – to sustain the unity – that is the practical fact – it is a hard fact for people with bitter division in the wake of the strike to accept – I understand that – but it is still the hard fact – and secondly *I* can't play ducks and drakes with the constitution – I can't shuffle it round the board and I can't make general presumptions on the basis of that – that's not democratic and it's not consistent and if there w…anyone who ran a country tried to do that then of course they would be rightly accused of being undemocratic – and the point that I put to you is we have a constitution – it is a satisfactory constitution – as the leader of the party I uphold that constitution.

4 *I.:* You are nevertheless (uh) making use of your constitutional duties (uh) as a reason – perhaps a good reason – for not speaking out on this issue.

    P.: Why are you talking about not speaking out? – how can you do anything more clearly than to prepare to appear on any media – to give an interview – to make a direct speech at a very large gala with the (uh) television cameras there and put your point of view very directly – now if it doesn't (uh) amount to speaking out and speaking your mind I don't know what does – I may not be saying what you want me to say – now of course that's something entirely different.

(from BBC2, 'Newsnight', 1985)

10 Demographic survey questions
(from Lucas 1985)

Questions about Identity

1 *Household.* (a) What are the names of members of this household who usually live here, and who slept here last night? (b) Could you please tell me about everyone who is living with you and eating with you?

2 *Name.* (a) What are the names of the people living here? (b) What is the full name of this person?

3 *Sex.* Is this person male or female? (*Be careful to get the sex of children right – ask, do not guess.*)

4 *Age.* In what month and year were you born? (if 'don't know':) How old are you?

5 *Nuptuality.* (a) What is your present marital status? (b) During the course of the last month did your husband stay in this house for at least one day? (c) Does your husband presently have any other wives besides you?

Questions about population change

6 *Fertility.* (a) How many births have you had? (b) How many were born, even if born dead? (*or:* even if they lived only a little while; *or:* even if they went to live with someone else)

7 *Birth intervals.* In what year was that child born?

8 *Breast-feeding.* (a) Did you feed (*name of most recent child*) at the breast? (b) For how many months did you breast-feed?

9 *Contraception.* (a) Do you know of or have you heard of any ways or methods to delay a pregnancy or avoid pregnancy? (b) (*Even if 'No':*) Have you or your partner ever used any of these methods of birth control? (*list methods*)

10 *Mortality.* (a) Has anybody died in this house since (*an easily identifiable date around 12 months ago*)? (b) Have you ever given birth to any boy or girl who later died, even if the child lived only for a short time?

11 *Migration.* (a) Where was each person's usual residence one year ago? (b) Why did this person leave the village?

Questions about background

12. *Education.* (a) Have you ever attended school? (b) What was the highest level of school you attended?

13. *Occupation.* What kind of work do you do?

14. *Ethnicity.* (a) What is your ethnic group? (*List groups.*) (b) What is each person's ancestry? (*List ancestries.*)

11   Informational discussion

1a   Someone else want to address themselves? What were the patterns of behaviour in your family in regards to these three things? (Tony) (teacher – 6 secs)

b   In my house, they were very strict on the kids, they didn't wanna talk about sex or nothing like that. They did touch each other, express affection. (b-11) (boy – 11 sec)

2a   They would do that. (t-1)

b   Yeah. But they wouldn't talk about it with us. We learned it off the street. (b-6)

3a   So you're saying that your parents never sat you down and talked to you about sex. (t-4)

b   (–) You know, I learned it off the street. (b-7)

4a   OK, we'll talk about that. That's another question – What did you learn about sex off the street – What about nudity? (t-6)

b   That was nothing, like – ah, you know (–) (b-12)

5a   That was sort of natural. (t-1)

b   *NO RESPONSE* (7 secs) (Larry)

c   Are you talking about when we were kids? (b-1)

6a   Or even today, though. It's safer to talk about ten years ago, you know. (t-4)

b   Because – well, what was it? (b-5)

7a   Nudity, talk about sex, and physical affection. (t-7)

b   Yeah, talking about sex, that was – it was there, but it was controlled (b-6)

8a   Controlled? (t-1)

b   I mean, it was kinda, you know, like – it wasn't like now, you know, when you couldn't even mention anything about sex. It wasn't like that. (b-9)

9a   It wasn't that strict. (t-1)

b   Because my cousin would make jokes and all that. (–) Like I was saying, it was always under control. (–) little kids. (b-13)

10a It was more open. Is that what you were saying? Were you saying there was more freedom to talk about it the older you got? (t-7)

b   No, it's just what we talked about. (b-3)

11a The kinds of things you talked about. (t-2)

b   Yeah... (b-3)

12a What about affection? (t-1)

b   Yeah. I mean, it's not like I'd see my folks naked on the couch, no. *(Laughter)* (b-9)

13a   Right. So, quickly, one problem I know I have when I think about this question, I can't ever imagine my parents having sex, or whatever. But the thing is, you know, at least the kids – my parents had 10 kids, so I know they went to bed together at least 10 times, you know. *(Laughter)* You know, but I still have this trouble connecting that – the reality. (t-25)

b   Yeah, I have that trouble, too. I just couldn't – remember I was saying that they showed signs of affection. But (–) children. (Right. OK, Marilyn.) (b-11)

c   In our family, you know, we have something like, we sit down and talk about sex. (–) to understand it, the way the oldest ones – (g-12)

14a   You all do this together. (t-1)

b   Yeah, my mother and father and all the rest of us. And just like he said, 'Control'. In a way I understand, because you have to specialize what you mean, you can't use slang, like vulgar language (or street language). Yeah, you can't use that. But you can express, 'What do you mean? What is this?' (g-21)

15a   So there's a time, you're saying, for questions and answers? (t-3)

b   Um-hm. (g-1)

16a   I don't know, you seem to feel good about that. (t-2)

b   In a way, yes, 'cause (–).(Larry) (g-11)

c   That's – something like that I think is good, too, because it makes for more openness amongst members of the family also, in a sense, you know. (–) (b-10)

17a   Helps to tie it up. ... *(Laughter)* (John) (t-1)

b   My parents talked – *(Talk louder).* They talked to me about this, you know. They'd discuss about sex and all that. But I feel like – a lot of times I feel uncomfortable talking about sex. I know that (–) takes place. *(Laughter)* (b-23)

18a   You're saying they're willing to talk to you, though (t-2)

b   Right. (b-1)

c   See, and in my case, what they're telling me, I know something that they don't know. Because, they have (–) and you look at them seriously and all that. (–) And I want to get their attention. 'Cause if I try to correct her, she doesn't believe me. (b- 20)

19a   She won't listen. (t-1)

b   Right. So I feel, I get angry with her, you know. (b-5)

20a   So, even though she's willing to talk about it, it still sounds strained, right? (Jackie) (t-4)

b   (–) talk about sex (–) (Among themselves.) (–) You know what I mean? *(Name)* (g-25) c   In my family situation, (–) (b-10)

21a Like you were saying, you learn a lot from your older brothers and sisters. (Alvin, are you agreeing? OK, Shawn) (t-4)

b   One thing I don't understand, you know, like in my family, even though my mother – I know my father is different – but my mother and my sister are all real close, you know. I mean, talking about sex is nothing in my house – (g-17)

22a Pardon me, Shawn. *(Messenger interruption)* OK, I'm sorry for that, Shawn. Hey, let's settle down. I'm sorry for that interruption. (t-19)

b   That's OK. I don't understand why (–) talk about. My mother talked about it like talking about going to a dance or something. (Like the weather.) It's no big deal. (Right.) I mean, I can remember she telling me about sex when I was about 8 years old. (g-16)

23a How did you react as an 8-year-old? (t-2)

b   I think I was curious, you know. (g-3)

24a Did you ask her? (t-1)

b   I think I used to ask her questions. And my mother, she says, 'Look–' she – she rather for me to ask her than ask somebody off the street. Because she said, now if I come home pregnant, she said, 'I told you so'. I mean – *(Laughter)* (g-12)

c   My mother – it's no big deal. I'll go home and talk about it tonight, you know. (g-5)

25a You talk with her about the class? (t-1)

b   Oh, yeah, all the time. (g-2)

26a What did she say? (t-1)

b   She didn't say nothing. She just say, 'Oh, yeah?' *(Laughter)* (Sharee) (g-3)

c   Like, in my house there's not too much talk about it. Like, if you bring it up, you know, like my father, he'll go back into the (–). You know, and stuff like that. He'd never bring it up. When they did bring it up to me, I didn't hardly know about it, so I just sat there and listened. *(Laughter)* (g-26)

27a So you're saying that your dad goes off on these tangents, talking – what? – telling stories, or – (t-7)

b   Yeah, or (–) (g-11)

28a OK, so you're saying they're not so willing to listen or hear your story. (t-3)

b   Well, my mother, she like, she's sort of open, she realizes that she can't go back (–) everything. So she's real different from my father. (–) (Shan) (g-17)

c   It's just like sort of – (Speak up.) Just like, sort of like Shawn (–) When I was young, (–) hospital. OK? So I was pregnant, OK? (–) They told me 'To get circumcised'. And I said, 'What's circumsised?'

(Laughter) You know, I was real, awful young, you know? (–) She
said, 'OK, sit down', so we talked about it, you know? (–) We talk
about it. (–) We don't have no certain time. (g-66)

29a It's not a traumatic event. (t-1)
  b It becomes a little bit lighter, that's what I want to say. (g-3)
30a Let's go on to the last topic.

12   Dialectical discussion

1a I don't think they're totally incompatible, the things you're saying,
I just think there are two different ways of looking at them, OK? I
mean, I think when you say that you're being led to really kinda
make your own way more, I think that's a response to that you really
are being influenced by a lot of forces beyond – you have to respond
to a lot of things beyond your family, beyond the small society. You
know? And I think that's what he was saying, that in the past we
tended to be limited in those sorts of situations, whereas now we
really do need to go beyond our family, to be able to deal with those
situations, those influences for growing earlier on, maybe. Does that
fit, do you think? OK, good. (Regina) (Teacher-46 secs)

  b I don't see what Paul and Steve said as two separate ideas. I think that
both of them approve of the way things have happened in the past
and the future. And that's why I said that in the past, you know, I
think that our generation was led to believe that, well, the teen-
agers, they were young adults, like. The parents were very strict on
them. At that point, I remember my father telling me that people
were never allowed to contradict their parents, whatever they say, it
was accepted, and you weren't able to ask or even think on your own
to see if it fit. And I think that, well, I do think that they had a little
bit more respect for not only their elders but their peers, too. You
know what I mean? (uh-hm) And like today, I feel as though we've
made some improvements, but we still like, slip back in a slump because, well now our communication is more open, we are able to
question, you know, what our parents say, and disagree with it, and
everything like that. I'm not saying that it'll work, but you know we
can bring it up, not that we're backed down. And we have – even
though we improved it that way, we still, we don't have as much respect as for other people or our friends. So I don't look at it as a separate idea, I think both of them are, you know, a combination. (g-83)

2a All right, in a way you're taking it in a different element, you know. I
think more kinda personal relationships, – for one another. But not
in the (–) case, because you're saying that there's more – could I ask

you why do you think – I mean, I would presume that you think it is good that there is some more opportunity for young people to really voice their own opinion. Why do you think that's important, or necessary, now? (t-32)

b   I think so because, well, in that way, as being taught something, you understand it. There's a difference in being told to do something, understanding it, and being told to do something and doing it because you're afraid of what might happen if you don't. And I feel as though my parents, they were told to do different things then, certain situations were good for them, because this was their parents talking to them, you know, and they weren't going to defy them. Well, if I have another way of thinking, and my mother or father told me to do something, I'm going to question them. Even if I end up doing it, or if I don't, I still have the priority to question, to think through it. (g-39)

3a   Good, OK, good. I think that's, you know, a really clever analysis. Do you feel – do your parents themselves even agree that they think maybe it's better that you be able to really question them at times? (t-16)

b   In my family situation? (g-1)

4a   Well, yeah, our parents in general, if you want. (t-3)

b   It's kinda difficult, because my mother seems to be more of a liberal, I guess you would say, and she goes along with me more and I learn an awful lot from her. But my father – and I can't blame him for it – is like, he can only do what he's been taught. And from his parents I know some things I can't say to him, a lot of things I can't question him on. He's more a 'I said it, you do it'. (g-23)

5a   OK, good. That's a really good illustration there. (Steve) (t-4)

b   I agree with her almost all the way up until the end, where she said it should be partly a responsibility of ours. I think the parent should have – there's not enough respect, is what I was trying to say. I feel it should be back the other way. The other way you don't figure out – you lose respect for the parents, let's see, by – you question them. The other way, if you don't question them, you always have somebody to look up to for an answer. (All right. Anna.) (b- 30)

c   (–) But I wasn't arguing with (father). *(Laughter)* (–) And he said 'No'. And I just wanted to know why, you know, what he thought. And he started yelling at me, like, why am I arguing with him? 'I'm not arguing with you, father, I really want to know why'. (–) (g-50)

6a   How do you mean? (t-1)

b   I was wondering 'why?' (–) It's OK, that's human nature. (g-7)

7a   OK, yeah, I mean I don't think that it necessarily is disrespectful. I think it's probably good. I think some people might be just kinda protective. People do try to get into arguments. But – it's human. But there's sometimes people do this want to egg somebody on, to see how they would answer something. But at the same time it's legitimate sometimes to just want to know what they think. But that's not like other people do it, so – apparently with her father there are certain limits. (Tommy) (t-45)

b   You can have all the respect in the world for your parents, but there's no reason why you shouldn't be able to voice your opinion on what you think is right, if your parents don't agree with you. Or sometimes the only reason for talking like that is you're at the age where you should be able to, like if you don't agree with your parents, ask them why. You're not little kids where you have to snap to do everything that they say. (b-24)

8a   All right, how do you maintain the respect? Steve was – you know, that's another problem. Is there a way to really ask for the reasons and that sort of thing without being disrespectful? And where your parents can really maintain their decision as your parents without having to simply say, 'Well, I said so, that's gotta be the way it is' –? (Do you want to talk about that?) (t-26)

b   You don't really lose no respect for them by questioning them. If they tell you to do something, you could ask them why you want to do it and they'll tell you. But if they still want to do it, you still gotta do it no matter what. No matter what the reasons, if they tell you to do it, you gotta do it. (b-14)

9a   So in the end, the respect might come from accepting their wisdom, whether you understand it or not, huh? (t-7)

b   My parents will say (–) (b-12)

10a   OK. And yet, you know, as Regina was saying, in the past it did tend to be more like that, that parents were considered kinda total authorities, and I mean, it seemed like it wasn't a completely impossible situation for people to live like that, for long times. And yet for us, it just doesn't seem quite right if you don't have at least the opportunity to hear the reasons why your parents do what they do, or – (t-32)

b   (–) (OK. Chris) (s-4)

c   (–) our family has respect and all that kind of thing. When my parents ask us to do something, like housework, there's no question, because you know housework has to be done. Well, if it does come to questioning why do they do things they do, you're free (School Bell). Both my parents, they didn't have, when they were children, they didn't have the strict parents, 'you have to do this, that's it'. My mother was in the hospital all her life, my father was in an orphanage. They never had the strict parents. So when it came to us, we were just like, they treated us as little people (–) I dunno, there was always respect. And yet whenever we wanted it (–), you know, they like to hear what we didn't understand. (OK, good. Tommy). (g- 66)

d   Like, most parents when they say, 'Don't question whatever I say', I think that's a cop-out, because there could be fault in what they're saying and they don't want to find fault because they want the human authority. (OK. Regina) (b-17)

I think he has a point of view or whatever, but I think, taking from what Chris said, that that shows the point of view that parents are human too. And they relate to situations only from what they have been taught. And the way Chris' parents were brought up, it's easy for them to relate to her and understand her feelings, because it sounds like a situation they were in, they probably, you know, had a lot of care and understanding given to them. And just like – I don't know what his name is – but just like he said, some parents are, 'Listen to what I say, and you have to do what I say', and everything – this is because that's the kind of atmosphere they were brought up when they were children. And if you just keep harping at your parents, what else they going to do? They've been living like that for – what? – 30–40 some odd years. You can't bring them up all over again. So, like it's a situation you have to bear with. You have to try and deal with it on your own. (g- 60)

11a   All right. I think this is really a good illustration of how the family, let's say, really shows the differences partly just in historical development.

13   Problematical discussion

10a   So, Eve White the quiet introvert, was the most dominant. OK, now we're back to the question. We're trying to solve, with the little bit of psychology that we have – we know it's dysfunctional to have three personalities – we want to help this woman to have one personality. How – what might we do? (Gabriella) (teacher – 21 secs)

b   I think that you could try to, ah, get Eve White to see herself as Eve Black, and ah, once she sees herself like this, then, whatever's causing this, split personality, she might try and deal with both of them, and make both one personality, and change it. Because, I wouldn't knock them out, I would combine them. (g-28)

11a   Do you think there'd be an advantage of knocking them out? (t-3)

b   Yeah, if you knocked both out. (g-4)

12a   If you knocked Eve White and Eve Black out, and left Jane? (t-4)

b   Well, aren't Eve White and Eve Black Jane? (b-3)

c   (–) (s-3)

13a   What would be the danger of that? Why not, as one solution, why not destroy the first two – if you had the psychological tools – and leave Jane? (t-11)

  b   That's what we want to do. (g-5)

14a   That's what you want to do? (t-1)

  b   That's why I'd combine them, you know – Eve Black and Eve White. But you can't do that. (g-6)

15a   Well, supposing you have the tools? In other words, supposing you have the psychological know-how to knock out two personalities. Now, from what you know, is that a good idea? (t-9)

  b   Yeah, I think so/I don't think so. (Duane) (s-3)

  c   Wouldn't she gain another personality? (Say that again) Wouldn't she gain another personality? (b-9)

16a   How do you know – that's a good question – how do you know she wouldn't gain another personality? You got rid of Black and White; you got Jane left; how do you know she wouldn't get another one? (t-11)

  b   (–) (Mitchell) (s-3)

  c   I said, how do you know that the two that you knocked out, and the one that you left, are suitable? – the one that's left is – the original one? (b-9)

17a   I don't know. (Yvonne) (t-3)

  b   OK, now, first I would – if I was the psychiatrist, I would go all the way back to her childhood. And I'd find out from her how she was – not from her but, you know, through other sources – ask them exactly how was she as a child, even when she was one or two years old, because it did say that, in the book, that her split personality started as far back as a child. I mean, as far back as when she was a child, she used to do, you know – get into different things. Then I would – I wouldn't knock out – (g-42)

18a   Stop there for a moment, Yvonne. Supposing you take this approach – what do you expect to find? If you have a grown woman winding up in your office with three personalities – what do you expect to find back there in her childhood? (t-16)

  b   Something that could have flared up or something. (g-4)

19a   Like what? (t-1)

  b   I don't know! That's what we're looking for! (g-3)

20a   OK, come on, let's find it! (Mike) (t-2)

  b   You'd probably expect to find problems she had at home, you know – like mistreatment from her parents. (b-7)

21a   How would that – (t-1)

b 'Cause, ah, like it set up, like, insecurity – and she might look for something else inside herself to compensate for that, so she developed a new personality. (OK. Darryl) (b-12)

c OK, like getting back to the childhood thing – like see who her idols were. See where the person had her idols. (b-12)

22a OK, but how would that – if you found out who her heroes or her idols were, what would that have to do with splitting off into two personalities? (Terrence) (t-9)

b Wouldn't you want to try and be like your idol? You know, if you were idolized, you know, you were more or less one of the big idols, to a certain point. Then like, ah, she had an auntie that was shot, and you know, she admired her for the way she was – maybe she'd be shot down as long as she's like her auntie. She'll go home and see that her mother is a nice housewife. She'd want to be like that. Or somebody else – her friends – something like that. (b-35)

23a We all experience what you just said! How come – so it – don't we? (Yeah.) How come she wound up in such a, such a dump? (t-11)

b Well, wouldn't that be some kind of restrictions in her background that wouldn't allow her to do that, such as her parents not letting her do something, to the point that she had to, like, ah – (g-14)

24a Did you see the movie? (t-1)

b No. (g-1)

25a No. OK, something like that is suggested in the movie – that the trauma was so great that it caused the creation of a new personality. (Duane) (t-10)

b It could be like – you want to do something like that, (–) go with the stronger personality. (–) a person, you know, like is reading a lot of books and stuff like that. (–) 'I want to be just like her'. (b-26)

26a OK, I think you'd have to put that together with trauma. That kind of idea, that several of you have expressed, put that together with trauma. In other words, if you try to imitate as a little child, your idols, and you were severely punished for it – this is just one general example – then, for whatever reasons, you might be forced to split in two. I think that's the only way I can put it together – it's been a long time since I read that. (Yvonne) (t-33)

b OK. Isn't it true that whatever your conscious mind turns out, your subconscious reacts, don't it, right? Now, say she's saying to herself – she's getting it in her mind that she wants to be just like that lady, and her subconscious mind's gonna pick up on that and react on that, and she's gonna start acting like a certain person, doing the same kind of things that certain person do, you know – she's gonna pick up that personality, act that person. (g-37)

27a   You're working – we're working on one model now, aren't we? We're
       working on the idol model. I wonder if there are others. (Mike)
       (t-10)

 b   There's got to be others, 'cause you can have a personality that you
       develop under, you know, constant conflict. Like a child might be ex-
       posed to two opposites and it's always rehearsing, it's always going
       on, over and over and over again. OK? The child might be split into
       each one of those worlds, in order to deal with it. (b-22)

28a   OK, good. That wasn't in the book, either. If there's so much conflict
       – if there's so much conflict, you might have to shift gears without
       even knowing it, just to protect the self – is the model that he's
       using, the conflict model. (Anthony) (t-15)

 b   What about like, an overprotective parent and stuff? Like, you can be
       very shy and things like that. And maybe she had parents that told
       her, you know, that she shouldn't go out with no guys, or nothing
       like that. (–) that wasn't the kind of person she was. She was a little
       more outgoing. And maybe when she was young and that, maybe
       that (–) her parents had a real overpowering effect on her. That
       could change her. (b-31)

29a   OK, how many of you read *I Never Promised You a Rose Garden?* –
       Hannah Green's book.

References

Chapter one   The world of questioning

Baldwin, C. (1987) 'A question classification scale for marriage and family therapy', *Journal of Marital and Family Therapy 13*: 375–86.

Bastian, H-D. (1970) *Theologie der Frage* (Theology of questions), Munich: Kaiser.

Belnap, N. and Steel, T. (1976) *The Logic of Questions and Answers*, New Haven, CT: Yale University Press.

Bolc, L. (ed.) (1980) *Natural Language Question Answering Systems*, Munich: Hanser.

Brennan, M. and Brennan, R. (1988) *Strange Language: Child Victims under Cross-examination*, Wagga Wagga, Australia: Riverina Murray Institute of Higher Education.

Buckwalter, A. (1983) *Interviews and Interrogations*, Stoneham, MA: Butterworth.

Campbell, J., Daft, R., and Hulin, C. (1982) *What to Study: Generating and Developing Research Questions*, Beverly Hills, CA: Sage.

Carlson, L. (1983) *Dialogue Games: An Approach to Discourse Analysis*, Dordrecht: Reidel.

Chester, D. and Bowring, N. (1962) *Questions in Parliament*, Oxford: Clarendon Press.

Chisholm, W. (ed.) (1984) *Interrogativity: a Colloquium on the Grammar, Typology and Pragmatics of Questions in Seven Diverse Languages*, Amsterdam: Benjamins.

Churchill, L. (1978) *Questioning Strategies in Sociolinguistics*, Rowley, MA: Newbury.

Clark, M. (1972) *Perplexity and Knowledge: an Inquiry into the Structures of Questioning*, The Hague: Nijhoff.

Dillon, J.T. (1981) 'Categories of literature on questioning in various enterprises: an introduction and bibliography', *Language Sciences 3*: 337–58.

— (1988a) *Questioning and Teaching: A Manual of Practice*, London: Croom Helm.

— (ed.) (1988b) *Questioning and Discussion: a Multidisciplinary Study*, Norwood, NJ: Ablex.

Dillon, J.T., Golding, J., and Graesser, A. (1988) 'Annotated bibliography on question-asking', *Questioning Exchange 2*: 81–5.

Egli, U. and Schleichert, H. (1976) 'Bibliography of the theory of questions and answers', in N. Belnap and T. Steel, *The Logic of Questions and Answers*, New Haven, CT: Yale University Press, pp. 155–200.

Feldstein, L. (1978) *Homo Quaerens: the Seeker and the Sought*, New York: Fordham.

Fischer, D. (1987) 'Questioning and management', *Questioning Exchange 1*: 171–6.

Goody, E. (ed.) (1978) *Questions and Politeness: Strategies in Social Interaction*, Cambridge: Cambridge University Press.

Graesser, A. and Black, J. (eds) (1985) *The Psychology of Questions*, Hillsdale, NJ: Erlbaum.

Hintikka, J. (1976) *The Semantics of Questions and the Questions of Semantics*, Amsterdam: North-Holland.

— (ed.) (1981) *Scientific Method as a Problem-solving and Question-answering Technique*, Dordrecht: Reidel (*Synthèse*, vol. 47, no. 1).

Hiz, H. (ed.) (1978) *Questions*, Dordrecht: Reidel.

Howarth, P. (1956) *Questions in the House: the History of a Unique British Institution*, London: Bodley Head.

Jucker, A. (1986) *News interviews: a Pragmalinguistic Analysis*, Amsterdam: Benjamins.

Kaiser, A. (1979) *Questioning Techniques*, Pomona, CA: Hunter.

Kestler, J. (1982) *Questioning Techniques and Tactics*, Colorado Springs, CO: Shepard/McGraw-Hill.

Kiefer, F. (ed.) (1983) *Questions and Answers*, Dordrecht: Reidel.

Lazarescu, M. (1988) 'The role of the question in medical psychiatric diagnosis', *Questioning Exchange 2:* 263-73.

Leeds, D. (1987) *Smart Questions*, New York: McGraw-Hill.

Long, L., Paradise, L., and Long, T. (1981) *Questioning: Skills for the Helping Process*, Monterey, CA: Brooks/Cole.

Lynch, M. (1978) 'Reference interviews in public libraries', *Library Quarterly 48*: 119–42.

Maier, N. (1958) *The Appraisal Interview: Objectives, Methods, Skills*, New York: Wiley.

Merritt, M. (1976) 'On questions following questions in service encounters', *Language in Society 5*: 315–57.

Metzler, K. (1988) *Creative Interviewing: the Writer's Guide to Gathering Information by Asking Questions*, Englewood Cliffs, NJ: Prentice-Hall (1st edn, 1977)

Meyer, M. (1983) *Meaning and Reading: A Philosophical Essay on Language and Literature*, Amsterdam: Benjamins.

— (ed.) (1988) *Questions and Questioning: an Interdisciplinary Reader*, Berlin: De Gruyter.

Mishler, E. (1984) *The Discourse of Medicine: Dialectics of Medical Interviews*, Norwood, NJ: Ablex.

Pope, E. (1976) *Questions and Answers in English*, The Hague: Mouton.

Rescher, N. (1982) *Empirical Inquiry*, London: Athlone.

Robinson, W. (1980) *Questions are the Answer: Believing Today*, New York: Pilgrim.

Romero, A. (1985) *Multidisciplinary Perspectives on the Question-answer Exchange,* Los Alamitos, CA: National Center for Bilingual Research.

Schuman, H. and Presser, S. (1981) *Questions and Answers in Attitude Surveys: Experiments on Question Form, Wording, and Context*, New York: Academic.

Slavens, T. (ed.) (1978) *Informational Interviews and Questions*, Metuchen, NJ: Scarecrow.

Stenstroem, A-B. (1984) *Questions and Responses in English Conversation*, Malmoe, Sweden: Gleerup.

Stock, G. (1987) *The Book of Questions*, New York: Workman.

Sudman, S. and Bradburn, N. (1982) *Asking Questions: a Practical Guide to Questionnaire Design*, San Francisco: Jossey- Bass.

Taylor, L. (1984) *Scientific Interrogation*, Charlottesville, VA: Michie.

Tengler, C. and Jablin, F. (1983) 'Effects of question type, orientation, and sequencing in the employment screening interview', *Communication Monographs 50*: 245–63.

Xerox Corporation (1976) *Professional selling skills II*, Greenwich, CT: Xerox Learning Systems.

Chapter two   Classroom questioning

Berliner, D. (1983) 'Developing conceptions of classroom environments', *Educational Psychologist 18*: 1–13.

Dillon, J.T. (1985) 'Using questions to foil discussion', *Teaching and Teacher Education 1*: 109–21.

— (1988a) *Questioning and Teaching: a Manual of Practice*, London: Croom; New York: Teachers College.

— (1988b) 'The remedial status of student questioning', *Journal of Curriculum Studies 20*: 197–210.

Doyle, W. (1986) 'Classroom organization and management', in M. Wittrock (ed.) *Handbook of Research on Teaching* (3rd edn), New York: Macmillan, pp. 392–431.

Hyman, R. (1979) *Strategic Questioning*, Englewood Cliffs, NJ: Prentice-Hall.

Rowe, M. (1974) 'Wait-time and rewards as instructional variables', *Journal of Research in Science Teaching 11*: 81–94.

Stevens, R. (1912) 'The question as a measure of efficiency in instruction', *Teachers College Contributions to Education*, no. 48, New York: Teachers College Press.

Stodolsky, S., Ferguson, T., and Wimpelberg, K. (1981) 'The recitation persists, but what does it look like?' *Journal of Curriculum Studies 13*: 121–30.

Susskind, E. (1969) 'The role of questioning in the elementary school classroom', in F. Kaplan and S. Sarason (eds) *The Psycho-educational Clinic*, New Haven, CT: Yale University Press, pp. 130–51.

Winne, P. (1979) 'Experiments relating teachers' use of higher cognitive questions to student achievement', *Review of Educational Research 49*: 13–50.

Chapter three   Courtroom questioning

Brennan, M. and Brennan, R. (1988) *Strange Language: Child Victims under Cross-examination*, Wagga Wagga, Australia: Riverina Murray Institute of Higher Education.

Brown, P. (1987) *The Art of Questioning: Thirty Maxims of Cross Examination*, New York: Macmillan.

Busch, F. (1961) *Trial Procedure Materials*, Indianapolis, IN: Bobbs-Merrill.

Fordham, E. (ed.) (1970) *Notable Cross-examinations*, Connecticut: Greenwood Press.

Harris, S. (1984) 'Questions as a mode of control in Magistrates' Courts', *International Journal of the Sociology of Language 49*: 5–27.

Keeton, R. (1954) *Trial Tactics and Methods*, New York: Prentice-Hall.

Kestler, J. (1982) *Questioning Techniques and Tactics*, Colorado Springs, CO: Shepard-McGraw-Hill.

Loftus, E. (1979) *Eyewitness Testimony*, Cambridge, MA: Harvard University Press.

Philips, S. (1984) 'The social organization of questions and answers in courtroom discourse: a study of Changes of Plea in an Arizona court', *Text 4*: 225–48.

— (1985) 'Wh-questions in courtroom language use', in L. Kedar (ed.) *Power through Discourse*, Norwood, NJ: Ablex.

Romer, J. (1984) *Ancient Lives*, New York: Holt, Rinehart and Winston.

Tierney, K. (1971) *How to be a Witness*, Dobbs Ferry, NY: Oceana.

Wellman, F. (1936) *The Art of Cross-examination* (4th edn, rev.), New York: Macmillan (lst edn, 1903).

Woodbury, H. (1984) 'The strategic use of questions in court', *Semiotica 48*: 197–228.

Chapter four Clinic questioning: psychotherapy

Arbuckle, D. (1950) *Teacher Counseling*, Reading, MA: Addison-Wesley.
— (1975) *Counseling and Psychotherapy: an Existential-humanistic View*, Boston: Allyn & Bacon.
Baldwin, C. (1987) 'A question classification scale for marriage and family therapy', *Journal of Marital and Family Therapy 13*: 375–86.
Benjamin, A. (1977) *The Helping Interview*, Boston: Houghton Mifflin.
Collins, A. and Stevens, A. (1982) 'Goals and strategies of inquiry teachers', in R. Glaser (ed.) *Advances in Instructional Psychology II*, Hillsdale, NJ: Erlbaum, pp. 65–119.
Curran, C. (1952) *Counseling in Catholic Life and Education*, New York: Macmillan.
Dillon, J.T. (1979) 'Curiosity as non-sequitur of Socratic questioning', *Journal of Educational Thought 14*: 17–22.
— (1980) '*Paper Chase* and the Socratic method of teaching law', *Journal of Legal Education 30*: 529–35.
Ellis, A. (1977) 'The rational-emotive facilitation of therapeutic goals', in A. Ellis and R. Grieger (eds) *Handbook of Rational-Emotive Therapy*, New York: Springer, pp. 189–97.
Long, L., Paradise, L., and Long, T. (1981) *Questioning: Skills for the Helping Process*, Monterey, CA: Brooks/Cole.
Neimeyer, R. (1988) 'The origin of questions in the clinical context', *Questioning Exchange 2*: 75–80.
Olinick, S. (1954) 'Some considerations of the use of questioning as a psychoanalytic technique', *Journal of the American Psychoanalytic Association 2*: 57–66.
— (1957) 'Questioning and pain, truth and negation', *Journal of the American Psychoanalytic Association 5*: 302–24.
Rogers, C. (1942) *Counseling and Psychotherapy*, Boston: Houghton-Mifflin.
— (1951) *Client-centered Therapy*, Boston: Houghton Mifflin.
Santas, G. (1979) *Socrates: Philosophy in Plato's Early Dialogues*, London: Routledge & Kegan Paul.
Snyder, W. (1963) *Dependency in Psychotherapy*, New York: Macmillan.
Stiles, W. (1987) 'Verbal response modes as intersubjective categories', in R. Russell (ed.) *Language in Psychotherapy*, New York: Plenum, pp.131–70.
Wessler, R. and Wessler, R. (1980) *The Principles and Practices of Rational-emotive Therapy*, San Francisco: Jossey-Bass.

Chapter five Clinic questioning: medicine

Lazarescu, M. (1988) 'The role of the question in psychiatric medical diagnosis', *Questioning Exchange 2*: 263-73.
Mishler, E. (1984) *The Discourse of Medicine: Dialectics of Medical Interviews*, Norwood, NJ: Ablex.
Stiles, W., Putnam, S., Wolf, M., and James, S. (1979) 'Verbal response mode profiles of patients and physicians in medical screening interviews', *Journal of Medical Education 54*: 81–9.
West, C. (1983) '"Ask me no questions ..." An analysis of queries and replies in physician–patient dialogues', in S. Fisher and A. Todd (eds) *The Social Organization of Doctor–Patient Communication*, Washington, DC: Center for Applied Linguistics, pp. 75–106.
Woolliscroft, J. (1988) 'Patient–physician communication', *Questioning Exchange 2*: 255-62.

References

Woolliscroft, J., Calhoun, J., Billiu, G., Stross, J., MacDonald, M., and Templeton, B. (1986) 'House officer interview techniques: impact on data elicitation and patient perceptions', Paper presented at the annual meeting of the American Educational Research Association, San Francisco.

Chapter six   Personnel interviewing

Arvey, R. and Campion, J. (1982) 'The employment interview: a summary and review of recent research', *Personnel Psychology 35*: 281–322.
Babbitt, L. and Jablin, F. (1985) 'Characteristics of applicants' questions and employment screening interview outcomes', *Human Communication Research 11*: 507–35.
Jablin, F. and McComb, K. (1984) 'The employment screening interview: an organizational assimilation and communication perspective', in R. Bostrom and B. Westley (eds) *Communication Yearbook 8,* Beverly Hills, CA: Sage, pp.137-63.
McComb, K. and Jablin, F. (1984) 'Verbal correlates of interviewer empathic listening and employment interview outcomes', *Communication Monographs 51*: 353–71.
Tengler, C. and Jablin, F. (1983) 'Effects of question type, orientation, and sequencing in the employment screening interview', *Communication Monographs 50*: 245–63.

Chapter seven   Criminal interrogation

Buckwalter, A. (1983) *Interviews and Interrogations*, Boston: Butterworth.
Inbau, F. and Reid, J. (1962) *Criminal Interrogation and Confessions*, Baltimore, MD: Williams & Wilkins.
Royal, R. and Schutt, S. (1976) *The Gentle Art of Interviewing and Interrogation: a Professional Manual and Guide*, Englewood Cliffs, NJ: Prentice-Hall.
Taylor, L. (1984) *Scientific Interrogation*, Charlottesville, VA: Michie.
Yeschke, C. (1987) *Interviewing: an Introduction to Interrogation*, Springfield, IL: Thomas.

Chapter eight   Journalistic interviewing

Greatbatch, D. (1986) 'Some standard uses of supplementary questions in news interviews', *Belfast Working Papers in Language and Linguistics 8*: 86–123.
Harris, S. (1989) 'Questions in political broadcast interviews', *Communication and Cognition*.
Jucker, A. (1986) *News Interviews: a Pragmalinguistic Analysis*, Amsterdam: Benjamins.
Metzler, K. (1977) *Creative Interviewing: the Writer's Guide to Gathering Information by Asking Questions*, Englewood Cliffs, NJ: Prentice-Hall. (2nd edn, 1988).

Chapter nine   Survey questioning

Belson, W. (1981) *The Design and Understanding of Survey Questions*, Aldershot: Gower.
Billiet, J. (1989) 'Question wording effects in survey interviews', *Questioning Exchange 3*.
Blankenship, A. (1940) 'The influence of the question form upon the response in a public opinion poll', *Psychological Record 3*: 345–422.
Bradburn, N. and Sudman, S. (1979) *Improving Interview Method and Questionnaire Design: Response Effects to Threatening Questions in Survey Research*, San Francisco: Jossey-Bass.
Converse, J. and Presser, S. (1986) *Survey Questions: Handcrafting the Standardized Questionnaire*, Beverly Hills, CA: Sage.

Lucas, D. (ed.) (1985) *Asking Demographic Questions*, Canberra: Australian National University, National Centre for Development Studies.

Molenaar, N. (1989) 'Recent methodological studies on survey questioning', *Questioning Exchange 3*.

Oppenheim, A. (1966) *Questionnaire Design and Attitude Measurement*, New York: Basic Books.

Payne, S. (1951) *The Art of Asking Questions*, Princeton, NJ: Princeton University Press.

Roslow, S., Wulfeck, W., and Corby, P. (1940) 'Consumer and opinion research: experimental studies on the form of the question', *Journal of Applied Psychology 24*: 334–46.

Schuman, H. and Presser, S. (1981) *Questions and Answers in Attitude Surveys: Experiments on Question Form, Wording, and Context*, New York: Academic Press.

Stenstroem, A-B. (1984) *Questions and Responses in English Conversation*, Lund, Sweden: Gleerup.

Sudman, S. and Bradburn, N. (1982) *Asking Questions: a Practical Guide to Questionnaire Design*, San Francisco: Jossey-Bass.

— (1974) *Response Effects in Surveys: a Review and Synthesis*, Chicago: Aldine.

Chapter ten   Notions of questioning

Belnap, N. (1969) 'Questions: their presuppositions, and how they can fail to arise', in K. Lambert (ed.) *The Logical Way of Doing Things*, New Haven: Yale University Press, pp. 23–37.

Belnap, N. and Steel, T. (1976) *The Logic of Questions and Answers*, New Haven, CT: Yale University Press,

Berry-Rogghe, G., Kolvenbach, M., and Lutz, H. (1980) 'Interacting with PLIDIS, a deductive question answering system for German', in L. Bolc (ed.) *Natural Language Question Answering Systems*, Munich: Hanser, pp. 137–216.

Bradburn, N. and Sudman, S. (1979) *Improving Interview Method and Questionnaire Design: Response Effects to Threatening Questions in Survey Research*, San Francisco: Jossey-Bass.

Buckwalter, A. (1983) *Interviews and Interrogations*, Stoneham, MA: Butterworth.

Churchill, L. (1978) *Questioning Strategies in Sociolinguistics*, Rowley, MA: Newbury.

Cronbach, L. (1982) *Designing Evaluations of Educational and Social Programs*, San Francisco: Jossey-Bass.

Davis, J. and Schiffman, H. (1985) 'The influence of the wording of interrogatives on the accuracy of eyewitness recollections', *Bulletin of the Psychonomic Society 23*: 394–6.

Davis, M. (1971) 'That's interesting!' *Philosophy of the Social Sciences 1*: 309–44.

Dillon, J.T. (1986) 'Student questions and individual learning', *Educational Theory 36*: 333–41.

— (1988) *Questioning and Teaching: a Manual of Practice*, London: Croom Helm; New York: Teachers College.

Greatbatch, D. (1986) 'Some standard uses of supplementary questions in news interviews', *Belfast Working Papers in Language and Linguistics 8*: 86–123.

Grewendorf, G. (1983) 'What answers can be given?' in F. Kiefer (ed.) *Questions and Answers*, Dordrecht: Reidel, pp. 45–84.

Harrah, D. (1985) 'The logic of questions', in F. Guenthner and D. Gabbay (eds) *Handbook of Philosophical Logic*, vol. 2, Dordrecht: Reidel.

Hintikka, J. (1983) 'New foundations for a theory of questions and answers', in F. Kiefer (ed.) *Questions and Answers*, Dordrecht: Reidel, pp. 159–90.

Johnson, M. (1979) *Discussion Dynamics*, Rowley, MA: Newbury.

Joshi, A. (1982) 'Mutual beliefs in question–answer systems', in N. Smith (ed.) *Mutual Knowledge*, London: Academic Press, pp. 181–97.

Joshi, A. (1983) 'Varieties of cooperative responses in question–answer systems', in F. Kiefer (ed.) *Questions and Answers*, Dordrecht: Reidel, pp. 229–40.

Jucker, A. (1986) *News Interviews: a Pragmalinguistic Analysis*, Amsterdam: Benjamins.

Kaplan, S. (1981) 'Appropriate responses to inappropriate questions' in A. Joshi, B. Webber, and I. Sag (eds) *Elements of Discourse Understanding*, Cambridge: Cambridge University Press, pp. 127–44.

Keenan, E. and Hull, R. (1973) 'The logical presuppositions of questions and answers', in J. Petoefi and D. Franck (eds) *Praesuppositionen in Philosophie und Linguistik*, Frankfurt: Athenaeum, pp. 441–66.

Kestler, J. (1982) *Questioning Techniques and Tactics*, Colorado Springs, CO: Shepard/McGraw-Hill.

Loftus, E. (1979) *Eyewitness Testimony*, Cambridge, MA: Harvard University Press.

— (1982) 'Interrogating eyewitnesses – good questions and bad', in R. Hogarth (ed.) *Question Framing and Response Consistency*, San Francisco: Jossey-Bass, pp. 51–63.

Muscio, B. (1916) 'The influence of the form of a question', *British Journal of Educational Psychology 8*: 351–89.

Olinick, S. (1954) 'Some considerations of the use of questioning as a psychoanalytic technique', *Journal of the American Psychoanalytic Association 2*: 57–66.

Reisman, D. and Benney, M. (1956) 'Asking and answering', *Journal of Business 29*: 225–36.

Rescher, N. (1982) *Empirical Inquiry*, London: Athlone Press.

Rowe, M. (1974) 'Wait-time and rewards as instructional variables', *Journal of Research in Science Teaching 11*: 81–94.

Royal, R. and Schutt, S. (1976) *The Gentle Art of Interviewing and Interrogation: a Professional Manual and Guide*, Englewood Cliffs, NJ: Prentice-Hall.

Schuman, H. and Presser, S. (1981) *Questions and Answers in Attitude Surveys: Experiments on Question Form, Wording, and Context*, New York: Academic Press.

Stenstroem, A-B. (1984) *Questions and Responses in English Conversation*, Malmoe, Sweden: Gleerup.

Stevens, R. (1912) 'The question as a measure of efficiency in instruction: a critical study of class-room practice', *Teachers College Contributions to Education 48*, New York: Teachers College.

Stiff, J. and Miller, G. (1986) '"Come to think of it..." Interrogative probes, deceptive communication, and deception detection', *Human Communication Research 12*: 339–57.

Sudman, S. and Bradburn, N. (1974) *Response Effects in Surveys: a Review and Synthesis*, Chicago: Aldine.

— (1982) *Asking Questions: a Practical Guide to Questionnaire Design*, San Francisco: Jossey-Bass.

Swift, J. and Gooding, C. (1983) 'Interaction of wait-time feedback and questioning instruction on middle school science teaching', *Journal of Research in Science Teaching 20*: 721–30.

Tierney, K. (1971) *How to Be a Witness*, Dobbs Ferry, NY: Oceana Publications.

Weiser, A. (1975) 'How not to answer a question', in R. Grossman, L. San, and T. Vance (eds) *Papers from the 11th Regional Meeting of the Chicago Linguistic Society*, Chicago: Chicago Linguistic Society, pp. 649–60.

Wellman, F. (1936) *The art of cross-examination* (4th edn, rev.), New York: Macmillan (1st edn, 1903).

West, C. (1983) '"Ask me no questions": an analysis of queries and replies in physician–patient dialogues', in S. Fisher and A. Todd (eds) *The Social Organization of Doctor–*

Patient Communication, Washington, DC: Center for Applied Linguistics, pp. 75–106.

Yamada, S. (1913) 'A study of questioning', *Pedagogical Seminary [Journal of Genetic Psychology] 20*: 129–86.

Chapter twelve   Alternatives to questioning

Bougon, M. G. (1983) 'Uncovering cognitive maps: the Self-Q technique', in G. Morgan (ed.) *Beyond Method: Strategies for Social Research*, Beverly Hills, CA: Sage, pp. 173–88.

Colby, K. M. (1961) 'On the greater amplifying power of causal- correlative over interrogative inputs on free association in an experimental psychoanalytic situation', *Journal of Nervous and Mental Disease 133*: 233–9.

Dillon, J. T. (1988a) *Questioning and Teaching: a Manual of Practice*, London: Croom Helm; New York: Teachers College.

Frank, G. and Sweetland, A. (1962) 'A study of the process of psychotherapy: the verbal interaction', *Journal of Consulting Psychology 26*: 135–8.

Lopez, F. M. (1965) *Personnel Interviewing*, New York: McGraw-Hill.

McComb, K. B. and Jablin, F. M. (1984) 'Verbal correlates of interviewer empathic listening and employment interview outcomes', *Communication Monographs 51*: 353–71.

MacDonald, J. B. (1989) 'Using reacting moves to promote discourse', *Questioning Exchange 3*.

Mishler, E. G. (1984) *The Discourse of Medicine: Dialectics of Medical Interviews*, Norwood, NJ: Ablex.

Snow, D. A., Zurcher, L., and Sjoberg, G. (1982) 'Interviewing by comment: an adjunct to the direct question', *Qualitative Sociology 5*: 385–411.

Chapter thirteen   Research on questions vs alternatives

Adana, B.S. (1979) 'Effects of counselor's silence and nonverbal behavior on the perception of the counseling interview', Unpublished doctoral dissertation, West Virginia University, *Dissertation Abstracts*, 40–7: 3775-A.

Arnold, D., Atwood, R., and Rogers, V. (1974) 'Question and response levels and lapse time intervals', *Journal of Experimental Education 43*: 11–15.

Boggs, S.T. (1972) 'The meaning of questions and narratives to Hawaiian children', in C. Cazden, V. John, and D. Hymes (eds) *Functions of Language in the Classroom*, New York: Teachers College.

Chafe, W. (1985) 'Some reasons for hesitating', in D. Tannen and M. Saville-Troike (eds) *Perspectives on Silence*, Norwood, NJ: Ablex, pp. 77–89.

Colby, K.M. (1961) 'On the greater amplifying power of causal-correlative over interrogative inputs on free association in an experimental psychoanalytic situation', *Journal of Nervous and Mental Disease 133*: 233–9.

Cook, J.J. (1964) 'Silence in psychotherapy', *Journal of Consulting Psychology 11*: 42–6.

Dillon, J.T. (1981) 'Duration of response to teacher questions and statements', *Contemporary Educational Psychology 6*: 1–11.

— (1982) 'Cognitive correspondence between question/statement and response', *American Educational Research Journal 19*: 540–51.

— (1983) 'Cognitive complexity and duration of classroom speech', *Instructional Science 12*: 59–66.

— (1985) 'Using questions to foil discussion', *Teaching and Teacher Education 1*: 109–21.

References

— (1986) 'Student questions and individual learning', *Educational Theory 36*: 333–41.

— (1988a) *Questioning and Teaching: a Manual of Practice*, London: Croom Helm; New York: Teachers College.

— (ed.) (1988b) *Questioning and Discussion: a Multidisciplinary Study*, Norwood, NJ: Ablex.

— (1988c) 'The remedial status of student questioning', *Journal of Curriculum Studies 20:* 197-210.

— (1988d) 'Discussion vs. recitation', *Tennessee Educational Leadership 15*: 52–64.

— (1989) 'Question asking and human development', paper presented at the Conference on Developmental Psychology, Bern, Switzerland, Sept. 1988.

Ellis, A. (1977) 'The rational-emotive facilitation of psychotherapeutic goals', in A. Ellis and R. Grieger (eds) *Handbook of Rational-emotive Therapy*, New York: Springer, pp. 189–97.

Frank, G. and Sweetland, A. (1962) 'A study of the process of psychotherapy: the verbal interaction', *Journal of Consulting Psychology 26*: 135–8.

Goldman-Eisler, F. (1968) *Psycholinguistics: Experiments in Spontaneous Speech*, New York: Academic Press.

Gorden, R.L. (1954) 'An interaction analysis of the depth-interview'. Unpublished doctoral dissertation, University of Chicago.

Hubbell, R.D. (1977) 'On facilitating spontaneous talking in young children', *Journal of Speech and Hearing Disorders 42*: 216–31.

Hunter, C.K. (1957) 'An experimental study of the pause analysis technique in interviewing', unpublished doctoral dissertation, Indiana University, *Dissertation Abstracts 17–10*: 2208.

Jaffe, J. and Feldstein, S. (1970) *Rhythms of Dialogue*, New York: Academic Press.

Levin, H., Silverman, I., and Ford, B. (1967) 'Hesitations in children's speech during explanation and description', *Journal of Verbal Learning and Verbal Behavior 6*: 560–4.

Lief, H.I. (1962) 'Silence as intervention in psychotherapy', *American Journal of Psychoanalysis 22*: 80–3.

Long, L., Paradise, L., and Long, T. (1981) *Questioning: Skills for the Helping Process*, Monterey, CA: Brooks-Cole.

McComb, K.B. and Jablin, F.M. (1984) 'Verbal correlates of interviewer empathic listening and employment interview outcomes', *Communication Monographs 51*: 353–71.

MacDonald, J.B. (1989) 'Using reacting moves to promote discourse', *Questioning Exchange 3*.

Matarazzo, J., and Wiens, A. (1972) *The Interview: Research on its Anatomy and Structure*, Chicago: Aldine.

Matarazzo, J., Wiens, A., Matarazzo, R., and Saslow, G. (1968) 'Speech and silence behavior in clinical psychotherapy and its laboratory correlates', in J. Shlien (ed.) *Research in Psychotherapy*, vol. 3, Washington, DC: American Psychological Association.

Matarazzo, J., Wiens, A., Saslow, G., Allen, B., and Weitman, W. (1964) 'Interviewer mm-hm and interviewee speech duration', *Psychotherapy 1*: 109–14.

Mishler, E.G. (1978) 'Studies in dialogue and discourse: III, Utterance structure and utterance function in interrogative sequences', *Journal of Psycholinguistic Research 7*: 279–305.

Roby, T.W. (1988) 'Models of discussion', in J. T. Dillon (1988b) *Questioning and Discussion: a Multidisciplinary Study*, Norwood, NJ: Ablex.

Rogers, C.R. (1942) *Counseling and Psychotherapy*, Boston: Houghton Mifflin.

— (1961) *On Becoming a Person*, Boston: Houghton Mifflin.

Rowe, M.B. (1974a) 'Pausing phenomena: influence on the quality of instruction', *Journal of Psycholinguistic Research 3*: 203–33.

— (1974b) 'Wait-time and rewards as instructional variables, their influence on language, logic, and fate control. Part One – Wait-time', *Journal of Research in Science Teaching 11*: 81–94.

Susskind, E. (1969) 'The role of question-asking in the elementary school classroom', in F. Kaplan and S. Sarason (eds) *The Psycho-educational Clinic*, New Haven, CT: Yale University Press.

Taylor, I. (1969) 'Content and structure in sentence production', *Journal of Verbal Learning and Verbal Behavior 8*: 170–5.

Tobin, K. (1987) 'The role of wait time in higher cognitive level learning', *Review of Educational Research 57*: 69–95.

Weisman, A.D. (1955) 'Silence and psychotherapy', *Psychiatry 18*: 241–60.

Wood, D. and Wood, H. (1988) 'Questioning versus student initiative', in J.T. Dillon (ed.) *Questioning and Discussion: a Multidisciplinary Study*, Norwood, NJ: Ablex, pp. 280–305.

Wood, D., Wood, H., Griffiths, A., Howarth, S., and Howarth, C. (1982) 'The structure of conversations with 6- to 10-year old deaf children', *Journal of Child Psychology and Psychiatry 23*: 295–308.

Wood, H. and Wood, D. (1983) 'Questioning the pre-school child', *Educational Review 35*: 149–62.

— (1984) 'An experimental evaluation of the effects of five styles of teacher conversation on the language of hearing-impaired children', *Journal of Child Psychology and Psychiatry 25*: 45–62.

Index

questioning techniques *see* scheme of practice; *see also* alternatives to questioning

recruiter questions 66–74
respondent questions: applicant 66–73; client in therapy 37–8; defendant 18; interviewee 103; patient 55–6; partner or speaker 192–6, 205–6, 215–17; student 7, 205–6, 215–17, 230–5; witness 83
responding strategies: acquiescing 121, 126, 162–3; co-operating 158–60; distorting 120, 161–2; evading 97–104, 155–6; lying 23, 156–7; stonewalling 157; withholding 78–9, 88, 160–1
response type: answer responses 150–4; non-answer responses 96–105, 147–50; non-responses 147; *see also* answers, responding
responses: to non-questions *see* alternatives to questioning; to question form 117–19; question structure 122–6; question topic 119–22; question words 114–17; questioner status 20; *see also* answers, responding, response

scheme of practice 166–75
signals: fillers 197–8, 217–18; pass 198–9; phatics 197, 218–19
silences 199–203, 219–27
speaker questions 192–6, 205–6, 215–17; *see also* respondent questions
statements: declarative 177–83; of interest 188–9; of mind 186–8; reddition 190–2; referral 189–90; reflective 183–6; research on 208–15; various 203–7
survey questions 109–27

teacher questions 7–15, 230–6
therapist questions 36–53